Computational Economics

Computational Economics: A concise introduction is a comprehensive textbook designed to help students move from the traditional and comparative static analysis of economic models to a modern and dynamic computational study. The ability to equate an economic problem, to formulate it into a mathematical model and to solve it computationally is becoming a crucial and distinctive competence for most economists.

This vital textbook is organised around static and dynamic models, covering both macro- and microeconomic topics, exploring the numerical techniques required to solve those models. A key aim of the book is to enable students to develop the ability to modify the models themselves so that, using the MATLAB/Octave codes provided in the book and on the website, they can demonstrate a complete understanding of computational methods.

This textbook is innovative, easy to read and highly focused, providing students of economics with the skills needed to understand the essentials of using numerical methods to solve economic problems. It also provides more technical readers with an easy way to cope with economics through modelling and simulation. Later in the book, more elaborate economic models and advanced numerical methods are introduced that will prove valuable to those in more advanced study.

This book is ideal for all students of economics, mathematics, computer science and engineering taking classes on Computational or Numerical Economics.

Oscar Afonso is an Associate Professor at the Faculty of Economics, University of Porto, Portugal.

Paulo B. Vasconcelos is an Assistant Professor at the Faculty of Economics, University of Porto, Portugal.

Routledge Advanced Texts in Economics and Finance

1 **Financial Econometrics**
   Peijie Wang

2 **Macroeconomics for Developing Countries 2nd edition**
   Raghbendra Jha

3 **Advanced Mathematical Economics**
   Rakesh Vohra

4 **Advanced Econometric Theory**
   John S. Chipman

5 **Understanding Macroeconomic Theory**
   John M. Barron, Bradley T. Ewing and Gerald J. Lynch

6 **Regional Economics**
   Roberta Capello

7 **Mathematical Finance: Core Theory, Problems and Statistical Algorithms**
   Nikolai Dokuchaev

8 **Applied Health Economics**
   Andrew M. Jones, Nigel Rice, Teresa Bago d'Uva and Silvia Balia

9 **Information Economics**
   Urs Birchler and Monika Bütler

10 **Financial Econometrics (Second Edition)**
   Peijie Wang

11 **Development Finance**
   Debates, dogmas and new directions
   Stephen Spratt

12 **Culture and Economics**
   On values, economics and international business
   Eelke de Jong

13 **Modern Public Economics Second Edition**
   Raghbendra Jha

14 **Introduction to Estimating Economic Models**
   Atsushi Maki

15 **Advanced Econometric Theory**
   John Chipman

16 **Behavioral Economics**
   Edward Cartwright

17 **Essentials of Advanced Macroeconomic Theory**
   Ola Olsson

18 **Behavioral Economics and Finance**
   Michelle Baddeley

19 **Applied Health Economics – Second Edition**
Andrew M. Jones, Nigel Rice, Teresa Bago d'Uva and Silvia Balia

20 **Real Estate Economics**
A point to point handbook
Nicholas G. Pirounakis

21 **Finance in Asia**
Institutions, regulation and policy
Qiao Liu, Paul Lejot and Douglas Arner

22 **Behavioral Economics – Second Edition**
Edward Cartwright

23 **Understanding Financial Risk Management**
Angelo Corelli

23 **Empirical Development Economics**
Måns Söderbom and Francis Teal with Markus Eberhardt, Simon Quinn and Andrew Zeitlin

24 **Strategic Entrepreneurial Finance**
From value creation to realization
Darek Klonowski

25 **Computational Economics**
A concise introduction
Oscar Afonso and Paulo B. Vasconcelos

Computational Economics
A concise introduction

Oscar Afonso and Paulo B. Vasconcelos

LONDON AND NEW YORK

First published 2016
by Routledge
2 Park Square, Milton Park, Abingdon, Oxon OX14 4RN

by Routledge
711 Third Avenue, New York, NY 10017

Routledge is an imprint of the Taylor & Francis Group, an informa business

© 2016 Oscar Afonso and Paulo B. Vasconcelos

The right of Oscar Afonso and Paulo B. Vasconcelos be identified as the authors of this work has been asserted by them in accordance with the Copyright, Designs and Patent Act 1988.

All rights reserved. No part of this book may be reprinted or reproduced or utilised in any form or by any electronic, mechanical, or other means, now known or hereafter invented, including photocopying and recording, or in any information storage or retrieval system, without permission in writing from the publishers.

Trademark notice: Product or corporate names may be trademarks or registered trademarks, and are used only for identification and explanation without intent to infringe.

British Library Cataloguing in Publication Data
A catalogue record for this book is available from the British Library

Library of Congress Cataloging in Publication Data
Afonso, Oscar.
Computational economics: a concise introduction/
Oscar Afonso and Paulo Vasconcelos.
    1. Economics, Mathematical. 2. Economics–Mathematical models.
    3. Economics–Data processing. 4. Economics–Computer programs.
    I. Vasconcelos, Paulo. II. Title.
HB135.A36 2015
330.01'13–dc23   2015006110

ISBN: 978-1-138-85965-4 (hbk)
ISBN: 978-1-138-85966-1 (pbk)
ISBN: 978-1-315-71699-2 (ebk)

Typeset in Bembo
by Sunrise Setting Ltd, Paignton, UK

Contents

List of figures   xi
Preface   xiii
Using the book   xvi
Introduction   xix

PART I
Static economic models   1

1 Supply and demand model   3
   Introduction 3
   Economic model in autarky 4
   First computer program 7
   First numerical results and simulations 8
   Economic model with international-trade policy 11
   Numerical solution: linear systems of equations 14
   Numerical results and simulation 16
   Highlights 24
   Problems and computer exercises 24

2 IS–LM model in a closed economy   26
   Introduction 26
   Economic model 26
   Numerical solution: linear systems of equations 29
   Computational implementation 31
   Numerical results and simulation 33
   Highlights 37
   Problems and computer exercises 37

3 IS–LM model in an open economy   38
   Introduction 38
   Economic model 38
   Numerical solution: linear systems of equations 41
   Computational implementation 44

viii   Contents

    Numerical results and simulation 46
    Highlights 48
    Problems and computer exercises 48

4   AD–AS model   49
    Introduction 49
    Economic model 49
    Numerical solution: nonlinear systems of equations 52
    Computational implementation 55
    Numerical results and simulation 57
    Highlights 61
    Problems and computer exercises 61

5   Portfolio model   64
    Introduction 64
    Economic model 65
    Numerical solution 65
    Computational implementation 67
    Numerical results and simulation 72
    Highlights 73
    Problems and computer exercises 74

PART II
Dynamic economic models   77

6   Supply and demand dynamics   79
    Introduction 79
    Cobweb model 79
    Market model with inventory 82
    Numerical solution: difference equations 83
    Computational implementation 85
    Numerical results and simulation 88
    Highlights 90
    Problems and computer exercises 91

7   Duopoly model   93
    Introduction 93
    Cournot, Stackelberg and Bertrand models of duopoly markets 93
    Discrete dynamics Cournot duopoly game 95
    Numerical solution: systems of difference equations 96
    Computational implementation 99
    Numerical results and simulation 100
    Highlights 101
    Problems and computer exercises 102

Contents ix

8 SP–DG model 103
    Introduction 103
    Economic model 103
    Numerical solution 106
    Alogrithm 106
    Computational implementation 106
    Numerical results and simulation 110
    Highlights 111
    Problems and computer exercises 111

9 Solow model 113
    Introduction 113
    Economic model 113
    Numerical solution: initial value problems 119
    Computational implementation 121
    Numerical results and simulation 122
    Highlights 125
    Problems and computer exercises 127

10 Skill-biased technological change model 129
    Introduction 129
    Economic model 130
    Numerical solution: initial value problems 134
    Computational implementation 138
    Numerical results and simulation 139
    Highlights 141
    Problems and computer exercises 142

11 Technological-knowledge diffusion model 143
    Introduction 143
    Economic model 144
    Numerical solution: initial value problems 147
    Computational implementation 150
    Numerical results and simulation 151
    Highlights 154
    Problems and computer exercises 154

12 Ramsey–Cass–Koopmans model 156
    Introduction 156
    Economic model 156
    Numerical solution: boundary value problems 163
    Computational implementation 166
    Numerical results and simulation 168
    Highlights 170
    Problems and computer exercises 170

x Contents

Afterword 173

PART III
Appendices 175

Appendix A: Projects 177
Supply–demand model with trade: export taxes 177
Product differentiation model 178
Some variants on the Mundell–Fleming model 180
Nonlinear supply–demand model 186
Dynamic continuous duopoly game 186
Dynamic IS–LM model 189
Dynamic AD–AS model 190
Extensions to the neoclassic growth model 191
Effects of public intervention on wage inequality 197
Migratory movements and directed technical change 199
Skill-structure, high-tech sector and economic growth dynamics model 200
Multiple equilibria in economic growth 204

Appendix B: Solutions 207
Supply and demand 207
IS–LM in a closed economy 209
IS–LM in an open economy 211
AD–AS 214
Portfolio 218
Supply and demand dynamics 222
Duopoly 228
SP–DG 229
Solow 234
Skill-biased technological change 239
Technological-knowledge diffusion 244
Ramsey–Cass–Koopmans 249

Bibliography 257
Index 261

Figures

I.1	Short–medium run stability	xx
I.2	Long-run path: country with small growth rate (A) and with high growth rate (B)	xxi
1.1	Supply and demand diagram	9
1.2	Consumer and producer surplus	10
1.3	Effects of a demand shock (negative)	12
1.4	Supply and demand curves for all markets	19
1.5	Supply and demand curves, with tariff, for all markets	21
1.6	Supply and demand curves, with subsidy, for all markets	24
2.1	IS–LM diagram	34
2.2	Decrease in T	35
2.3	Increase in G	36
2.4	Decrease in M	36
4.1	AD–AS diagram	58
4.2	Increase in $\overline{G}$	60
4.3	Increase in $\overline{M}$	61
4.4	Increase in $\overline{A}$	62
5.1	Monte Carlo convergence path for the portfolio with minimum variance	72
5.2	Efficient frontier, minimum variance portfolio, portfolio with return equal to the asset with greater return and the assets	73
6.1	Cobweb plots	90
6.2	Price phase diagram for the inventory market model	91
7.1	Quantity phase diagram for the dynamic duopoly Cournot game	101
8.1	SP-DG disinflation process	111
9.1	Solow diagram	116
9.2	Golden rule savings rate	118
9.3	Transition dynamics to steady state	123
9.4	Transition dynamics and Solow diagram: variation on δ	125
9.5	Transition dynamics and Solow diagram: variation on A	126
9.6	Direction field and paths to steady state	126
10.1	Path of variables D and W	140

10.2	Path of variable $D = Q_H/Q_L$ for several values of H	141
11.1	Transitional dynamics for $\hat{N}$ and χ_2	151
11.2	Increase in ν_2	152
11.3	Decrease in ν_2	153
12.1	Golden rule, equilibrium point, steady state	162
12.2	Transition dynamics to steady state	169
12.3	Phase diagram, RCK model	169
12.4	Numerical estimates of the dynamic paths in the RCK model	171
B.1	Divergent processes ($\lvert -\frac{b}{a} \rvert \geq 1$)	224

Preface

There is consensus that computational approach to economics is a growing field. The large majority of economists, or students in economics, are not aware of numerical computing, although the ubiquity of numerical methods is known. On the other hand, professionals or students in mathematics, physics and engineering increasingly require economic knowledge.

This book blends economics with the numerical techniques required for the solution of the problems, providing explained codes. It is precise and concise, meaning that it balances theory and practice. The textbook provides and explains, with detail, the MATLAB/Octave implementation of the algorithms. The intuition and central ideas of the numerical methods required to deal with the mathematical theory underlying the economic problem are pedagogically provided. The topics covered also prepare the reader to undertake more complex models and/or to develop new research. They give economic readers the skills needed to understand the essentials about numerical methods to solve economic problems, and provide more technical readers with an easy way to cope with economics through modelling and simulation.

The main ingredients of the book are seminal economic models, relevant and efficient numerical methods and (explained) software solutions. The aim behind this choice is twofold. First, the book should be suitable for those who do not have skills in either economics or in scientific programming. Second, the book should be instructive, providing the basics and skills to deal with this multidisciplinary topic.

Economic models A set of micro and macroeconomic models were selected to be included in this book.

Regarding the short–medium run stability of the macroeconomic models, the classical IS–LM model, in closed and open economy, is presented. Then the book covers flexible prices and the determinants of inflation. Following on from the former models, the AD curve from the IS–LM model is introduced along with the short- and long-run AS curve. In addition, the SP–DG model to explain the ups and downs of inflation is introduced. For the long-run macroeconomic growth models, the book presents the seminal Solow model, which is extended by the general equilibrium model called the Ramsey–Cass–Koopmans model.

Two other models are also considered: one is a general equilibrium economic growth model to explain the path of intra-country wage inequality; and the other, a general equilibrium economic growth model as well, tackles the international technological-knowledge diffusion from developed to developing countries.

The chapters on microeconomic models start by examining how the behaviour of individual agents affect the supply and/or demand for goods and services, which determines prices, and how prices, in turn, determine the quantity supplied and/or quantity demanded of goods and services. The proposed models meet exactly this outline, by first considering a static supply–demand model, which is extended to consider international trade policy, and then a dynamic cobweb model, which in turn is derived from the previous static one. In this sequence, afterwards a dynamic duopoly game model, through which firms compete by quantities, is analysed. Finally, to accommodate optimisation problems, a portfolio model resulting from the setup originally proposed by Markowitz is presented and solved using different approaches.

Numerical methods and software The economic models are presented emphasising the underlying mathematical problems that must be solved. A brief presentation of some of the most common and state-of-the-art numerical methods to solve these problems is provided. Emphasis is given to numerical methods to solve systems of linear and nonlinear equations, to solve systems of differential equations (both initial and boundary value problems), and to solve optimisation problems.

For the numerical implementation of the models as well as of the numerical methods, MATLAB and Octave are used. Our choice was primarily based on their adequacy for the purposes of the book, mainly due to ease of code writing, availability of a plethora of functions programmed on state-of-the-art methods, nice and rich plotting capabilities and ease of debugging.

MATLAB is a high-level language and interactive environment that enables computationally intensive tasks. The codes were tested on several MATLAB releases. A trial license can be obtained from the MathWorks (leading developer of mathematical computing software for engineers and scientists) website. Additionally, MATLAB can be enlarged with toolboxes, which provide functions for specific development areas.

GNU Octave is a high-level language, primarily intended for numerical computations, mostly compatible with MATLAB. The codes were also tested on the more recent Octave versions. It is freely redistributable software, under the terms of the GNU General Public License (GPL) as published by the Free Software Foundation. Octave-Forge provides a set of packages for GNU Octave, to extend its functionalities.

To run the files provided in the book, the *Optimization Toolbox* is required for MATLAB, and two packages, *optim* and *odepkg*, are needed for Octave. Some, but few, functionalities may differ between the two software packages, but the tendency is that newer versions of Octave tend to diminish these differences.

Project proposals The textbook proposes, at the end, a set of projects for further development. These projects aim at consolidating and expanding the skills gained as a result of studying this book.

Book prerequisites The textbook was conceptualised to be as much as possible self-contained. Some knowledge or at least general interest that the reader certainly has of economics will prove helpful. It also helps to have some mathematical background, mainly related to the basics of linear algebra and calculus. Some familiarity with programming techniques may be advantageous. A quick introduction to MATLAB (or Octave) programming is recommended by reading one of the many short courses available in the world wide web.

Acknowledgments Many students assisted, by experiencing the contents of this book and by preparing some reports, in the production of this book. We are particularly grateful to Carlos Seixas, Diana Aguiar, Duarte Leite, José Gaspar, Mariana Cunha, Pedro Gonzaga and Sofia Vaz for their efforts in preparing outstanding reports that inspired some of the projects proposed in the book.

The influence of our colleagues at the Faculty of Economics was also important: in particular, Pedro Gil for carefully reading some of the projects.

We acknowledge all anonymous referees for their careful reviews and valuable comments which helped to improve the manuscript. We would also like to thank the Editor since without his professional procedure and helpful guidance this book never would have come to be produced in its present form. The editorial team was also meticulous and unsurpassed.

The work of brilliant economists and mathematicians has been inspiring for us, namely: Beresford Parlett, Cleve Moler, Daron Acemoglu, Gene Golub, Mario Ahues, Robert Barro and Xavier Sala-i-Martin.

We would like to thank the Faculty of Economics at University of Porto (FEP.UP) for believing and supporting our Computational Economics course in the economics PhD program and our Numerical Methods course in the MSc program.

We dedicate this book to our children, Nuno Vasconcelos, Ana Afonso, Tiago Vasconcelos and João Afonso. We have always hoped to be an inspiration to them, and still do. They are surely very inspiring to us.

Using the book

Notation Throughout this work, we generally adopt the Householder (1964) notation. Greek letters indicate scalars, upper case letters indicate matrices and lower case letters indicate vectors or scalar indices (namely, i, j, and k). For vectors and matrices, subscripts are used in the following ways.

- v_k denotes a term in a sequence of vectors $v_0, v_1, \ldots, v_k, v_{k+1}, \ldots$.
- The element or component i of vector v is denoted by $v(i)$ (or simply by v_i when there is no conflict of notation with the previous convention).
- M_k denotes a term in a sequence of matrices $M_0, M_1, \ldots, M_k, M_{k+1}, \ldots$.
- The element or coefficient in row i and column j of matrix A is denoted by $a(i, j)$ (or simply by $a_{i,j}$ or a_{ij} when there is no conflict of notation with the first convention above).

A note to students We strongly advise students to replicate the codes provided and to introduce slight modifications of the values of the parameters. Being acquainted with the sensitivity of the numerical methods and economic models is fundamental. We also encourage the development of some of the projects. They follow an increasing level of difficulty, to cope with everyone's needs and pace.

A note to instructors The book can be used in several different types of courses, such as the following.

- Title: Introduction to Computational Macroeconomics (1 semester)
  - Syllabus: Chapters 2–4 and 8–12 plus some of the projects (Appendix A); part of the course should be planned by the students to develop their models or extend existing ones. Research skills regarding how to investigate existing literature (books and papers) should be explored.

- Title: Introduction to Computational Microeconomics (1 semester)
  - Syllabus: Chapters 1, 5–7 followed by some of the projects (Appendix A); students are encouraged to plan and develop their

models taking into consideration the ones exposed. Research skills regarding how to investigate existing literature (books and papers) should be explored.

- Title: Introduction to Computational Economics (1 semester)
  - Syllabus: Chapters 1–2, 4–7, 9 and some of the proposed projects (Appendix A); part of the course should/could exploit further the programming skills as well as the numerical methods.
- Title: Topics on Computational Economics (1 semester)
  - Syllabus: Chapters 3, 8, 10–12 with emphasis in the projects (Appendix A); the course should be complemented by dynamic programming models, either deterministic or stochastic, and optimisation procedures.

We strongly recommend that the evaluation process should be performed using modelling and computing assignments to be developed during the semester. Two can be done individually and a third can be performed individually or in a small numbered group. Each assignment should be answered in a report, following a working paper format, and presented briefly inside the class room, so all students can profit from the work of their colleagues. This methodology will enforce and strengthen the class cohesion as well as the students' capability and motivation to develop their own work, learning also from others. The teacher should assume only an arbitrary role in this process, allowing students to lead the presentations and the answers/responses period. The teacher's role, at least during these periods, should be to stimulate, mentor and monitor; a course learner-driven instead of one teacher-driven should be more appreciated by students allowing them to better stimulate their learning pace.

Enjoy the book.

Introduction

The computational approach to economics is a growing field. Without this skill it is not possible to simulate policy effects in today's complex economic models. However, there is a gap between the usual preparation in economics and the computational tools. This book aims at bridging the gap between economics and numerical computing. It enables economists or students in economics to enrich their knowledge by endowing them with the required numerical and computational skills. With equal interest, it allows the specialist in mathematics and in computation to become familiar with economic problems.

The material covered gives the reader the skills needed to understand the essentials about numerical methods to solve economic problems, by using standard economic models. The textbook provides and explains, with detail, the MATLAB/Octave implementation of the algorithms. The intuition and central ideas of the numerical methods required to deal with the mathematical theory underlying the economic problems are pedagogically provided. The topics covered also prepare the reader to undertake more complex models and/or to develop their own research.

The chapters are modular. They begin with a brief presentation of the economic problem, followed by its mathematical formulation and computational implementation. As a result, the economic problem can be simulated in various scenarios and therefore enables economic interpretation of the results. The reader is challenged to modify the computational programs following proposals to change the baseline models. Through this book, the reader acquires the necessary computational skills to understand and analyse economic models with ease, overcoming limitations such as the size of the problem and/or the nonexistence of an explicit solution. This skill may then be used to produce their own research.

The provided learning outcomes and competencies are thus: to offer a vision of numerical methods in economics and its importance to the professional and academic practice; to provide knowledge and understanding of concepts, methods, and application topics in numerical methods and computing relevant to the economy; to support the development in the field of numerical methods and economics, analytical skills, communication and learning appropriate to the practice of the profession; to develop critical capacities, in particular in modelling, analysis and treatment of data and results.

xx *Introduction*

The book consists of two parts: the first deals with static economic models and the second with dynamic economic models. Both parts incorporate macro and microeconomic models, which are numerically solved. The required numerical methods are presented throughout the book, illustrating how to solve efficiently the models and providing the necessary knowledge to tackle other problems with similar mathematical needs.

Macroeconomic themes dominate the news since directly or indirectly they affect our well-being. Each of these themes involves the overall economic performance of the nation rather than whether one particular economic agent earns more or less than another. Thus, macroeconomics deals with *aggregate* economic variables.

In the *short–medium run* the three most important aspects are the *output level*, the *unemployment rate* and *inflation*. More output level implies lower unemployment rate, but a higher rate of inflation (and vice versa). The output level is measured by the *real gross domestic product*, GDP, which includes all currently produced goods and services of an economy sold in the market in a certain time period. The term *real* means that increases of the output reflect only increases in the quantities produced; in general terms, a variable measured in *real* term is free of changes in prices. It can be cast in *actual* (or effective) and *natural* (or potential) *real* GDP. The former is the level indeed produced by an economy and the latter is the real GDP when the inflation rate is constant. Figure I.1 illustrates the relations between these variables.

In this period of time, macroeconomists aim at minimising the fluctuations in unemployment and in the inflation rate, which requires also the minimisation of real GDP fluctuations. Nevertheless, to achieve an increasing

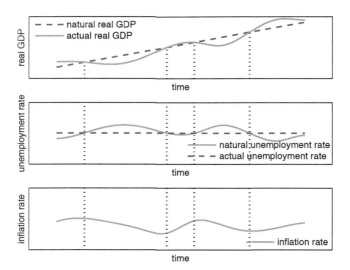

Figure I.1 Short–medium run stability.

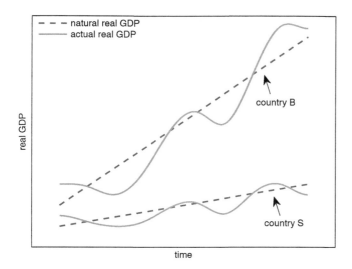

Figure I.2 Long-run path: country with small growth rate (A) and with high growth rate (B).

standard of living the real GDP must grow, which is the *long-run* concern of macroeconomists. Figure I.2 schematises two different economies with their own gap between actual and natural real GDP but with different growth rates (higher in economy B).

In turn, microeconomics analyses the market behaviour of individual consumers and firms in an attempt to understand the decision-making processes of households and firms. It examines how these decisions and behaviours influence the supply and demand for goods and services, which determines prices, and how prices determine the quantity supplied and demanded of goods and services. Thus, it is concerned with the interaction between individual buyers and sellers and the factors that affect the choices made by them. It includes several areas: in particular, the supply–demand model of price determination in a market, the consumer demand theory, the production theory, perfect and imperfect competition, game theory, labour economics, international trade policy, welfare economics and economics of information.

Specifically, the structure of the book is as follows. Part I, related to static economic models, includes the following chapters.

- Chapter 1 presents and solves a static supply–demand model, finding the competitive economic equilibrium for price and quantity of a particular good or service, which occurs when the quantity demanded by consumers will equal the quantity supplied by producers. The model is extended to include international trade policy and is solved by the Gaussian elimination method, a direct method for linear systems.

- Chapter 2 presents and solves the standard IS–LM model, which relates the real output and the interest rate in the goods and services market (IS curve) and in the money market (LM curve). Computations are then performed through the LU factorisation (where L stands for lower and U for upper), as part of the solution of systems of linear equations, introduced along with stability issues.
- Chapter 3 extends the previous IS–LM model to a scenario of an open economy. As a result, the effects of both fiscal and monetary policies are analysed in the setting of an open economy. An introduction to iterative methods for the solution of linear systems is provided.
- Chapter 4 introduces the AS–AD variable-price-level model. The AD curve comes from the IS–LM equilibrium and the AS curve reflects the labour market. Iterative numerical methods for the solution of nonlinear systems of equations are introduced.
- Chapter 5 is used to treat optimisation problems, by revisiting the problem of portfolio optimisation originally proposed by Markowitz. The aim is to implement a model that uses both a Monte Carlo optimisation and other numeric techniques available in MATLAB/Octave.

Part II, dealing with dynamic economic models, comprises the following chapters.

- Chapter 6 deals with the dynamic cobweb model derived from the static supply–demand model, by assuming that the supply reacts to price with a lag of one period, while demand depends on current price. Numerical computations for difference equations are presented.
- Chapter 7 addresses the dynamic duopoly game model, through which firms compete by quantities. The model allows us to analyse the strategic interaction between firms. The computational implementation provides additional insights into iterative processes and introduces numerical methods for eigenvalue problems.
- Chapter 8 explains the SP–DG model through which the dynamics of inflation and output gap under disinflation strategies can be analysed, as well as permanent demand shocks and temporary supply shocks. The computational implementation provides insights to iterative processes.
- Chapter 9 summarises the seminal Solow growth model, which highlights a number of very useful insights about the dynamics of the growth process. The Euler numerical method is presented to solve the related initial-value problem.
- Chapter 10 presents a dynamic growth model that explains the direction of technological knowledge, which, in turn, drives intra-country wage inequality. The Runge–Kutta family of numerical methods is used to reach the solution of the respective initial value problem.
- Chapter 11 analyses international technological-knowledge diffusion from developed to developing countries through cheaper imitative R&D. As a

result, developing countries grow more than developed ones during the transitional dynamics phase towards the steady state. Numerical methods with memory and methods to tackle stiff initial value problems are mentioned.
- Chapter 12 extends the Solow growth model in Chapter 9, by considering an endogenous saving rate – the usually called Ramsey–Cass–Koopmans model – which includes the rational behaviour of utility maximising by individuals. To solve the boundary value problems for systems of ordinary differential equations by the collocation method, some specific MATLAB/Octave functions are referenced.

Finally, Appendix A proposes, through projects, either additional economic models or extensions of the studied ones. These projects allow for knowledge sedimentation, reflection on the topics covered, exploitation of new extensions and features. Appendix B provides solutions for the proposed project exercises.

Part I
Static economic models

1 Supply and demand model

Introduction

In microeconomics, the supply–demand model is required to understand the determination of the price and of the quantity of a good sold on the market. The mechanism depends on the interaction of two different groups: buyers and sellers. The model assumes a high degree of competition, meaning that there are many buyers and sellers in the market for bidding to take place. Buyers bid against each other and thereby raise the price, and sellers bid against each other and thereby lower the price. The equilibrium is a point at which all the bidding has been done and nobody has an incentive to offer higher prices or accept lower prices. This is a partial equilibrium because it ignores the connections between markets and only studies the way individual markets work.

The assumed perfect competition assumption is an abstraction, because no market is actually perfectly competitive, but the framework still provides a good approximation for what is happening much of the time. Thus, the model, initially approached by Smith (1776), Ricardo (1817) and Cournot (1838), is simplified to regard the quantity demanded and the quantity supplied as functions of the price of the goods. The standard graphical representation, usually attributed to Marshall (1890), has price on the vertical axis and quantity on the horizontal axis. Since determinants of demand and supply other than the price of the goods in question are not explicitly represented, changes in the values of these variables are represented by moving the supply and demand curves. In turn, responses to changes in the price of the good are represented as movements along unchanged demand and supply curves.

This model is defined in a closed economy. It is then extended to an open context to accommodate international trade policy, by considering tariffs to imports and subsidies to exports. The market effects as well as social welfare effects are analysed.

In this chapter, the model is described by a system of linear equations (for a nonlinear version, see Appendix A). The solution provides the market equilibrium price and quantity. With an automatic procedure, it is straightforward to evaluate the impacts of changes in some exogenous factors that affect demand or supply and, also, to measure those impacts on social welfare.

The description of the economic model follows Varian (1992, ch. 1, 3, 9–10), Perloff (2013, ch. 1–5), Mas-Colell *et al.* (1995, part I) and

4   Static economic models

Krugman et al. (2011, part II). In turn, the numerical methods are explained according to Golub and Van Loan (1996, ch. 3), Demmel (1997, ch. 2) and Dahlquist and Björck (2008, ch. 1).

Economic model in autarky

Variables, parameters and functional forms

As in any model, the supply–demand model is composed of endogenous and exogenous variables, parameters and functional forms, which link variables and parameters.

The standard equations that characterise the economy are:

- demand, $Q_d = \overline{Q}_d - aP$;
- supply, $Q_s = \overline{Q}_s + bP$.

The endogenous variables are: quantity demanded, Q_d; quantity offered, Q_s; price of the good, P.

The exogenous variables are: independent/autonomous quantity demanded, $\overline{Q}_d$; independent/autonomous quantity offered, $\overline{Q}_s$.

In the functional forms above, a and b are parameters: $a > 0$ is the sensitivity of the demand to price and $b > 0$ is the sensitivity of the supply to price.

Demand

Quantity demanded, Q_d, is the total amount of a good (or of a service) that buyers would choose to purchase under given conditions, which include the price of the good, P, as well as other variables, represented by the exogenous variable $\overline{Q}_d$, such as income and wealth, prices of substitutes and complements, population, preferences (tastes) and expectations of future prices. That is, all of these things are considered, with the exception of the price of the good, as determinants of demand. Indeed, when we refer to the demand, we are focusing on the relationship between quantity demanded and price (while holding all the others fixed).

The Law of Demand states that when the price of a good rises, the quantity of the good demanded falls, considering that everything else remains constant, *ceteris paribus*, (i.e. income, wealth, prices of other goods, population, and preferences). In the real world this assumption is rarely satisfied but the point is to analyse the effects of the change in P without being confused or distracted by other things.

A demand curve (or line) is a graphical representation of the relationship between price and quantity demanded (*ceteris paribus*). Each point shows the amount of the good buyers would choose to buy at that specific price. Changes or shifts in demand occur when at least one of the determinants of demand other than price changes; i.e. 'when the *ceteris* is not *paribus*'.

It is important to note that quantity demanded is a specific amount associated with a specific price, whereas demand is a relationship between price and quantity demanded, involving quantities demanded for a range of prices. Hence, change in quantity demanded means a movement along the demand curve, while change in demand refers to a shift of the demand curve, caused by something other than a change in price.

Supply

Quantity supplied, Q_s, is the total amount of a good (or of a service) that sellers would choose to produce and sell under given conditions, which include the price of the good, P, as well as other variables, represented by the exogenous variable $\overline{Q}_s$, such as prices of factors of production, prices of alternative products the firm could produce, technology, productive capacity and expectations of future prices. All of these things, with the exception of the price of the good, are considered as determinants of supply. Again, when we refer to the supply, we are focusing on the relationship between quantity supplied and the price of the good, while holding everything else constant.

The Law of Supply states that when the price of a good rises, the quantity of the good supplied will also rise, assuming that everything else remains constant.

A supply curve (or line) is a graphical representation of the relationship between price and quantity supplied (*ceteris paribus*). Each point shows the amount of the good sellers would choose to sell at that specific price. Changes or shifts in supply occur when at least one of the determinants of supply other than price changes.

Analogous to the demand versus quantity demanded distinction, change in quantity supplied means a movement along the supply curve, whereas change in supply refers to a shift of the supply curve, caused by something other than a change in price.

Putting the demand and the supply curves together

The equilibrium is reached when the supply and demand curves

$$\begin{cases} Q_d + aP = \overline{Q}_d \\ Q_s - bP = \overline{Q}_s \end{cases} \quad (1.1)$$

cross ($Q_d = Q_s$), determining the equilibrium price P_e and the equilibrium quantity Q_e

$$\begin{cases} P_e = \dfrac{\overline{Q}_d - \overline{Q}_s}{a+b} \\ Q_e = \overline{Q}_d - aP_e = \overline{Q}_s + bP_e. \end{cases} \quad (1.2)$$

6 *Static economic models*

If price is below P_e, then there is 'excess demand' or 'shortage', $Q_d > Q_s$, and the quantity that actually occurs will be Q_s. For this quantity, buyers are willing to pay much more, and thus they will start bidding against each other and raising the price. In turn, if price is above P_e, then there is 'excess supply' or 'surplus', $Q_d < Q_s$, and the suppliers will start competing against each other for customers by lowering the price. Hence, when there is a disequilibrium price, the actually quantity that gets sold is given by $Q = \min\{Q_d, Q_s\}$.

In this context, four basic laws of supply and demand are stressed.

- If demand increases (demand curve shifts to the right) and supply remains unchanged, a shortage occurs, leading to a higher equilibrium price.
- If demand decreases (demand curve shifts to the left) and supply remains unchanged, a surplus occurs, leading to a lower equilibrium price.
- If demand remains unchanged and supply increases (supply curve shifts to the right), a surplus occurs, leading to a lower equilibrium price.
- If demand remains unchanged and supply decreases (supply curve shifts to the left), a shortage occurs, leading to a higher equilibrium price.

Social welfare

To measure social welfare first it is required to study what is the *consumer surplus*, C_s, and the *producer surplus*, P_s. The former is the consumers' utility gain when what they are willing to pay for the good is higher than what they really have to pay. The latter is the gain that producers' obtain when the price of the good that they sell in the market is higher than what they would be willing to sell at.

Graphically, the consumer surplus is the area below the market inverse demand curve and above the equilibrium price. The producer surplus is the area above the supply curve and below the equilibrium price. Mathematically, for a linear demand function, the consumer surplus is the area given by

$$C_s = \frac{Q_e(P_{\max} - P_e)}{2},$$

where $P_{\max} \equiv \overline{Q}_d/a$ is the price in which the quantity demanded is zero. Similarly, for a linear supply function, the producers' surplus is the area of

$$P_s = \begin{cases} P_e \overline{Q}_s + \dfrac{(Q_e - \overline{Q}_s)P_e}{2}, & \text{if } \overline{Q}_s \geq 0 \\ \dfrac{Q_e(P_e - P_{\min})}{2}, & \text{otherwise} \end{cases}$$

where $P_{\min} \equiv -\overline{Q}_s/b$. The *social welfare*, S_w, is the sum of the consumer surplus and the producer surplus: $S_w = C_s + P_s$.

First computer program

To implement the model (1.1) the following baseline values for a generic industry G are considered: $\overline{Q}_d = 1000$, $\overline{Q}_s = 250$, $a = 10$ and $b = 5$.

MATLAB/Octave code

Program files are written as scripts, executing a series of MATLAB/Octave statements, or as functions, also accepting input arguments and producing output. Both contain lines of code and are stored in text files with a .m extension, called m-files.

In the next script, supply_demand.m, the first m-file is delivered, which allows for a first insight on the use of MATLAB/Octave. Since the analytical solution is known, the equilibrium point can be obtained just by programming equations (1.2). MATLAB and Octave can also be manipulated at the command line as powerful calculators.

```
%% Supply-demand model
% Implemented by: P.B. Vasconcelos and O. Afonso
disp('──────────────────────────────────────────');
disp('Supply-demand model in autarky             ');
disp('──────────────────────────────────────────');

%% parameters
a = 10; % sensitivity of the demand to price
b =  5; % sensitivity of the supply to price

%% exogenous variables
Qd_bar = 1000; % independent/autonomous quantity demanded
Qs_bar =  250; % independent/autonomous quantity offered

%% endogenous variables
% Qd, quantity demanded
% Qs, quantity offered
% P,  price

%% model
fprintf('Qd = %g - %g*P \n',Qd_bar,a) % demand
fprintf('Qs = %g + %g*P \n',Qs_bar,b) % supply

%% compute the endogenous variables
% solving analitically
Pe = (Qd_bar-Qs_bar)/(a+b); Qe = Qd_bar-a*Pe;
disp('computed endogenous variables: (equilibrium point)')
fprintf('    quantity, Q:    %g \n', Qe);
fprintf('    price, P:       %g \n', Pe);

%% show the curves (in this case the lines)
Q = 0:2*Qe;
plot(Q,(Qd_bar-Q)/a,'b',Q,(Q-Qs_bar)/b,'r--');
title('demand and supply curves'); legend('demand','supply');
```

8 *Static economic models*

```
xlabel('quantity, Q'); ylabel('price, P');
ylim([0,Qd_bar/a]); xlim([0,2*Qe])
```

Some short comments on the code

The code begins by providing information about its purpose. This is accomplished by using the special character %, which designates a comment (not interpreted by the software), and by the input/output command `disp`, which displays contents of an array or string. Values for parameters and exogenous variables are then assigned. For MATLAB, the use of %% indicates a section on the file that can be explored in the editor to execute only that part of the code. Then, the model is displayed to the user making use of the command `fprintf`, which combines characters with data, formatted according to the specifications. To obtain information on a specific command, at the command line type (in this case) `help fprintf`. The equilibrium point is computed using the analytical solution provided and its content is displayed.

It is interesting to access what goes on in the neighbourhood of the equilibrium point. For that a vector Q is built, which contains the ticks, equidistant values from 0 to two times the value for Q_e, on the x-axis. Then, both curves, demand and supply, are plotted with the `plot` function. The `plot` function plots the vectors $(\overline{Q}_d - Q)/a$ and $(Q - \overline{Q}_s)/b$ against Q (specifying line properties); a title and a legend are provided and axes are labelled. Again, for further information on these functions type `help plot`, `help title`, `help legend`, `help xlabel` or `help ylabel`.

To execute this script three possibilities can be used: (i) type the name of the script at the MATLAB/Octave command prompt; (ii) select and drag the file from the current folder to the command prompt; or (iii) press the run button on the software editor.

First numerical results and simulations

The output is as follows.

```
----------------------------------------------------
Supply-demand model in autarky
----------------------------------------------------
Qd = 1000 - 10*P
Qs =  250 +  5*P
computed endogenous variables: (equilibrium point)
    quantity, Q:    500
    price, P:        50
```

Figure 1.1 displays the supply–demand diagram.

From Figure 1.1, as it was expected, the demand curve is negatively sloped and the supply curve is positively sloped. When both functions intersect the market equilibrium price and quantity is obtained.

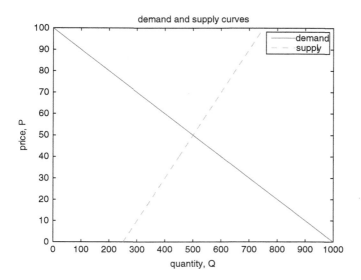

Figure 1.1 Supply and demand diagram.

To illustrate the consumer and producer surplus, another m-file, `surplus.m` is developed.

```
%% Supply−demand model: surplus and welfare
%  Implemented by: P.B. Vasconcelos and O. Afonso

hold on; % freezes the generated figure

%% consumer surplus
Pmax = Qd_bar/a;
Cs = Qe*(Pmax−Pe)/2;
% area: (0,Pe), (0,Pmax), (Qe,Pe)
fill ([0,0,Qe],[Pe,Pmax,Pe],'c');
annotation('textbox',[0.15,0.55,0.1,0.1],...
    'String','Consumer Surplus','EdgeColor','none')
fprintf('    Consumer surplus, Cs:    %g \n', Cs);

%% producer surplus:
Pmin = −Qs_bar/b;
if Qs_bar>=0
    Ps = Pe*Qs_bar+(Qe−Qs_bar)*Pe/2;
    % area: (0,0), (0,Pe), (Qe,Pe), (Qs_bar,0)
    fill ([0,0,Qe,Qs_bar],[0,Pe,Pe,0],'y')
    annotation('textbox',[0.15 0.35 0.1 0.1],...
        'String','Producer Surplus','EdgeColor','none')
else
    Ps = Qe*(Pe−Pmin)/2;
    % area: (0,Pmim), (0,Pe), (Qe,Pe)
```

10 Static economic models

```
    fill([0,0,Qe],[Pmin,Pe,Pe],'y')
    annotation('textbox',[0.15 0.35 0.1 0.1],...
        'String','Producer Surplus','EdgeColor','none')
end
fprintf('    Producer surplus, Ps:    %g \n', Ps);

hold off;
```

The code begins by invoking the previous script followed by a set of commands to depict and compute the surplus areas. First, the `hold on` command retains the generated plot in the current axis so that new plots added do not delete the existing one. Two instructions are called, `fill` and `annotate`, the former is used to fill polygons and the latter to write an annotation inside the plot at a specific point. Before leaving, do `hold off` resetting the default. The computation of the values of the areas depends on the value of $\overline{Q}_s$: if positive (negative) the producer surplus area is a trapezium (triangle). To accommodate these two situations, statements following an `if/else` condition are executed.

At the command line just do `supply_demand; surplus;` and the output is

```
    Consumer surplus, Cs:     12500
    Producer surplus, Ps:     18750
```

and Figure 1.2 displays the consumer and producer surplus.

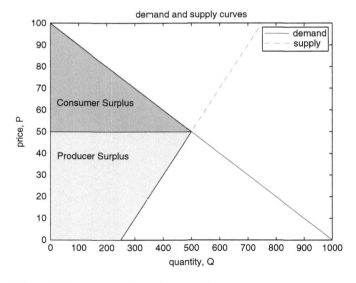

Figure 1.2 Consumer and producer surplus.

Supply and demand model 11

The consumer surplus is the area below the demand curve and above the equilibrium price, whereas the producer surplus is the area above the supply curve and below the equilibrium price. The total social welfare is then given by the sum of the two areas.

Let us consider a decrease in the consumer's income and wealth which induces a decrease in exogenous demand of 250.

```
% Qd_bar decreases 250

supply_demand            % reproduce baseline model
Qd_bar = Qd_bar-250; % perform shock
fprintf('Qd_bar changes to %g \n',Qd_bar)

Pe = (Qd_bar-Qs_bar)/(a+b); Qe = Qd_bar-a*Pe;
disp('new computed endogenous variables: (equilibrium point)')
fprintf('     quantity, Q:     %g \n', Qe);
fprintf('     price, P:        %g \n', Pe);

% show the curves (in this case the lines)
Q = 0:2*Qe;
hold on;
plot(Q,(Qd_bar-Q)/a,'b','LineWidth',3);
title('demand and supply curves');
legend('demand','supply','new demand');
xlabel('quantity, Q'); ylabel('price, P');
ylim([0,Qd_bar/a]); xlim([0,2*Qe]);

% compute surplus and welfare
surplus;
```

The output is as follows.

```
new computed endogenous variables:
     (equilibrium point)
    quantity, Q:     416.667
    price, P:        33.333
    Consumer surplus, Cs:    8680.56
    Producer surplus, Ps:    11111.10
```

When the consumer's income and wealth decreases, the demand curve shifts to the left (Figure 1.3), leading to a decrease in the equilibrium quantity and price. The consumer's and producer's surplus also decrease, along with a consequent decrease in the social welfare.

Economic model with international-trade policy

Following Krugman and Obstfeld (2011), it is now considered that there are two big countries, Home (H) and Foreign (F), which produce and consume the final good, G. This good can be costlessly transported between countries, the exchange rate between currencies is fixed and in each country G

12 Static economic models

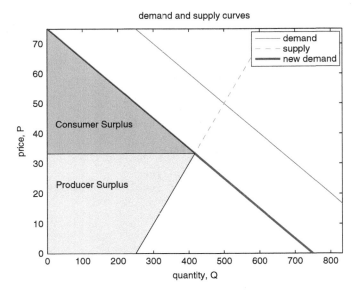

Figure 1.3 Effects of a demand shock (negative).

is produced under perfect competition. Thus, the supply and demand curves are functions of the market price:

- Home demand, $Q_{d,H} = \overline{Q}_{d,H} - a_H P_H$;
- Home supply, $Q_{s,H} = \overline{Q}_{s,H} + b_H P_H$;
- Foreign demand, $Q_{d,F} = \overline{Q}_{d,F} - a_F P_F$; and
- Foreign supply, $Q_{s,F} = \overline{Q}_{s,F} + b_F P_F$.

If, without international trade (autarky), prices of G are different between countries, then trade emerges whenever barriers are removed. Let us assume that, in this case, the price of G is higher in H, which under free trade implies that producers of G in F begin to export it to H. The exports of G raises its price in F and lowers its price in H until the elimination of the difference in prices. When prices become equal in both countries, there is no additional advantage to trade more quantity of G, and the prices and quantities traded stabilise. To find the world price, P_w, and the quantity traded, Q_w, two new curves need to be defined: the import demand curve by H, M_H, and the export supply curve by F, E_H. The former is the excess of what H consumers demand over what H producers supply, the latter is the excess of what F producers supply over what F consumers demand:

- Home import demand curve, $M_H = Q_{d,H} - Q_{s,H}$; and
- Foreign export supply curve, $E_F = Q_{s,F} - Q_{d,F}$.

The Home import demand curve intercepts the price axis at P_e in H in which import demand equals zero; from then on, M_H is downward sloping because as price increases, the quantity of imports demanded declines since Home consumers decrease their demand and Home producers increase their supply. The Foreign export supply curve also intercepts the price axis at P_e in F in which export supply equals zero; from then on, E_F is upward sloping since if price increases, Foreign producers raise the quantity supplied and Foreign consumers lower the amount demanded. Hence, the world equilibrium occurs when M_H equals E_F, which occurs at price P_w.

This framework can also be used to determine the effects on markets and agents' welfare due to the imposition of some instrument of trade policy as in for example a tariff on imports or an export subsidy.

Effects of a tariff on imports

A tariff is a tax on imports and can be either specific (a fixed sum per unit) or *ad valorem* (a proportion of the value imported). The effects of a specific tariff t per unit of G are now analysed, starting by considering a scenario without tariff. In this case, the price of G would be equalised at P_w in both H and F.

With the tariff, however, shippers are not willing to move G from F to H unless the H price exceeds the F price by at least t. If no G is being shipped there will be an excess demand for G in H and an excess supply in F. Thus, the H price will rise and it will fall in F until the price difference is t. The tariff raises the H price and lowers the F price. In H, producers supply more at the higher price, while consumers demand less, so that fewer imports are demanded; therefore, the producer surplus increases and the consumer surplus falls. In F, the lower price leads to a reduction in supply and an increase in demand, and thus a smaller export supply; thus, the producer surplus decreases and the consumer surplus increases. Hence, the volume of G traded declines. The increase in the H price is less than the amount of the tariff, because part of the tariff is reflected in a decline in F price and thus is not passed on to H consumers. Moreover, the government's welfare is also affected; it gains from collecting tariff revenue, which are given by t times the volume of imports.

Since the welfare gains and losses accrue to different agents, the overall cost–benefit evaluation of a tariff depends on how much consumers, producers and government are affected. In the importing country, a tariff distorts the incentives of both producers and consumers by inducing them to act as if imports were more expensive than they actually are. Since the tariff raises the domestic price above the world price, consumers reduce their consumption, which imposes a consumption distortion loss, and producers expand production, which generates a production distortion loss. Moreover, a gain in the terms of trade emerge because the tariff lowers foreign export prices; this gain relies on the ability of the tariff-imposing country to drive down foreign export

14 *Static economic models*

prices: if the country cannot affect world prices, it is then clear that the tariff reduces welfare. In country F, consumers gain because they buy more quantity of the good at a lower price, and the reverse occurs with foreign producers: they need to export the good at a higher price, being less competitive, and domestically they are forced to sell the good at a lower price. Thus, the net welfare in a foreign country is negative. In terms of the world, the gain in trade terms in H is offset by the loss in trade terms in F and the distortions in H will prevail. The imposition of a tariff has therefore negative effects on worldwide welfare.

These are the normal market and welfare results of a tariff and of any trade policy that limits imports.

Effects of an export subsidy

An export subsidy is a payment to an agent that ships a good abroad, which can also be either specific (a fixed sum per unit) or *ad valorem* (a proportion of the value exported). When the government offers an export subsidy, the effect on prices is exactly the reverse of those of a tariff: the price in the exporting country rises, but because the price in the importing country falls, the price increase is less than the subsidy. In the exporting country, consumers loss (they buy less quantity at a higher price), producers gain (they produce more at a higher price), and the government loses because it must expend money on the subsidy (the amount of exports times the amount of the subsidy). In net terms, the welfare of the exporting country is penalised; i.e. an export subsidy unambiguously leads to costs that exceed its benefits: as in the case of a tariff, consumption and production distortion arise and, in contrast to a tariff, the export subsidy worsens the terms of trade since it lowers the price of the export in the foreign market. In the Foreign importing country, consumers gain because they buy more quantity of the good at a lower price, and the reverse occurs with foreign producers. Thus, the net welfare in the Foreign country is positive. In terms of the world, now the loss in trade terms in H is offset by the gain in trade terms in F and the distortions will prevail. The imposition of a subsidy has therefore negative effects on worldwide welfare.

Numerical solution: linear systems of equations

The equilibrium solution is affected by any change in the value of either an exogenous variable or parameter. A comparative static analysis can be done by recalculating the (new) equilibrium. For the simple problem at hand, the process is also simple. However, for larger systems this process can be tedious or even impracticable if no closed form solution can be obtained. Therefore, a numerical implementation is mandatory.

The model, as defined in (1.1), is linear with respect to the endogenous variables and can therefore be defined by a system of linear equations.

Matrix representation

A system of linear equations

$$\begin{cases} a_{11}x_1 + a_{12}x_2 + \cdots + a_{1n}x_n = d_1 \\ a_{21}x_1 + a_{22}x_2 + \cdots + a_{2n}x_n = d_2 \\ \vdots \\ a_{n1}x_1 + a_{n2}x_2 + \cdots + a_{nn}x_n = d_n \end{cases}$$

can be represented in matrix form by

$$\begin{bmatrix} a_{11} & a_{12} & \cdots & a_{1n} \\ a_{21} & a_{22} & \cdots & a_{2n} \\ \vdots & \vdots & \ddots & \vdots \\ a_{n1} & a_{n2} & \cdots & a_{nn} \end{bmatrix} \times \begin{bmatrix} x_1 \\ x_2 \\ \vdots \\ x_n \end{bmatrix} = \begin{bmatrix} d_1 \\ d_2 \\ \vdots \\ d_n \end{bmatrix}$$

or in short by

$$Ax = d, \tag{1.3}$$

where A $(n \times n)$ is the coefficient matrix, x $(n \times 1)$ is the vector of unknowns and d $(n \times 1)$ is a given vector (right-hand side, rhs).

Thus for the problem in hand

$$A = \begin{bmatrix} 1 & a \\ 1 & -b \end{bmatrix}, \quad x = \begin{bmatrix} Q \\ P \end{bmatrix} \quad \text{and} \quad d = \begin{bmatrix} Q_d \\ Q_s \end{bmatrix}. \tag{1.4}$$

Gaussian elimination

In general, systems of linear equations are solved by the *Gaussian elimination method*. The basic idea is to transform the original system to an equivalently simpler one using operations that do not change the solution. These are called *elementary row operations*: (i) interchanging two equations; (ii) multiplying any equation by a nonzero scalar; (iii) adding a multiple of one equation to another. By performing these operations, zero entries can be inserted into matrix A in order to produce an upper triangular matrix U. Then, system $Ux = \overline{d}$ (note that d is also changed with these operations) can be easily solved by *back-substitution*:

$$x_n = \overline{d}_n/u_{nn}, \quad x_i = \left(\overline{d}_i - \sum_{j=i+1}^{n} u_{ij} x_j\right)\bigg/u_{ii}, \quad i = n-1, \ldots, 1.$$

16   *Static economic models*

Alternatively, one can compute a lower triangular matrix L and solve $Lx = \hat{d}$ by *forward-substitution*:

$$x_1 = \hat{d}_1/\ell_{11}, \qquad x_i = \left(\hat{d}_i - \sum_{j=1}^{i-1} \ell_{ij} x_j\right) \bigg/ \ell_{ii}, \quad i = 2, \ldots, n.$$

Gaussian elimination in practice

Using MATLAB/Octave, the solution for $Ax = d$ only requires the command A\d (*backward slash*), which performs Gaussian elimination.

The implementation of the method is, however, not straightforward, and the algorithm under *backward slash* is implemented using partial pivoting to ensure stability, and manages data efficiently in today's computers' hierarchical memory. Depending on the properties of A, different algorithms in *backward slash* are used to solve the problem. For rectangular linear systems, where the number of rows is different from the number of columns, algorithms for over(under)-determined system are used. For square systems, it distinguishes algorithms according to the data structure (for instance, sparse, band, triangular or dense matrix) and according to the type of matrix (for instance, symmetric, unsymmetrical). Some of these features will be addressed in Chapters 2 and 3.

Additional comments

If A is nonsingular (i.e. its determinant is nonzero, $|A| \neq 0$) then multiplying both sides of (1.3) by A^{-1} gives rise to the unique solution $x = A^{-1}d$. However, this is not numerically appropriate since inverting is very expensive and prone to numerical errors; in fact A^{-1} is computed as the solution of $AX = I$, where I is the identity matrix. Thus, for an $n \times n$ matrix, instead of the solution of one linear system, we are, at least theoretically, computing the solution of n systems of equations followed by a matrix vector multiplication $A^{-1}d$.

Numerical results and simulation

As a numerical example, the industry G in two countries, H (the country in the previous autarky case) and F is considered. Three cases are considered: autarky (in which a country is self-sufficient); free international trade; and restricted trade imposed by the tariff or the subsidy. The domestic equations are $\overline{Q}_{d,H} = 100$, $a_H = 20$, $\overline{Q}_{s,H} = 20$, $b_H = 20$, $\overline{Q}_{d,F} = 80$, $a_F = 20$, $\overline{Q}_{s,F} = 40$ and $b_F = 20$.

To answer this problem, consider the following supply_demand_open.m script.

```
%% Supply-demand model with trade
%  Implemented by: P.B. Vasconcelos and O. Afonso
disp('-------------------------------------------------------------');
disp('Supply-demand model with international trade policy          ');
```

```
disp('————————————————————————————————————');

%% parameters
aH = 10; bH = 5; aF = 20; bF = 25;

%% exogenous variables
Qd_barH = 1000; Qs_barH = 250; Qd_barF = 1400; Qs_barF = 500;

%% model
% solution for each country
AH = [1 aH; 1 -bH]; dH = [Qd_barH; Qs_barH]; xH = AH\dH;
AF = [1 aF; 1 -bF]; dF = [Qd_barF; Qs_barF]; xF = AF\dF;
disp('computed endogenous variables (autarky):')
fprintf('   quantity (Home), QH:       %7.2f \n', xH(1));
fprintf('   price (Home), PH:          %7.2f \n', xH(2));
fprintf('   quantity (Foreign), QF:    %7.2f \n', xF(1));
fprintf('   price (Foreign), PF:       %7.2f \n', xF(2));

% Home Import Demand and Foreign Export Supply
% HID = QdH-QsH; FES = QsF-QdF
aW = aH+bH; bW = bF+aF;
Qd_barW = Qd_barH-Qs_barH; Qs_barW = Qs_barF-Qd_barF;
A = [ 1  aW ; 1  -bW ]; d = [Qd_barW; Qs_barW];
x = A\d; QW = x(1); PW = x(2);
disp('computed endogenous variables (free international trade):')
fprintf('   quantity (World), QW:      %7.2f \n', QW);
fprintf('   price (World), PW:         %7.2f \n', PW);
QdHW = Qd_barH-aH*x(2); QsHW = Qs_barH+bH*x(2);
QdFW = Qd_barF-aF*x(2); QsFW = Qs_barF+bF*x(2);
fprintf('   Home eq. demand at PW, QdHW:    %7.2f \n', QdHW);
fprintf('   Home eq. supply at PW, QsHW:    %7.2f \n', QsHW);
fprintf('   Foreign eq. demand at PW, QdFW: %7.2f \n', QdFW);
fprintf('   Foreign eq. supply at PW, QsFW: %7.2f \n', QsFW);

%% plots
Qmax = max([xH(1),xF(1),x(1)]); Q = 0:1.5*Qmax;
Pmax = max([xH(2),xF(2),x(2)]);

% Home country
subplot(1,3,1);
plot(Q,(Qd_barH-Q)/aH,'b',Q,(Q-Qs_barH)/bH,'r—');
title('Home market');
xlabel('quantity, Q'); ylabel('price, P');
ylim([0,2*Pmax]); xlim([0,1.2*Qmax])

% World
subplot(1,3,2);
plot(Q,(Qd_barW-Q)/aW,'b',Q,(Q-Qs_barW)/bW,'r—');
title('World market');
xlabel('quantity, Q'); ylabel('price, P');
ylim([0,2*Pmax]); xlim([0,1.2*Qmax])
```

18 Static economic models

```
% foreign country
subplot(1,3,3);
plot(Q,(Qd_barF-Q)/aF,'b',Q,(Q-Qs_barF)/bF,'r—');
title('Foreign market');
xlabel('quantity, Q'); ylabel('price, P');
ylim([0,2*Pmax]); xlim([0,1.2*Qmax])
```

The output is as follows.

```
-----------------------------------------------------
Supply-demand model with international trade policy
-----------------------------------------------------
computed endogenous variables (autarky):
    quantity (Home), QH:                    500.00
    price (Home), PH:                        50.00
    quantity (Foreign), QF:                1000.00
    price (Foreign), PF:                     20.00
computed endogenous variables
        (free international trade):
    quantity (World), QW:                   337.50
    price (World), PW:                       27.50
    Home eq. demand at PW, QdHW:            725.00
    Home eq. supply at PW, QsHW:            387.50
    Foreign eq. demand at PW, QdFW:         850.00
    Foreign eq. supply at PW, QsFW:        1187.50
```

Figure 1.4 displays the supply and demand curves for all markets. By solving the system for each country in autarky, the results are that the price of G is higher in H, $P_H = 50$, than in F, $P_F = 20$. Hence, there are conditions to establish international trade, since, under free trade, the worldwide price, P_W, is given by 27.50: H is the importing country and F is the exporting country. With international trade, the quantity demanded by H is higher (725 units vs 500 units in autarky) while the quantity produced is smaller (387.5 units vs 500 units in autarky). The excess of 337.5 units produced in F is exported to H and the worldwide equilibrium is attained.

The equilibrium in the presence of international trade is represented in Figure 1.4: 337.5 units of G are traded on the world market at price 27.50; at this price, the excess demanded by H consumers coincide with the excess supplied by F producers. For a price below (above) 27.50, H consumers want to import more (less) quantity than F producers are willing to export.

In the next two subsections, the structure of the industry G market in terms of equilibrium price and quantity (market effects) and agents' welfare (welfare analysis) with free trade and restricted trade are studied. The first instrument considered is the tariff, used by the importing country to protect domestic producers and increase public revenues, while the second is the export subsidies, used by the exporting country to provide incentive to exports.

Supply and demand model 19

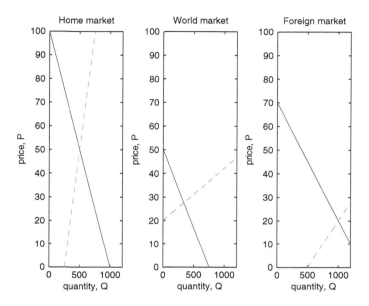

Figure 1.4 Supply and demand curves for all markets.

Free trade vs restricted trade: tariff

H, as an importing country, imposes a (specific) tariff to limit imports to 250. The program determines the effects on the structure of both markets and on agents' welfare.

```
%% Supply-demand model with a tariff to international trade
%  Implemented by: P.B. Vasconcelos and O. Afonso
clc; clear; supply_demand_open;

disp('——————————————————————————————————');
disp('Supply-demand with international trade policy   ');
disp('                    tariff'                     );
disp('——————————————————————————————————');

% H limits imports to 250 units
Qt = 250;
fprintf('H limits imports to %d units\n', Qt);
PHt = ((Qd_barH-Qs_barH)-Qt)/(aH+bH);
PFt = (Qt-(Qs_barF-Qd_barF))/(aF+bF);
tariff = PHt-PFt;

%% new H and F for Qs and Qd
QdHt = Qd_barH-aH*PHt;  QsHt = Qs_barH+bH*PHt;
QdFt = Qd_barF-aF*PFt;  QsFt = Qs_barF+bF*PFt;
disp('computed endogenous variables (tariff): ')
fprintf('    Home price, PHt:              %7.2f \n', PHt);
```

20 *Static economic models*

```
fprintf('    Foreign price, PFt:           %7.2f \n', PFt);
fprintf('    tariff:                       %7.2f \n', tariff);
fprintf('    Home quantity demanded, QdHt: %7.2f \n', QdHt);
fprintf('    Home quantity supplied, QsHt: %7.2f \n', QsHt);
fprintf('    Foreign quantity demanded, QdFt: %7.2f \n', QdFt);
fprintf('    Foreign quantity demanded, QsFt: %7.2f \n', QsFt);

%% surplus computations at H and F
CSH_var =  -(PHt-PW)*QdHt-(PHt-PW)*(QdHW-QdHt)/2;
PSH_var =   (PHt-PW)*QsHW+(PHt-PW)*(QsHt-QsHW)/2;
TAX_var =   (PHt-PFt)*(QdHt-QsHt);
WH_var  =   CSH_var+PSH_var+TAX_var;
CSF_var =   (PW-PFt)*QdFt-(PW-PFt)*(QdFt-QdFW)/2;
PSF_var =  -(PW-PFt)*QsFW+(PW-PFt)*(QsFW-QsFt)/2;
WF_var  =   CSF_var+PSF_var;
disp('computed welfare variation:')
fprintf('    Home, WH_var:                 %7.2f \n', WH_var);
fprintf('    Foreign, WF_var:              %7.2f \n', WF_var);

%% plots

% Home country
subplot(1,3,1); hold on;
% ... effect of the terms of trade gain in the welfare
%     (QsHt,PFt), (QsHt,PW), (QdHt,PW), (QdHt,PFt)
fill([QsHt,QsHt,QdHt,QdHt],[PFt,PW,PW,PFt],'g');
% ... effect of the distortion in production in the welfare
%     (QsHW,PW), (QsHt,PHt), (QsHt,PW)
fill([QsHW,QsHt,QsHt],[PW,PHt,PW],'m');
% ... effect of the distortion in consumption in the welfare
%     (QdHt,PW), (QdHt,PHt), (QdHW,PW)
fill([QdHt,QdHt,QdHW],[PW,PHt,PW],'m');
ylim([15,55]); hold off;

% World
subplot(1,3,2); hold on; ylim([15,55]); hold off;

% Foreign country
subplot(1,3,3); hold on;
% ... effect of the terms of trade loss in the welfare
%     (QdFt,PFt), (QdFW,PW), (QsFW,PW), (QsFt,PFt)
fill([QdFt,QdFW,QsFW,QsFt],[PFt,PW,PW,PFt],'m');
ylim([15,55]); xlim([500,1500]); hold off;
```

The output is as follows.

```
--------------------------------------------------------
Supply-demand model with international trade policy
                       tariff
--------------------------------------------------------
H limits imports to 250 units
computed endogenous variables (tariff):
```

```
Home price, PHt:                           33.33
Foreign price, PFt:                        25.56
tariff:                                     7.78
Home quantity demanded, QdHt:             666.67
Home quantity supplied, QsHt:             416.67
Foreign quantity demanded, QdFt:          888.89
Foreign quantity demanded, QsFt:         1138.89
computed welfare variation:
Home, WH_var:                             230.90
Foreign, WF_var:                         -571.18
```

Figure 1.5 displays the supply and demand curves, with tariff, for all markets.

The tariff is 7.78 and, as expected from the theory, when compared with the free trade case, it raises the price of G in the importing country H from 27.50 to 33.33 and lowers it in the exporting country F from 27.5 to 25.56: the difference in prices between the countries is the amount of the tariff. As a result, the quantity traded between H and F decreases by $337.5 - 250 = 87.50$ units. In terms of welfare, consumers in H lose and gain in F, whereas producers gain in H and lose in F; the government in H gains the tariff × imports ($7.78 \times 250 = 1945$). In this case, the net effects on welfare of H agents are positive at the level 230.90, which means that the gain in the terms of trade offsets the costs associated with the distortions in production and consumption. As expected, the net effects on welfare of F agents are negative in the amount of

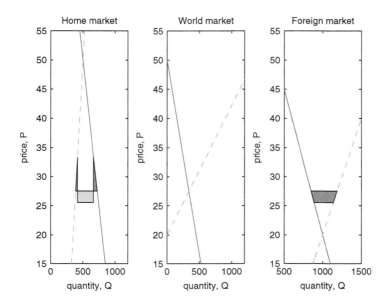

Figure 1.5 Supply and demand curves, with tariff, for all markets.

22 Static economic models

−571.18. Hence, the total impact of the tariff in worldwide welfare is negative, which represents the distortions in *H* production and consumption: producers produce more than the optimal, while consumers demand less than the optimal.

Free trade vs restricted trade: export subsidies

Consider a (specific) subsidy imposed by *F* in order to export 400 units. A new code is now developed which is similar to the previous one.

```
%% Supply-demand model with a subsidy to exports
%  Implemented by: P.B. Vasconcelos and O. Afonso
clc; clear; supply_demand_open;

disp('——————————————————————————————');
disp('Supply-demand model with international trade policy:    ');
disp('                        subsidy'                         );
disp('——————————————————————————————');

% F applies a subsidy to exports to trade of 400 units
Qs  = 400;
fprintf('F applies a subsidy to exports to trade of %d units\n', Qs);
PHs = ((Qd_barH-Qs_barH)-Qs)/(aH+bH);
PFs = (Qs-(Qs_barF-Qd_barF))/(aF+bF);

%% new H and F for Qs and Qd
QdHs = Qd_barH-aH*PHs;  QsHs = Qs_barH+bH*PHs;
QdFs = Qd_barF-aF*PFs;  QsFs = Qs_barF+bF*PFs;
subsidy = PFs-PHs;
disp('computed endogenous variables (subsidy):')
fprintf('    Home price , PHs:               %7.2f \n', PHs);
fprintf('    Foreign price , PFs:            %7.2f \n', PFs);
fprintf('    subsidy:                        %7.2f \n', subsidy);
fprintf('    Home quantity demanded, QdHs:   %7.2f \n', QdHs);
fprintf('    Home quantity supplied , QsHs:  %7.2f \n', QsHs);
fprintf('    Foreign quantity demanded, QdFs:%7.2f \n', QdFs);
fprintf('    Foreign quantity demanded, QsFs:%7.2f \n', QsFs);

%% surplus computations at H and F
CSF_var = -(PFs-PW)*QdFs-(PFs-PW)*(QdFW-QdFs)/2;
PSF_var =  (PFs-PW)*QsFW+(PFs-PW)*(QsFs-QsFW)/2;
SUB_var = -(PFs-PHs)*(QsFs-QdFs);
WF_var  = CSF_var+PSF_var+SUB_var;
CSH_var =  (PW-PHs)*QdHW+(PW-PHs)*(QdHs-QdHW)/2;
PSH_var = -(PW-PHs)*QsHs-(PW-PHs)*(QsHW-QsHs)/2;
WH_var  = CSF_var+PSF_var;
disp('computed welfare variation:')
fprintf('    Home, WH_var:                   %7.2f \n', WH_var);
fprintf('    Foreign , WF_var:               %7.2f \n', WF_var);

%% plots

% Home country
subplot(1,3,1); hold on;
```

Supply and demand model 23

```
%  ...  effect  of  the  terms  of  trade  gain  in  the  welfare
%       (QsHs,PHs),  (QsHW,PW),  (QdHW,PW),  (QdHs,PHs)
fill ([QsHs,QsHW,QdHW,QdHs],[PHs,PW,PW,PHs],'g');
ylim ([15,75]);  hold  off;

% World
subplot(1,3,2);  hold  on;  ylim ([15,75]);  hold  off;

% Foreign  country
subplot(1,3,3);  hold  on;
%  ...  effect  of  the  distortion  in  consumption  in  the  welfare
%       (QdFs,PW),  (QdFs,PFs),  (QdFW,PW)
fill ([QdFs,QdFs,QdFW],[PW,PFs,PW],'m');
%  ...  effect  of  the  distortion  in  production  in  the  welfare
%       (QsFW,PW),  (QsFs,PFs),  (QsFs,PW)
fill ([QsFW,QsFs,QsFs],[PW,PFs,PW],'m');
%  ...  effect  of  the  terms  of  trade  loss  in  the  welfare
%       (QdFs,PHs),  (QdFs,PW),  (QsFs,PW),  (QsFs,PHs)
fill ([QdFs,QdFs,QsFs,QsFs],[PHs,PW,PW,PHs],'r');
ylim ([15,75]);  xlim ([500,1500]);  hold  off;
```

The output is as follows.

```
--------------------------------------------------------
Supply-demand model with international trade policy
                    subsidy
--------------------------------------------------------
F applies a subsidy to exports to trade of 400 units
computed endogenous variables (subsidy):
    Home price, PHs:                        23.33
    Foreign price, PFs:                     28.89
    subsidy:                                 5.56
    Home quantity demanded, QdHs:          766.67
    Home quantity supplied, QsHs:          366.67
    Foreign quantity demanded, QdFs:       822.22
    Foreign quantity demanded, QsFs:      1222.22
computed welfare variation:
    Home, WH_var:                          512.15
    Foreign, WF_var:                     -1710.07
```

Figure 1.6 displays the supply and demand curves, with subsidy, for all markets.

The subsidy required is 5.56 and its effects on prices are the reverse of the tariff. In the H equilibrium, price decreases from 27.5 to 23.33 and in the F equilibrium, price increases from 27.5 to 28.89. The difference in price between the countries is the level of the subsidy. In quantities, the amount of G traded between countries increases from 337.50 to 400 units. In terms of welfare, in the exporting country F consumers lose utility and producers gain;

24 *Static economic models*

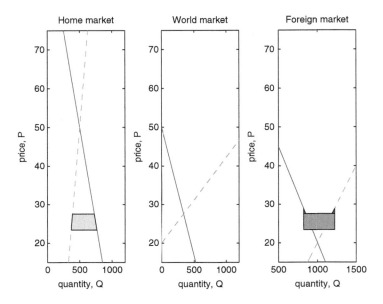

Figure 1.6 Supply and demand curves, with subsidy, for all markets.

government loses subsidy × exports $(5.56 \times 400 = 2224)$. In the importing country H, consumers benefit and producers lose. In net terms, F agents lose -1710.07 and H agents gain the amount of 512.15. Hence, the total impact in worldwide welfare is negative. This numerical example shows that export subsidies unambiguously lead to costs that exceed the benefits.

Highlights

- The supply–demand model provides a practical and simple explanation of how markets work.
- In competitive markets, the model allows for the determination of price and quantity traded, along with the social welfare.
- The framework is extended to consider international trade policy; the effects of a tariff to imports and of a subsidy to exports are analysed.
- This chapter introduces the Gaussian elimination method for the solution of a system of linear equations.

Problems and computer exercises

1. Consider the basic supply–demand model in autarky. Analyse numerically the implications for the new equilibrium price and quantity, for the new consumer surplus and producer surplus, from:

    (a) an increase of exogenous demand value to 1250;

(b) an increase of exogenous supply to 500;
   (c) a combination of both the previous shocks.
2. In autarky, assume a legal minimum price of 60 defined by the government.
   (a) What is the excess of supply?
   (b) What are the implications if the government sets a legal maximum price of 60?
3. Consider the model with trade. With respect to market effects, analyse numerically the implications for the new equilibrium prices and quantities resulting from:
   (a) an increase of exogenous demand value in H to 1250;
   (b) an increases of exogenous supply in H to 500;
   (c) a combination of both the previous shocks.
4. In trade, assume that country H wants to import only 200 units. Analyse numerically the implications for the new tariff, market and welfare effects in both countries. Comment on the results.
5. Again in trade, assume that country F aims to export 500 units. Analyse numerically the implications for the new subsidy, market and welfare effects in both countries. Comment on the results.

2 IS–LM model in a closed economy

Introduction

The standard *IS–LM model, Investment Saving–Liquidity preference Money supply*, is a macroeconomic set-up that illustrates the relationship between real output (production) and interest rates in the goods and services market (IS side) and in the money market (LM side). When the IS curve crosses the LM curve the equilibrium is achieved.

In this model the economy is described by static equations, where generally it is assumed that prices are fixed and where the relationships between aggregate variables such as production, consumption, investment, government/public spending and money supply are well established. It is a business cycle model based on the assumption that there are barriers to the instantaneous adjustment of nominal prices. Hence, purely monetary disturbances and/or governmental policies affect variables like production, interest rate, consumption and investment.

In this chapter, MATLAB/Octave is used to solve the model in closed the economy (autarky case). The analysis is based on the IS–LM model presented in the seminal books by Romer (2006, ch. 5), Barro (2008, ch. 6), Mankiw (2009, ch. 9–11), Burda and Wyplosz (2009, ch. 10), Carlin and Soskice (2006, ch. 1) and Gordon (2011, ch. 3–5). The numerical method used for the solution of the problem is the well known Gauss elimination, and the description follows the preeminent works by Golub and Van Loan (1996, ch. 3), Demmel (1997, ch. 2) and Dahlquist and Björck (2008, ch. 1).

Economic model

The set-up of the typical IS–LM model specifies relationships among aggregate variables. Such a simple model can be used to study the effect of changes either in policy variables or in the specification of the interaction between endogenous variables.

A general description of the relationships between variables permits us to get qualitative results; for example, both consumption and investment increase

IS–LM model in a closed economy 27

with increased supply of money. Nevertheless, usually it is interesting to obtain quantitative results, to access both the path and the level of the effects. In order to do so, mathematical forms of the interaction across variables must be specified.

Variables, parameters and functional forms

In this version of the model, the standard equations that characterise the economy are:

- product equals aggregate demand, $Y = C + I + G$;
- consumption function, $C = \overline{C} + c(Y - T)$;
- investment function, $I = \overline{I} - bR$;
- public spending function, $G = \overline{G}$;
- income taxes function, $T = \overline{T}$;
- monetary equilibrium, $\overline{M}/\overline{P} = kY - hR$;
- money supply function, $M = \overline{M}$; and
- price level function, $P = \overline{P}$.

The endogenous variables are: product, Y; consumption, C; investment, I; and interest rate, R.

The exogenous variables are: government/public spending, $\overline{G}$; independent/autonomous consumption, $\overline{C}$; independent/autonomous investment, $\overline{I}$; income taxes, $\overline{T}$; money supply, $\overline{M}$; price level (fixed), $\overline{P}$.

In the functional forms above, c, b, k and h are parameters: c is the constant proportion of current disposable income that is consumed (or propensity to consume), $0 < c < 1$; $b > 0$ is the interest sensitivity of investment; $k > 0$ is the output sensitivity of the demand for money; and $h > 0$ is the interest sensitivity of the demand for money.

IS curve: goods and services market equilibrium

The *IS curve* shows the continuum of combinations of the interest and production level at which there is equilibrium in the goods and services market; i.e. the aggregate demand for goods and services equals the supply, $Y_d = Y$. Thus, taking into consideration the functional forms above, the IS curve is given by

$$Y = \frac{1}{1-c}(\overline{C} + \overline{I} + \overline{G} - c\overline{T} - bR). \qquad (2.1)$$

The use of a computational approach eliminates this explicit resolution, requiring only the equations of the set-up. In terms of additional comments concerning (2.1), considering a reference system where the output Y and the

28　*Static economic models*

interest rate R are represented by respectively in the x-axis and in the y-axis, the following can be stated.

- The position of the IS curve is affected by any factor that changes the position of (the line) $\overline{C} + \overline{I} + \overline{G}$; for example, the IS curve shifts to the right (left) when one of these elements increases (decreases).
- The slope of the IS curve is negative $\partial Y/\partial R < 0$, since $0 < 1 - c < 1$ ($1/(1-c)$ is the *Keynesian multiplier*); that is, to maintain goods and services market equilibrium, R and Y vary in the opposite direction. It is influenced by both the propensity to consume, c, and the interest sensitivity of investment, b. For example, a rise in c makes the IS curve flatter (it rotates counter-clockwise from the intercept on the vertical axis). Also, any change in b will lead to a consequent change in the slope of the IS curve, where a less interest-elastic investment function will be reflected in a steeper curve.
- Points on the left (right) side of the IS curve mean that there is excess demand (supply) for goods and services.

LM curve: money-market equilibrium

In the monetary–financial market there is a wide range of assets: money, commercial paper, bonds, and so on. For simplicity only two types of assets are considered: money (currency in circulation – notes and coins – and available deposits in banks) and the remaining ones. Both types evaluate wealth, but only money can be immediately used; however, money does not generate interest (or generates a very low level of interest).

The LM curve focuses on the denominated monetary (or money) market. However, it is easy to check that the equilibrium in one segment (e.g. in the money market) guarantees equilibrium in the other (e.g. the financial market).

The supply of money, $M_s = \overline{M}$, is considered a policy instrument, whose desired level the central bank can define exactly. In real terms, it is given by $M_s/P = \overline{M}/\overline{P}$. On the other hand, the demand for money, $kY - hR$, depends positively on Y to realise transactions and negatively on R due to the opportunity cost; thus, it is related with Y real and with R nominal.

As in any market, equilibrium requires equality between supply and demand; the *LM curve* shows the continuum of combinations of the interest and output level at which there is equilibrium in the money market (and, consequently of the financial/bonds market). Taking into consideration the functional forms above

$$\frac{\overline{M}}{\overline{P}} = kY - hR \qquad (2.2)$$

is the expression for the LM curve.

Additionally, the following can be stated.

- The position of the LM curve depends on $\overline{M}$ and $\overline{P}$; i.e. on $\overline{M}/\overline{P}$; *ceteris paribus*, an increase (decrease) in the money supply will shift the LM curve to the right (left).
- It has positive slope $\partial Y / \partial R > 0$; to maintain money market equilibrium, R and Y vary in the same direction. The slope is influenced by both the interest sensitivity of the asset demand for money, $h \equiv \partial L / \partial R > 0$, and for output, $k \equiv \partial L / \partial Y > 0$.
- Points in the left (right) side of the LM curve mean the existence of excess money supply (demand) or, in other words, excess bonds demand (supply).

Putting the IS and the LM curves together

To sum up, there is equilibrium in the goods and services market when the combination (Y, R) belongs to the IS curve (2.1) and in the money market when the combination (Y, R) belongs to the LM curve (2.2).

Hence, the global equilibrium interest rate and level of output will be determined by the intersection of both curves:

$$Y^* = \frac{\frac{h}{h+\frac{bk}{1-c}}}{1-c}\left(\overline{C}+\overline{I}+\overline{G}-c\overline{T}\right) + \frac{b}{(1-c)\left(h+\frac{bk}{1-c}\right)}\frac{\overline{M}}{\overline{P}},$$

$$R^* = -\frac{1}{h}\frac{\overline{M}}{\overline{P}} + \frac{k}{h}Y.$$

Regarding the points away from the global equilibrium, it is possible to state the following.

- Imbalance in the goods and services market occurs when there exists involuntary investment (as a result firms adjust production, thus changing Y).
- Imbalance in the money market provokes a pressure for interest rate adjustment.

It is easy to reach the analytical solution in this simple economic model; indeed, it does not require many mathematical considerations, just like the model in the previous chapter. However, any change in the value of one exogenous variable requires new evaluation of the analytical expression (which can be laborious). Through numerical implementation, shocks can be easily accommodated without requiring the analytical expressions for the curves.

Numerical solution: linear systems of equations

In the previous chapter a brief explanation of Gaussian elimination, which reduces a square matrix A $(n \times n)$ to an upper triangular matrix U, was

Static economic models

provided. Further and in depth details will now be presented, in particular sensitivity issues.

LU factorisation

To eliminate all entries below the *k*th position of the *k*th column-vector in matrix A, the product $M_k A$ is performed, where

$$M_k = \begin{bmatrix} 1 & \cdots & 0 & 0 & \cdots & 0 \\ \vdots & \ddots & \vdots & \vdots & \ddots & \vdots \\ 0 & \cdots & 1 & 0 & \cdots & 0 \\ 0 & \cdots & -\dfrac{a_{k+1\,k}}{a_{kk}} & 1 & \cdots & 0 \\ \vdots & \ddots & \vdots & \vdots & \ddots & \vdots \\ 0 & \cdots & -\dfrac{a_{nk}}{a_{kk}} & 0 & \cdots & 1 \end{bmatrix};$$

M_k is called the *elementary elimination matrix* (a lower triangular matrix), a_{kk} is called the *pivot*, and a_{ik}/a_{kk}, $i = k+1, \ldots, n$, are called the *multipliers*. Applying this procedure to all columns in A and multiplying both sides of $Ax = d$ (1.3) by nonsingular matrices M_j, $j = 1, \ldots, n-1$, the resulting system

$$MAx = Md,$$

where $M = M_{n-1} \cdots M_2 M_1$, can be cheaply solved by back-substitution. Noting that the inverse of each one of the matrices M_k is still lower triangular and nonsingular, let $L_k = M_k^{-1}$. Since the matrices are the same except the signs of the multipliers are reversed and the product of lower triangular matrices preserves the form, let $L = M^{-1} = M_1^{-1} \cdots M_{n-1}^{-1}$. Finally, since $MA = U$, the *LU factorisation* of A

$$A = LU \qquad (2.3)$$

is obtained, where L is unit lower triangular. To compute $Ax = d$, two triangular systems of equations, $Uy = d$ and $Lx = y$, are solved. The factorisation is independent of the right-hand side, and thus the same factorisation can be reused to solve linear systems for different values of d.

A problem occurs if the pivot element is zero. In this case one must apply a row interchange between row k and any row i, $i > k$, having a nonzero entry in column k (previously computed zero entries in columns $1, \ldots, k-1$ are kept unchanged). If all entries a_{ik}, $i = k+1, \ldots, n$, are zero, then U is singular. Moreover, to minimise the propagation error, one should choose for the pivot the element a_{ik}, $i = k, \ldots, n$, with the largest magnitude; as a consequence, all multipliers will be less than or equal to 1. This process is called *partial pivoting* and allows for a stable implementation of Gaussian elimination. A matrix performing a row interchange, *permutation matrix*, between rows i and j has the form of an identity matrix with rows i and j permuted. Letting $P = P_{n-1} \cdots P_2 P_1$,

$$PA = LU. \qquad (2.4)$$

LU factorisation in practice

Using MATLAB/Octave to factorise A as the product of L and U factors in (2.3) only requires the command `[L,U]=lu(A)` (note that L is the product of a lower triangular matrix with the appropriate permutation matrix) or the command `[L,U,P]=lu(A)` to compute the factors in (2.4); to obtain the solution for x just write, respectively, `x=U\(L\d)` and `x=U\(L\P*d)`.

Additional comments

As already stated, LU factorisation with partial pivoting is a numerically stable method. Nevertheless, an even more stable version can be achieved with complete pivoting, which applies the pivoting mechanism also to columns. However, this strategy is expensive; in practice, partial pivoting is usually adequate.

Pivoting avoids magnifying small errors, contributing to ensure the stability of the LU factorisation. On the other hand there is the *condition number* $cond(A) = \|A\| \|A^{-1}\| \geq 1$, which measures the sensitivity of the solution of the system of equations $Ax = d$ to errors in the data. The condition number yields the following error bounds: $\|\Delta x\|/\|x\| \leq cond(A) \|\Delta d\|/\|d\|$ and $\|\Delta x\|/\|x\| \leq cond(A) \|\Delta A\|/\|A\|$, for (small) perturbations Δd on d and ΔA on A. Small perturbations on d and/or A only produce small perturbations on the solution for small condition numbers. The lower the condition number the better.

Wrong solutions can result from the use of unstable algorithms for well-conditioned data or from the use of a stable algorithm for ill-conditioned data. In practice, type `cond(A)` or `cond(A,p)` for, respectively, the 2-norm and the p−norm condition number of matrix A.

Computational implementation

Here the script islm.m with the code to solve the problem is presented. The following baseline values are considered: $\overline{C} = 55$, $c = 0.63$, $\overline{I} = 75$, $b = 1500$, $k = 0.6$, $h = 2700$, $\overline{G} = 200$, $\overline{M} = 200$, $\overline{T} = 110$ and $\overline{P} = 1$.

MATLAB/Octave code

```
%% IS–LM model
%  A Closed Economy in the short−medium run
%  Implemented by: P.B. Vasconcelos and O. Afonso
```

32 Static economic models

```
disp('————————————————————————————————————————');
disp('IS–LM model: closed economy                                   ');
disp('————————————————————————————————————————');

%% parameters
c = 0.63;     % marginal propensity to consume
b = 1500;     % sensibility of the investment to the interest rate
k = 0.6;      % sensibility of the money demand to the product
h = 2700;     % sensibility of the money demand to the interest rate

%% exogenous variables
C_bar = 55;   % autonomous consumption
I_bar = 75;   % autonomous investment
G_bar = 200;  % government spending
T_bar = 110;  % tax on income
M_bar = 200;  % money supply
P_bar = 1;    % price level (fixed in the short-run)
disp('policy exogenous variables:')
fprintf('G = %d; T = %d; M = %d \n',G_bar,T_bar,M_bar);

%% endogenous variables
%  Y, product
%  C, consumption
%  I, investment
%  R, interest rate

%% matrix representation of the model: Ax=d
% A, coefficient matrix
%       Y   C   I   R
A = [  1  -1  -1   0    % Y=C+I+G
      -c   1   0   0    % C=C_bar+c(Y-T)
       0   0   1   b    % I=I_bar-bR
       k   0   0  -h];  % M/P=kY-hR
% x = [Y;C;I;R], vector of the endogeneous variables
% d, vector of the exogeneous variables
d = [G_bar; C_bar-c*T_bar; I_bar; M_bar/P_bar];

%% compute the endogenous variables
[L,U] = lu(A);  % LU factorization
x = U\(L\d);    % solution of the linear system

%% show the solution
disp('computed endogenous variables:')
fprintf('    product, Y:           %6.2f \n', x(1));
fprintf('    consumption, C:       %6.2f \n', x(2));
fprintf('    investment, I:        %6.2f \n', x(3));
fprintf('    interest rate (%%), R: %7.2f \n', x(4)*100);

%% plot the solution: IS–LM diagram (R against Y)
%  generate a grid on Y; in this case, since this is a line
%  only 2 points would have been required
Y = 0.95*x(1):1.05*x(1);
%  IS: I=Y–C–G and I=I_bar–bR expressed in terms of R
```

```
C = C_bar+c*(Y-T_bar);  I=Y-C-G_bar;  IS=(I_bar-I)/b;
% LM:  M_bar/P_bar=kY-hR  expressed  in  terms  of R
LM = 1/h*(k*Y-M_bar/P_bar);
plot(Y,IS,'—b',Y,LM,'r')
title('IS and LM curves');  legend('IS','LM');
xlabel('product, Y');  ylabel('interest rate, R');
```

Some short comments on the code

The code is written in the `islm.m` file. It begins by providing information about its purpose, and by assigning parameters and exogenous variables ($\overline{G}$, $\overline{T}$ and $\overline{M}$). The coefficient matrix A, according to the order of the endogenous variables in x, and the right-hand side vector d are built. The solution x is computed, using LU factorisation, and its components are shown. Finally, the IS–LM diagram is drawn.

Numerical results and simulation

The output is presented here, and Figure 2.1 displays the IS–LM diagram.

```
-----------------------------------------------------
IS-LM model: closed economy
-----------------------------------------------------
exogenous variables:
G = 200; T = 110; M = 200; P = 1
computed endogenous variables:
    product, Y:            528.64
    consumption, C:        318.74
    investment, I:           9.90
    interest rate (%), R:    4.34
```

Now it is intended to assess the results of shocks on the economy; as already stated, these shocks are performed on the exogenous variables. For that just change the vector d followed by a new call to the solver A\d. In order to overlap the curves from the baseline model with those resulting from the shock, the `hold` plot enhancement command is used. Let us now evaluate the result of some shocks on the output, interest rate, consumption and investment.

1. Consider the implementation of a fiscal policy where the government/public authorities decide to decrease taxes from 110 to 100.
   The code is as follows.

```
% T decreases 10

   islm  % reproduce baseline model
   T_bar = T_bar-10; % perform shock
   d = [G_bar; C_bar-c*T_bar; I_bar; M_bar/P_bar];
   fprintf('shock: new value for T = %6.2f \n',T_bar);
```

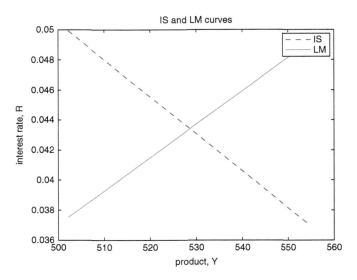

Figure 2.1 IS–LM diagram.

```
% compute new solution
xnew = U\(L\d);
disp ('new computed endogenous variables:')
fprintf('     product, Y:           %6.2f \n', xnew(1));
fprintf('     consumption, C:       %6.2f \n', xnew(2));
fprintf('     investment, I:        %6.2f \n', xnew(3));
fprintf('     interest rate (%%), R: %7.2f \n', xnew(4)*100);

% plot the solution: IS–LM diagram
Y = 0.95*xnew(1):1.05*xnew(1);
C = C_bar+c*(Y-T_bar); I = Y-C-G_bar; IS = (I_bar-I)/b;
LM = 1/h*(k*Y-M_bar/P_bar);
hold on; % to freeze baseline islm plot
plot(Y,IS,'—b','LineWidth',3);
plot(Y,LM,'  r','LineWidth',3);
legend('IS','LM','new IS','new LM');
T_bar = T_bar+10; hold off; % reset
```

The output is as follows.

```
shock: new value for T = 100.00
new computed endogenous variables:
    product, Y:           537.60
    consumption, C:       330.69
    investment, I:          6.91
    interest rate (%), R:   4.54
```

IS–LM model in a closed economy 35

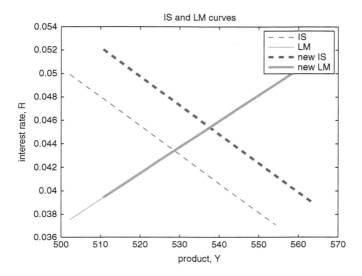

Figure 2.2 Decrease in T.

As expected, this shock increases the available income, thus increasing both consumption and output. The shift of the IS curve to the right (Figure 2.2) negatively affects the level of investment due to the increase of the interest rate. Note that the previously computed L and U factors are reused since only d changed with the shock and the solution for the endogenous variables can be obtained at the cost of two triangular solves.

2. Next consider a fiscal policy where the government/public authorities decide to increase public spending from 200 to 210.

```
shock: new value for G = 210.00
new computed endogenous variables:
    product, Y:              542.86
    consumption, C:          327.70
    investment, I:             5.16
    interest rate (%), R:      4.66
```

This increase in public spending affects the output directly, shifting the IS curve to the right (Figure 2.3). The additional resources increase consumption but the investment decreases since the effect on the interest rate dominates.

3. Lastly, consider a monetary policy in which monetary authorities decide to decrease the money supply from 200 to 180.

```
shock: new value for M = 180.00
```

36 Static economic models

```
new computed endogenous variables:
   product, Y:              512.84
   consumption, C:          308.79
   investment, I:             4.05
   interest rate (%), R:      4.73
```

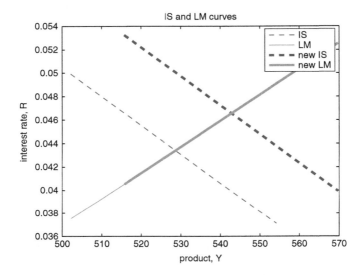

Figure 2.3 Increase in G.

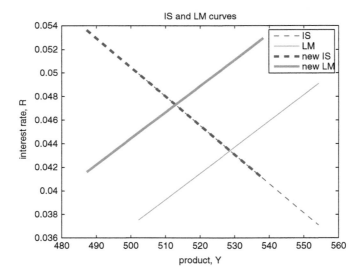

Figure 2.4 Decrease in M.

If M decreases, the LM curve goes to the left (Figure 2.4). In this context, the output decreases and the interest rate increases. Less resources have a negative impact on consumption. In turn, a higher interest rate has a negative effect on investment.

Highlights

- The IS–LM model, embodying Keynes' view, was developed in 1937 by the Nobel Laureate of 1972, John Hicks.
- The model allows us to study the effects of different fiscal and monetary policies on output and interest rates, as well as on consumption and investment.
- LU factorisation, as part of the solution of systems of linear equations, is introduced along with the notion of stability and conditioning. Stability measures the quality of the algorithm with respect to the problem whereas conditioning is a measure on the data with respect to the problem where the data is going to take part.

Problems and computer exercises

1. Display the Keynesian cross for the baseline parameters at the current equilibrium interest rate; that is, make a plot with Y on the horizontal axis and $C + I + G$, the planned expenditure, on the vertical axis; then include a 45° line in which effective and planned expenditures are equal.
2. Suppose that the government increases its spending by 10 and that the resulting deficit is covered by additional taxes. How much do output, consumption, investment and interest rate change to achieve a new equilibrium? (Note that the budget, B, is given by $B = T - G$.)
3. Repeat the previous exercise by considering that the government increases its transfers to consumers, TR, keeping $B = 0$ (note that now the budget B is given by $B = T - G - TR$). Compare the results.
4. Suppose that the government increases its spending by 10 and that the resulting budget deficit is financed by borrowing from the public.

   (a) How does the increase in government spending influence production?
   (b) How do the curves move in the IS–LM diagram?
   (c) Does the equilibrium change depend on the level of government spending?

5. Suppose that the money supply increases by 10. Analyse numerically the effects and explain how the monetary transmission mechanism works.

3 IS–LM model in an open economy

Introduction

In this chapter the IS–LM model is extended to a scenario of an open economy, with home and foreign countries, which may consider either: (i) perfect or imperfect capital mobility; or (ii) flexible or fixed exchange rate regime.

Through this model, the effects of both fiscal and monetary policies can also be analysed, but now in a setting of an open economy.

The model is based on the original version proposed by Fleming (1962) and Mundell (1963). Further insights can be obtained, for example, in Mankiw (2009, ch. 12), Burda and Wyplosz (2009, ch. 11), and Gordon (2011, ch. 7). The numerical methods follow Kelley (1995, ch. 1), Demmel (1997, ch. 6) and Saad (2003, ch. 4, 6, 7).

Economic model

In the proposed model, both economies are described by static equations of the standard IS–LM model, where generally: (i) prices are fixed; (ii) the relationships between aggregate variables – production, consumption, investment, government/public spending, exports, imports and money supply – are established; (iii) there is international mobility of assets as well as of goods and services, which must be paid in the country's currency; (iv) there is an exchange market; and (v) imports of one country are the exports of the other. This makes the model a very simplistic version of the IS–LM model in an open economy.

Moreover, as in the standard case, the net exports (i.e. exports minus imports) of the home country decrease with its own production, but rise with foreign, f, country's production. An increasing real exchange rate, which deteriorates the terms of trade, has negative effects on net exports. Due to the assumption of perfect capital mobility and bearing also in mind that agents do not expect changes in the exchange rate, the equilibrium interest rate must be equal in both countries. Otherwise, it would be profitable to borrow money in the country with the lowest interest rate and lend money in the other.

Variables, parameters and functional forms

In this version of the model, the general equations that characterise the economy(ies) are:

- product equals aggregate demand at home and foreign countries

$$Y = C + I + G + NX; \qquad Y_f = C_f + I_f + G_f + NX_f;$$

- consumption functions

$$C = \overline{C} + c(Y - T); \qquad C_f = \overline{C}_f + c_f(Y_f - T_f);$$

- investment functions

$$I = \overline{I} - bR; \qquad I_f = \overline{I}_f - b_f R_f;$$

- public spending functions

$$G = \overline{G}; \qquad G_f = \overline{G}_f;$$

- income tax functions

$$T = \overline{T}; \qquad T_f = \overline{T}_f;$$

- net exports

$$NX = \overline{NX} - j(Y - Y_f) + lE\frac{\overline{P}_f}{\overline{P}}; \qquad NX = -NX_f;$$

- monetary equilibrium

$$\frac{\overline{M}}{\overline{P}} = kY - hR; \qquad \frac{\overline{M}_f}{\overline{P}_f} = k_f Y_f - h_f R_f;$$

- interest rates

$$R = R_f.$$

The endogenous variables at home and abroad are respectively: product, Y and Y_f; consumption, C and C_f; investment, I and I_f; net exports, NX and NX_f; exchange rate (real and nominal, since prices are fixed) in terms of the home price for foreign currency, E, and interest rate, R and R_f. By considering $R = R_f$, either one of the two countries is small with respect to the other and/or there is perfect capital mobility.

40 Static economic models

The exogenous variables at home and abroad are respectively: government/public spending, $\overline{G}$ and $\overline{G}_f$; independent/autonomous consumption, $\overline{C}$ and $\overline{C}_f$; independent/autonomous investment, $\overline{I}$ and $\overline{I}_f$; income taxes, $\overline{T}$ and $\overline{T}_f$; independent/autonomous net exports, $\overline{NX}$ and $\overline{NX}_f$; money supply, $\overline{M}$ and $\overline{M}_f$; and price level (fixed), $\overline{P}$ and $\overline{P}_f$.

In the functional forms above, the following parameters are introduced (for the home and foreign countries respectively): c and c_f are the constant proportion of current disposable income that is consumed (or propensity to consume), $0 < c, c_f < 1$; $b, b_f > 0$ are the interest sensitivity of investment; $k, k_f > 0$ are the output sensitivity of the demand for money; $h, h_f > 0$ are the interest sensitivity of the demand for money; $j > 0$ is the output sensitivity of the net exports in the home country and $l > 0$ is the real exchange rate sensitivity of the net exports in the home country.

IS curve: goods and services market equilibrium

As stated in the previous chapter, the IS curve represents the continuum of combinations of the interest and output level at which aggregate demand for goods (and services) equals the supply, $Y_d = Y$. From the functional forms of the model, the goods and services market equilibrium at home, for example, is given by

$$Y = \frac{1}{1-c+j}\left(\overline{C} + \overline{I} + \overline{G} + \overline{NX} - c\overline{T} - bR + jY_f + lE\frac{\overline{P}_f}{\overline{P}}\right). \quad (3.1)$$

From (3.1), on the (Y, R) plane, the following can be stated.

- The position of the IS curve is affected by any factor that changes the position of (the line) $\overline{C} + \overline{I} + \overline{G} + \overline{NX}$: the IS curve shifts to the right (left) when (at least) one of these elements increases (decreases).
- Its slope is negative $\partial Y/\partial R < 0$; to maintain goods and services market equilibrium, R and Y vary in the opposite direction. The slope is affected by the parameters c, b and j.
- Points in the left (right) side of the IS curve mean that there is an excess of demand (supply) for goods and services.

LM curve: money-market equilibrium

The monetary–financial market is not affected by extending the model to the open scenario. Hence, the focus on the money market segment remains, since its equilibrium also guarantees the financial market equilibrium. The supply of money, $M_s = \overline{M}$, is a policy instrument defined by the central bank. The demand for money, $kY - hR$ and $k_f Y_f - h_f R_f$, depends positively on production and negatively on interest rate. It follows that equilibrium emerges when the supply of money is equal to the demand (3.2). From the functional forms considered, the LM (recall Chapter 2) curves are

$$\frac{\overline{M}}{P} = kY - hR \quad \text{and} \quad \frac{\overline{M}_f}{P_f} = k_f Y_f - h_f R_f. \tag{3.2}$$

Please note that the additional comments made for the closed economy also hold true here.

Putting the IS and the LM curves together

Considering, for example, the home country, it is assumed that: (i) the equilibrium in the goods and services market occurs when the combination (Y, R) belongs to the IS curve; (ii) the equilibrium in the money market is given by the combination (Y, R) that belongs to the LM curve; (iii) the equilibrium in the external market arises when the combination (Y, R) belongs to the external balance or $BP = 0$ curve (Balance of Payments, BP, reflects the record of a country's international transactions).[1] As a result, the global equilibrium interest rate and level of output will be determined by the intersection of all curves.

Concerning the points out of the global equilibrium, it is possible to state the following.

- Imbalance in the goods and services market occurs when variation in stocks takes place, leading firms to adjust production.
- Imbalance in the money market generates interest-rate adjustment.
- Imbalance in the external market provokes exchange-rate adjustment.

The equilibrium solution for the endogenous variables is affected by any change in the value of either an exogenous variable or parameter. A comparative static analysis can be done by recalculating the (new) equilibrium, which is now more tedious (larger system) than in the previous case. Therefore, a numerical implementation is useful.

Numerical solution: linear systems of equations

In the two previous chapters, the solution of the linear systems involved the factorisation of the coefficient matrix A. Methods of this type are known as *direct methods*. They compute the solution in a predictable finite number of steps and the answer is provided at the very end of the process. Direct methods are, however, not practical if A is large and sparse,[2] since the number of operations and memory requirements are high, and the factors of a sparse matrix can be dense. Alternatively, *iterative methods* are designed to generate a sequence of increasingly accurate approximations to the solution but do not provide the solution within a fixed number of steps. On the other hand, they can be stopped once the estimated error for the solution is below a prescribed tolerance.

42 Static economic models

An iterative method for solving a linear system $Ax = d$ constructs, beginning with an initial guess x_0, a sequence of approximate solutions, the *iterates* x_k, $k = 1, 2, \ldots$, convergent to the solution. The quality of the approximation can be assessed by the *residual* at iteration k, $r_k = d - Ax_k$. The iterative process can be stopped either by limiting the number of iterations, $k \leq k_{\max}$ and/or by imposing a required precision *tol* on the residual, $\|r_k\| < tol \times \|d\|$.

Stationary iterative methods

To obtain a recurrence, matrix A can be partitioned in two: $A = M - N$, $N = M - A$. The linear system $Ax = d$ becomes $Mx = Nx + d$, thus suggesting the iterative process (*fixed-point iteration*)

$$\begin{aligned} x_{k+1} &= M^{-1}Nx_k + M^{-1}d \\ &= M^{-1}(M - A)x_k + M^{-1}d \\ &= (I - M^{-1}A)x_k + M^{-1}d \\ &= Gx_k + f \text{ (}G\text{ is the \textit{iteration matrix})} \end{aligned} \quad (3.3)$$

for M nonsingular. It is crucial to ensure that the iterates x_k converge, after a certain number of iterations, to the approximate solution. If $\|G\| < 1$ then $I - G$ is nonsingular and the iteration (3.3) converges to the solution of $(I - G)x = f$ for any x_0. Indeed, the *preconditioned* system $M^{-1}Ax = M^{-1}d$ is being solved, where M is the *preconditioner*.

The methods of *Richardson*, *Jacobi*, *Gauss–Seidel* and *Successive Over-Relaxation* result, respectively, from the partitions

$$\begin{aligned} M_R &= I, & N_R &= I - A \\ M_J &= D, & N_J &= -E - F \\ M_{GS} &= D - E, & N_{GS} &= F \\ M_{SOR} &= D - \varpi E, & N_{SOR} &= (1 - \varpi)D + \varpi F \end{aligned} \quad (3.4)$$

with D, $-E$ and $-F$, respectively, the diagonal of A, the strictly lower and upper triangular parts of A. A *backward* Gauss–Seidel is obtained by just replacing E by F; the SOR with $\varpi = 1$ recovers the (*forward*) Gauss–Seidel method.

The Jacobi and Gauss–Seidel methods converge for strictly diagonal dominant matrices[3] and SOR does not converge outside the interval $]0, 2[$.

In the following, a function implementing the Jacobi stationary iterative method is provided, where the stopping criterion for the iterative loop controls both the number of iterations as well as the accuracy of the approximation.

```
function [x,k] = jacobi(A,d,x,maxit,tol)
% Jacobi iteration to solve a linear system Ax=d
```

```
% based on: Templates for the Solution of Linear Systems,
% R. Barrett, M. Berry, T. F. Chan, J. Demmel, J. Donato,
% J. Dongarra, V. Eijkhout, R. Pozo, C. Romine and
% H. Van der Vorst, SIAM, 1994
%   input:
%       A, coefficient matrix
%       d, right-hand side
%       x, initial vector
%       maxit, maximum number of iterations allowed
%       tol, tolerance to control the accuracy of the solution
%   output:
%       x, approximate solution (if convergent)
%       k, number of required iterations
if (norm(d)==0)
    disp('rhs should not be the zero vector'); return;
end
M = diag(diag(A)); N = M-A;
k = 0; r = d-A*x;
while (k<maxit && norm(r)>tol*norm(d))
    x = M\(N*x+d); r = d-A*x; k = k+1;
end
```

The methods defined by (3.3) are called *stationary iterative methods* since neither G nor f depends upon the iteration count. They are very simple and their convergence properties well studied. However, they may fail to converge on a wide range of problems. Computations in *nonstationary iterative methods* use information that changes at each iteration.

Nonstationary iterative methods

To solve $Ax = d$ for A, $n \times n$, sparse and large, a common technique is to project the problem onto a subspace $\mathcal{K}_m(A)$, $m \ll n$, of much smaller dimension than A, and to extract from $x_0 + \mathcal{K}_m(A)$ an approximate solution, imposing conditions on the residual.

Krylov subspace methods seek the approximate solution from

$$\mathcal{K}_m(A) \equiv \text{span}\{r_0, Ar_0, \ldots, A^{m-1}r_0\} \tag{3.5}$$

for $r_0 = d - Ax_0$ the initial residual.

Dating back to the late 1950s, the idea of Krylov subspace was developed by Lanczos and Arnoldi, and the intuition can be explained by the Cayley–Hamilton theorem, which states that the inverse of a matrix A of dimension $n \times n$ can be written as an $(n-1)^{\text{th}}$-order polynomial in A:

$$p(A) = A^n + c_{n-1}A^{n-1} + \cdots + c_1 A + (-1)^n \det(A) I_n = 0$$

and thus, since $\det(A) \neq 0$,

$$A^{-1} = \frac{(-1)^{n-1}}{\det(A)}(A^{n-1} + c_{n-1}A^{n-2} + \cdots + c_1 I_n).$$

44 *Static economic models*

Different classes of methods can be derived depending on the conditions imposed.

1. The *minimum residual* approach: find x_m for which $\|b - Ax\|_2$ is minimal over $\mathcal{K}_m(A)$. The well-known *GMRES (Generalised Minimum RESidual)* method is based on this approach.
2. The *Ritz–Galerkin* approach: approach find x_m for which the residual is orthogonal to $\mathcal{K}_m(A)$. The *CG (Conjugate-Gradient)* method method for symmetric definite-positive matrices belongs to this approach.
3. The *Petrov–Galerkin* approach: find x_m for which the residual is orthogonal to a subspace different from $\mathcal{K}_m(A)$. Among several methods, the most used may be the *BiCGstab (stabilised Bi-Conjugate Gradient)* iterative method.

Iterative methods in practice

MATLAB/Octave provide implementations for nonstationary iterative methods, in particular `pcg`, `gmres` and `bicgstab`. On the other hand, stationary iterative methods are seldom used as stand alone solvers, since they show good convergence properties only for a small set of problems. Thus, there are no implementations available in MATLAB nor Octave. However codes can be easily obtained from the web or the reader can also try to write them.

Additional comments

Two final notes are worth attention.

The matrix M in stationary iterative methods, or other matrices approximating A, can be used in Krylov subspace methods to improve the condition number of the coefficient matrix of the system to be solved.

Small relative residual only implies that the computed solution is accurate if A is well conditioned, since $\|\Delta x\|/\|x\| \leq cond(A)\|r\|/(\|A\|\|x\|)$. This is very important to point out, since the residual norm is often used to control the iterative process.

Computational implementation

The `mundell_fleming.m` script to solve the problem is now presented. In line with Hall and Papell (2005), the baseline parameter values and exogenous variables taken are $\overline{C} = \overline{C}_f = 55$, $c = c_f = 0.63$, $\overline{I} = \overline{I}_f = 47$, $b = b_f = 1500$, $k = k_f = 0.6$, $h = h_f = 2700$, $j = 0.1$, $l = 10$, $NX = -10$, $\overline{G} = \overline{G}_f = 150$, $\overline{M} = \overline{M}_f = 210$, $\overline{T} = \overline{T}_f = 150$ and $\overline{P} = \overline{P}_f = 1$.

Since countries have the same dimension, in the present case there is perfect mobility under $R = R_f$. Other scenarios, namely, the difference between perfect and imperfect capital mobility as well as a fixed and flexible exchange rate, will be explored in Appendix A.

MATLAB/Octave code

```
%% Mundell—Fleming Model
% An open Economy in the short—medium run: the Mundell—Fleming
      Model
% Implemented by: P.B. Vasconcelos and O. Afonso
disp('──────────────────────────────────');
disp('IS-LM model: open economy                      ');
disp('──────────────────────────────────');


%% parameters (f stands for foreign)
c  = 0.63; b  = 1500; k  = 0.6; h  = 2700;
cf = 0.63; bf = 1500; kf = 0.6; hf = 2700;
j  = 0.1;  l  = 10;

%% exogenous variables
C_bar  = 55;  I_bar  = 47;
Cf_bar = 55;  If_bar = 47;  NX_bar = -10;
G_bar  = 150; M_bar  = 210; T_bar  = 150; P_bar  = 1;
Gf_bar = 150; Mf_bar = 210; Tf_bar = 150; Pf_bar = 1;


%% endogenous variables
% Y, Yf, production;    C, Cf,   consumption
% I, If, investment;    NX, NXf, net exports
% R, Rf, interest rate; E,       exchange rate


%% matrix representation of the model: Ax=d
% A, coefficient matrix
% Y  C  I  NX  R  Yf  Cf  If  NXf  Rf  E
A = [ ...
  1 -1 -1 -1  0  0   0   0   0    0   0                      % Y=C+I+G+NX
 -c  1  0  0  0  0   0   0   0    0   0                      % C=C_bar+c(Y-T)
  0  0  1  0  b  0   0   0   0    0   0                      % I=I_bar-b*R
  k  0  0  0 -h  0   0   0   0    0   0                      % M/P=k*Y-h*R
  0  0  0  0  0  1  -1  -1  -1    0   0                      % Yf=Cf+If+Gf+NXf
  0  0  0  0  0 -cf  1   0   0    0   0                      % Cf=Cf_bar+cf(Yf-Tf)
  0  0  0  0  0  0   0   1   0    bf  0                      % If=If_bar-bf*Rf
  0  0  0  0  0  kf  0   0   0   -hf  0                      % Mf/Pf=kf*Yf-hf*Rf
  j  0  0  1  0 -j   0   0   0    0  -l*Pf_bar/P_bar         % NX=NX_bar-j(Y-Yf)+
                                                             %    l*E*Pf/P
  0  0  0  1  0  0   0   0   1    0   0                      % NX= -NXf
  0  0  0  0  1  0   0   0   0   -1   0 ];                   % R=Rf
% x = [Y,C,I,NX,R,Yf,Cf,If,NXf,Rf,E]', vector of the endogeneous
      variables
% d, vector of the exogenous variables
d = [G_bar  ; C_bar-c*T_bar   ; I_bar ; M_bar/P_bar   ; ...
     Gf_bar; Cf_bar-cf*Tf_bar; If_bar; Mf_bar/Pf_bar; ...
     NX_bar; 0; 0];

%% compute the endogenous variables
x = gmres(A,d,[],1e-10,11);
```

46 *Static economic models*

```
%% show the solution
disp('computed endogenous variables:')
fprintf(' product home/foreign      : %7.2f   %7.2f \n',x(1),x(6))
fprintf(' consumption home/foreign  : %7.2f   %7.2f \n',x(2),x(7))
fprintf(' investment home/foreign   : %7.2f   %7.2f \n',x(3),x(8))
fprintf(' net exports home/foreign  : %7.2f   %7.2f \n',x(4),x(9))
fprintf(' interest rate
   home/foreign (%%)                : %7.2f   %7.2f \n',...
                                      x(5)*100,x(10)*100)
fprintf(' exchange rate             : %7.2f             \n',x(11))
```

Some short comments on the code

The code follows closely the one presented in the previous chapter. The only difference is related with the use of the iterative solver gmres. For this method the tolerance required and maximum number of iterations allowed must be provided in addition to A and d. In this case they were set to, respectively, $1e-10$ and 11. Note that the third component of the call to function gmres is a [ ]; the function is expecting information about a possible restart of the Krylov basis, but here, due to the small dimension of the system, the default was not altered.

Numerical results and simulation

The output is presented here.

```
computed endogenous variables:
  product home/foreign            :   389.81    389.81
  consumption home/foreign        :   206.08    206.08
  investment home/foreign         :    33.73     33.73
  net exports home/foreign        :     0.00      0.00
  interest rate home/foreign (%)  :     0.88      0.88
  exchange rate                   :     1.00
```

The answers to the following questions can be easily obtained by changing the exogenous variables.

1. What is the impact on the model of a decrease in public tax by 20? The code is as follows.

    ```
    % T decreases 20

    mundell_fleming  % reproduce baseline model
    fprintf('T from %d to %d \n',T_bar,T_bar-20);
    T_bar=T_bar-20; % perform shock in home country
    d = [G_bar ; C_bar-c*T_bar  ; I_bar ; M_bar/P_bar   ; ...
         Gf_bar; Cf_bar-cf*Tf_bar; If_bar; Mf_bar/Pf_bar; ...
         NX_bar; 0; 0];
    ```

IS–LM model in an open economy

```
xnew = gmres(A,d,[],1e-10,11); % compute new solution
xdiff = xnew-x;
disp ('change in home / foreign countries')
fprintf (' in product      : %7.2f %7.2f \n', ...
    xdiff(1), xdiff(6))
fprintf (' in consumption  : %7.2f %7.2f \n', ...
    xdiff(2), xdiff(7))
fprintf (' in investment   : %7.2f %7.2f \n', ...
    xdiff(3), xdiff(8))
fprintf (' in net exports  : %7.2f %7.2f \n', ...
    xdiff(4), xdiff(9))
fprintf (' in interest rate : %7.2f %7.2f \n', ...
    xdiff(5), xdiff(10))
T_bar=T_bar+20; % reset
```

The output is as follows.

```
T from 150 to 130
change in home / foreign countries
  in product       :     8.96      8.96
  in consumption   :    18.24      5.64
  in investment    :    -2.99     -2.99
  in net exports   :    -6.30      6.30
  in interest rate :     0.00      0.00
```

In the present context, the interpretation of the results is similar to the one drawn in Chapter 2.

2. What is the impact of an increase in government spending by 20?

```
G from 150 to 170
change in home / foreign countries
  in product       :    14.22     14.22
  in consumption   :     8.96      8.96
  in investment    :    -4.74     -4.74
  in net exports   :   -10.00     10.00
  in interest rate :     0.00      0.00
```

3. What is the impact of an increase of money spending by 20?

```
M from 210 to 230
change in home / foreign countries
  in product       :    24.57     -8.77
  in consumption   :    15.48     -5.52
  in investment    :     2.92      2.92
  in net exports   :     6.17     -6.17
  in interest rate :     0.00      0.00
```

48 *Static economic models*

Highlights

- This model was developed in the early 1960s. Due to this development, Robert Mundell won the Nobel Prize in Economics in 1999.
- The open economy version of the IS–LM model enables the discussion of the equilibrium in an open economy and the impact of changes in fiscal and monetary policies in this context.
- Iterative methods (stationary and nonstationary) to compute approximate solutions of linear systems are shown emphasising on GMRES, BiCGstab and PCG.

Problems and computer exercises

1. What happens if home country embarks on an expansionary fiscal policy (increasing $\overline{G}$ by 10) while the central bank does not change the supply of money? Describe the effects.
2. How does your answer to the previous question change if the money supply also increases by 10?
3. Consider again the baseline model. What is the effect of an increase in taxes by 10?
4. Suppose that the home price level grows 5 per cent a year while the foreign price level grows 1 per cent. Which is the new exchange rate evaluated at PPP? (PPP stands for Purchasing Power Parity, and it is evaluated by $E(P_f/P)$).
5. Build a function implementing the Gauss–Seidel and SOR methods.
6. Solve the (baseline) problem applying:

    (a) Jacobi, Gauss–Seidel and SOR. Comment on the results (look for convergence results).
    (b) GMRES and BiCGstab for a tolerance on the residual of 10^{-6} and 10^{-12}. Comment on the results.
    (c) Gaussian elimination. Compare the results with GMRES and BiCGstab for a tolerance of 10^{-10}.

Notes

1 The external balance $BP = 0$ is reached when the supply of and the demand for foreign exchange are equal at the fixed exchange rate.
2 This is a matrix in which most of the elements are zero.
3 The matrix A, $n \times n$, is strictly diagonal dominant if $|a_{jj}| > \sum_{i=1, i \neq j}^{n} |a_{ij}|$, $j = 1, \ldots, n$.

4 AD–AS model

Introduction

The IS–LM model developed in Chapter 2 is a fixed-price-level model. This chapter introduces a variable-price-level model in which it is possible to simultaneously analyse changes in output, interest rate and price level. Moreover, it provides insights on inflation and unemployment.

The *AD–AS model, Aggregate Demand–Aggregate Supply* is an aggregation of the elementary microeconomic demand-and-supply model, resulting in *aggregate demand* (AD) and *aggregate supply* (AS) curves. The AD curve can be obtained from the IS–LM curves, by removing the fixed price level, and the AS curve requires the consideration of the productive firms capacity. Thus, in terms of standard representation, the AD curve is given by the set of output and price level combinations that guarantee equilibrium of both goods and services and monetary markets, whereas the AS curve is given by the set of output and price level combinations that maximise profits of firms.

The shapes of AD and AS curves and the forces causing them to shift are crucial to finding the equilibrium values of endogenous variables. Being a comparative static model, its insights are obtained by 'shocking' the initial equilibrium condition, by changing one or more of the parameters and exogenous variables, and then evaluating the resulting new equilibrium.

This chapter is based on Mankiw (2009, ch. 10–11, 13), Burda and Wyplosz (2009, ch. 13), and Gordon (2011, ch. 8) in terms of economic intuition and on Dahlquist and Björck (2008, ch. 6) and Kelley (1995, ch. 4–6) for the numerical solution of nonlinear systems of equations.

Economic model

In addition to the demand side, embodied in the AD curve, the AD–AS model considers the supply side, represented by the AS curve. In a closed economy, due to Pigou's wealth and Keynes' interest rate effects, the AD curve is downward sloping: the lower the price level is the higher is the demanded quantity. The Pigou effect relates the increase of the output to the increase of consumption due to higher wealth, in particular during disinflation. The Keynesian effect tells us that changes in interest rate affect expenditures more than savings.

50 *Static economic models*

On the other hand, the AS curve reflects how much output is supplied by firms at different price levels. The equilibrium levels of the main variables, annual national production, GDP, and price level, P, are determined by the interaction of the AD and AS curves.

Variables, parameters and functional forms

The general equations that characterise the economy are:

- product equals aggregate demand, $Y = C + I + G$;
- consumption function, $C = \overline{C} + cY(1-t)$;
- investment function, $I = \overline{I} - bR$;
- public spending function, $G = \overline{G}$;
- income taxes function, $T = tY$;
- money demand, $L = \overline{L} + kY - hR$;
- monetary supply, $\overline{M}/P$; and
- production function, $Y = \overline{A} K^\alpha H^{1-\alpha}$.

The endogenous variables are: product (output or income), Y; consumption, C; investment, I; interest rate, R; and prices, P.

The main exogenous variables are: government/public spending, $\overline{G}$; independent/autonomous consumption, $\overline{C}$; independent/autonomous investment, $\overline{I}$; independent/autonomous money demand, $\overline{L}$; money supply, $\overline{M}$; nominal wages, $\overline{W}$; capital, $\overline{K}$; labour (which is given), H, and total productivity of factors, $\overline{A}$.

Therefore, parameters are: marginal propensity to consume, $0 < c < 1$; tax rate, $t \geq 0$; interest sensitivity of investment, $b > 0$; interest sensitivity of the demand for money, $h > 0$; output sensitivity of the demand for money, $k > 0$; share of labour in production, $0 < \alpha < 1$; and share of capital in production, $1 - \alpha$.

AD curve: aggregate demand

The AD curve represents the various amounts of real GDP,[1] IS–LM equilibrium output, that buyers will desire to purchase at each possible price level.

Bearing in mind the equations that characterise the economy, the AD curve is given by

$$Y = \frac{\frac{1}{h}\left(\overline{L} - \frac{\overline{M}}{P}\right) - \frac{1}{b}\left(\overline{C} + \overline{I} + \overline{G}\right)}{\frac{c(1-t)-1}{b} - \frac{k}{h}}. \tag{4.1}$$

It shows an inverse relationship between price level and real domestic output. The explanation for the inverse relationship comes from: (i) real balances effect (indeed, when price level falls, the purchasing power of existing financial balances rise, which can increase spending); (ii) interest rate effect (in fact, a decline in price level means lower interest rates which can increase levels of certain types of spending); (iii) foreign purchases effect (when the price level falls, other things being equal, domestic prices will fall relative to foreign prices, which will tend to increase spending on domestic exports and also to decrease import spending in favour of domestic goods and services that compete with imports). Thus there is indeed an opposite relationship between Y and P to keep the equilibrium in both markets: goods and services, and monetary.

Determinants of AD are, besides the price level: changes in consumer spending, which can be caused by changes in several factors (consumer wealth, expectations, indebtedness and taxes); changes in investment spending, which can be also caused by changes in several factors (interest rates, profit expectations, business taxes, technology and the amount of excess capacity); changes in government spending; changes in net export spending unrelated to price level,[2] which may be caused by changes in other factors such as income abroad and exchange rates; and changes in money supply determined by the central bank.

To sum up, the position of the AD curve is affected by any factor that affects the position of IS and LM curves.

When there is a change in one of the determinants of the AD curve, there will be a change in the aggregate expenditures as well. If, for example, price level remains constant, then a change in aggregate expenditures is strongly multiplied and the real output rises by more than the initial change in spending.

A decrease in the AD curve, for instance, may imply a recession and cyclical unemployment, since prices do not fall easily. Indeed, (i) wage contracts are not flexible so businesses cannot afford to reduce prices; (ii) employers are reluctant to cut wages due to its impact on employee effort; (iii) minimum wage laws keep wages above that level; (iv) so-called menu costs are difficult to change;[3] and (v) fear of price wars keep prices from being reduced also.

Points on the left (right) side of the curve imply excess (scarcity) of aggregate demand.

AS curve: aggregate supply

The AS curve represents the real domestic output level that is supplied by the economy at different price levels. Basically, it is viewed as having three distinct segments.

- Horizontal range: where the price level remains constant with substantial output variation. In this range the economy is far from full-employment. This case is usually called the Keynesian (or short-run aggregate supply) curve (implicit in the IS–LM model), since it assumes that firms are willing to produce any quantity at the current P, which implies that the AS is horizontal. In this case the AS curve is given by $P =$ constant.
- Intermediate (up sloping) range: where the expansion of real output is accompanied by a rising price level, near to a full-employment level. In this stage per unit production costs rise because prices of resources will be bid up. This is usually denominated by the hybrid (or intermediate or medium-run aggregate supply) curve (AS_{mr}), since, Y and P are positively related.

52 Static economic models

In this case one can consider, for instance, a Cobb–Douglas production function $Y = \overline{A}\ \overline{K}^{\alpha} H^{1-\alpha}$. Under this function it is easy to derive the following expression for this AS curve,

$$Y = \overline{A}\ \overline{K}^{\alpha} \left(\frac{\overline{W}}{P} \frac{\overline{K}^{-\alpha}}{(1-\alpha)\overline{A}} \right)^{\frac{\alpha-1}{\alpha}}, \tag{4.2}$$

which takes into account that the marginal product of labour, $\partial Y / \partial H$, is equal to the real wage, $\overline{W}/P$.[4]

- Vertical range: where absolute full capacity is assumed, and any attempt to increase output will bid up resource and product prices. Full-employment occurs at the 'natural rate of unemployment'; as a result it is denominated the Classical AS (or long-run aggregate supply) curve (AS_{lr}), since regardless of P, the production fluctuates around the natural product.[5] Fiscal and monetary policies do not then affect Y. The long-run AS curve is given by the natural output, $Y = Y^N$.

Determinants of AS are (besides price level): (i) a change in input prices, which can be caused by changes in several factors (availability of resources such as land, labour, capital and entrepreneurial ability, prices of imported resources and market power of certain firms); (ii) change in productivity can cause changes in per-unit production cost (if productivity rises, unit production costs will fall. This can shift aggregate supply to the right and lower prices. The reverse is true when productivity falls. Productivity improvement is very important in business efforts to reduce costs); (iii) change in the legal institutional environment, which can be caused by changes in other factors (business taxes and/or subsidies, and government regulation).

A shifting AS curve occurs when a supply determinant changes. Leftward shift illustrates cost-push inflation, whereas rightward shift will cause a decline in price level.

Putting the AD and the AS curves together

Equilibrium price and quantity are found where the AD and AS curves intersect.

An AD curve shift changes the equilibrium. If the AD curve increases, in the intermediate and vertical AS curve ranges it will cause demand-pull inflation, whereas in the horizontal it will only cause output changes.

The multiplier effect is weakened by price-level changes in the intermediate AS curve range and is null in the vertical AS curve range. The more price-level increases the smaller the effect on real GDP.

Numerical solution: nonlinear systems of equations

Computing the zeros of a real function f, or equivalently the roots of the equation $f(x) = 0$, is a frequent problem in economics. Contrary to linear systems, this computation cannot be accomplished in a finite number of operations. Therefore, one must rely on iterative methods. Starting from an initial approximation x_0, an iterative method builds a sequence x_k, $k = 1, 2, \ldots$, that should converge to a zero of f. To assess the quality of the solution one can compute the residual, $\|f(x_k)\|$, or the error, $\|x_k - x^*\|$, where x^* is the solution sought. The convergence rate r of the iterative process is linear, super-linear or quadratic, if

$$\lim_{k \to \infty} \frac{\|x_{k+1} - x^*\|}{\|x_k - x^*\|^r} = c$$

for a nonzero constant c, respectively, $r = 1$, $r > 1$ or $r = 2$.

It is usual to specify a required precision *tol* such that, for instance, $\|f(x_k)\| <$ *tol* to stop the iterative process.[6]

Scalar nonlinear equations: Newton method and variants

Bisection method

Let us consider for now a scalar nonlinear equation, that is, f, a real-valued function defined and continuous on a bounded closed interval. If f on $[a_0, b_0]$ satisfies $f(a_0) f(b_0) < 0$, then it has at least one zero in the segment $]a_0, b_0[$. Taking $m_0 = (a_0 + b_0)/2$, new intervals can be iteratively defined by halving the previous one according to

$$]a_{k+1}, b_{k+1}[= \begin{cases}]a_k, m_k[, & f(m_k) f(b_k) > 0 \\ ]m_k, b_k[, & f(m_k) f(b_k) < 0 \end{cases}.$$

This is known as the *bisection method*, and after k bisection steps a root is contained in an interval of length $(b_0 - a_0)/2^k$. To achieve an error of tolerance of *tol* one must perform $\log_2((b_0 - a_0)/tol)$ iterations. This method is independent of the regularity of f and shows a low rate of convergence.

Newton method

If f is differentiable, a more efficient method can be constructed by exploiting the values at f and at its derivative f'. This is the case of the well-known *Newton method*, which computes the zero by locally replacing f by its tangent line

$$x_{k+1} = x_k - f'(x_k)^{-1} f(x_k), \qquad (4.3)$$

$k = 0, 1, 2, \ldots$, provided that $f'(x_k) \neq 0$. The rate of (local) convergence of this method is quadratic. The disadvantage is that it requires f' that is computationally expensive to compute and often it is not explicitly available. Numerically, (4.3) is done by computing the *Newton step* s_k, solving the linear system $f'(x_k) s_k = -f(x_k)$, followed by the computation of $x_{k+1} = x_k + s_k$.

54 Static economic models

Methods based on interpolation

To overcome the cost of $f'(x_k)$ one can approximate it by finite differences using two successive iterates, giving rise to the *secant method*

$$x_{k+1} = x_k - \frac{x_k - x_{k-1}}{f(x_k) - f(x_{k-1})} f(x_k),$$

$k = 1, 2, \ldots$, which has (local) super linear convergence. In other words, the secant method uses linear interpolation to approximate the function whose zero is sought. The rate of convergence can be improved by considering a higher-order interpolation polynomial. Alternatively, the secant method can be extended by using inverse interpolation. Robust methods combine some of the previous features.

Systems of nonlinear equations: Newton method and variants

Solving systems of nonlinear equations is much harder since, among other things computational overhead increases with the problem dimension.

Dealing with a system of n nonlinear equations, $f(x) = 0$ with $f: \mathbb{R}^n \longrightarrow \mathbb{R}^n$, the previous summary on the Newton method is similar, except that x_k is a vector with n components and

$$f'(x_k) = J(x_k) = \begin{bmatrix} \frac{\partial f_1}{\partial x_1}(x_k) & \cdots & \frac{\partial f_1}{\partial x_n}(x_k) \\ \vdots & \ddots & \vdots \\ \frac{\partial f_n}{\partial x_1}(x_k) & \cdots & \frac{\partial f_n}{\partial x_n}(x_k) \end{bmatrix} \quad (4.4)$$

is the Jacobian matrix at x_k.

Variants of the Newton method can also be developed. One possibility is to use the same Jacobian for several iterations; furthermore, one can compute the LU factorisation and solve the required linear system cheaply (modified Newton method). Other possibilities result in updating factorisation methods rather than re-factorising the Jacobian matrix.

The Newton method (or its variants) may not converge in cases where the initial approximation is far from the solution (or approximations jump between different zeros). In order to allow convergence from a large set of initial approximations (better global convergence) the so called *dumped Newton methods* were developed:

$$x_{k+1} = x_k + \alpha_k s_k,$$

where the length (scalar) α_k is computed by a *line search* (minimise the scalar function $\phi(\alpha) = \|f(x_k + \alpha s_k)\|_2^2$). This approach can fail if the Jacobian is singular (or near singular). Another possibility are the *trust-region methods*. In this approach,

$$x_{k+1} = x_k + d_k,$$

where d_k is the solution of constrained linear least squares problem. The *Powell hybrid method* uses a linear combination of the steepest descent and the Newton (or quasi-Newton) direction.

Solving nonlinear equations in practice

Using MATLAB/Octave to find the zeros of a continuous function of one variable only requires the command `fzero(f,x0)`, where f is the function and x_0 an initial approximation. In MATLAB a hybrid algorithm is used, which combines bisection, secant and inverse quadratic interpolation methods. For a system of nonlinear equations the command `fsolve(f,x0)` must be used. In MATLAB the algorithm is a trust region method, and is the Powell hybrid method in Octave.

Additional comments

The theory under the convergence properties of the iterative methods for the solution of nonlinear (systems of) equations relies on the fixed-point iteration, $x_{k+1} = \phi(x_k)$, $k = 0, 1, 2, \ldots$, for a continuous function ϕ and such that $\lim_{k \to \infty} x_k = \zeta$, where ζ is called a fixed point of mapping ϕ. Namely, if ϕ is differentiable in $[a, b]$ and $|\phi'(x)| < 1$ for $x \in [a, b]$ then ϕ has a unique fixed point $\zeta \in [a, b]$ and the fixed-point iteration converges to ζ, whatever choice is made for $x_0 \in [a, b]$.

Computational implementation

The following baseline values for the model are considered: $c = 0.6$, $b = 1500$, $k = 0.2$, $b = 1500$, $h = 1000$, $t = 0.2$, $\alpha = 0.5$, $\overline{A} = 1$, $\overline{K} = 30\,000$, $\overline{C} = 160$, $\overline{I} = 100$, $\overline{G} = 200$, $\overline{M} = 1000$, $\overline{W} = 50$ and $\overline{L} = 225$.

Here an m-file with the code to solve the problem (at the medium run) is presented.

MATLAB/Octave code

```
%% AD -AS model
%   Medium-run equilibrium
%   Implemented by: P.B. Vasconcelos and O. Afonso

function adas
global  C_bar I_bar G_bar M_bar W_bar L_bar A_bar K_bar ...
        c b t k h alpha aux
disp('————————————————————————————————————');
disp('AD-AS model                         ');
disp('————————————————————————————————————');
```

56 Static economic models

```
%% parameters
c = 0.6;       % marginal propensity to consume
b = 1500;      % sensibility of the investment to the interest rate
k = 0.2;       % sensibility of the money demand to the product
h = 1000;      % sensibility of the money demand to the interest rate
t = 0.2;       % tax on consumption
alpha = 0.5;   % capital share in production

%% exogenous variables (autonomous components)
A_bar = 1;         % exogenous productivity
K_bar = 30000;     % stock of capital
C_bar = 160;       % autonomous consumption
I_bar = 100;       % autonomous investment
G_bar = 200;       % government spending
M_bar = 1000;      % money supply
W_bar = 50;        % wage
L_bar = 225;       % autonomous money demand
disp('exogenous variables (autonomous components): ')
fprintf('G_bar = %d; M_bar = %d; W_bar = %d; L_bar = %d \n',...
        G_bar,M_bar,W_bar,L_bar);
%% endogenous variables
% Y, product; P, price

%% model solution: compute the endogenous variables
x0 = [500 5];              % initial approximation for Y and P, resp.
aux = (c*(1-t)-1)/b-k/h;   % auxiliary variable for AD curve
x = fsolve(@ADAS_system,x0);

%% show the solution
disp('computed endogenous variables:')
fprintf('    product, Y:          %6.2f \n', x(1));
fprintf('    price, P:            %6.2f \n', x(2));
% show variable of interest
R = 1/h*(L_bar-M_bar/x(2)+k*x(1));
fprintf('    interest rate (%%), R:   %6.2f \n', R*100);

%% plot the solution
P = 0:0.1:1.5*x(2);
AS = A_bar*K_bar^alpha*(W_bar./P * ...
    K_bar.^(-alpha)/((1-alpha)*A_bar)).^((alpha-1)/alpha);
AD = 1/h*(L_bar-M_bar./P)/aux-1/b*(C_bar+I_bar+G_bar)/aux;
plot(AS,P,'—b',AD,P,'r'); xlim([500 1200]);
xlabel('product'); ylabel('price'); legend('AS','AD');

%% AD-AS system
function f = ADAS_system(x)
global C_bar I_bar G_bar M_bar W_bar L_bar A_bar K_bar b h
       alpha ... aux;
    f = [x(1)-1/h*(L_bar-M_bar/x(2))/aux+1/b*(C_bar+I_bar+G_bar)/aux;
    x(1)-A_bar*K_bar^alpha*(W_bar/x(2)*...
    K_bar^(-alpha)/((1-alpha)*A_bar))^((alpha-1)/alpha)];
```

Some short comments on the code

The code begins by defining the parameters and exogenous variables. Then the model is built through a MATLAB function, ADAS_system, with arguments $x = [Y; P]$, the vector of endogenous variables. The system is composed by (4.1) and (4.2) written to have zero on the right-hand side. As explained, the solution x is obtained by solving the nonlinear system specified as a function handle for the file ADAS_system through the fsolve command. Since there are exogenous variables and parameters defined on the main program that must be accessed by the function, one way to deal with this situation is by considering them as global variables through the command global. Later it will be shown how to avoid the use of global variables, by passing them as function parameters. Also an initial solution x_0 must be provided before calling the fsolve. As usual the code ends by plotting the solution. In order to keep the function in the same file as the script, the script is taken as a function without input or output variables (this is required for MATLAB; Octave allows for functions inside scripts).

Numerical results and simulation

The output presents the equilibrium point and Figure 4.1 displays the corresponding AD–AS diagram.

```
------------------------------------------------------
AD-AS model
------------------------------------------------------
exogenous variables (autonomous components):
G_bar = 200; M_bar = 1000; W_bar = 50; L_bar = 225

computed endogenous variables:
    product, Y:              819.25
    price, P:                  2.73
    interest rate (%), R:      2.27
```

Let us now evaluate the result of some shocks on the output and price.

1. Consider an expansion of governmental spending of 20 per cent. Explore both IS–LM and AD–AS diagrams.
   The code is as follows.

```
% G_bar increases 20

function example1
global C_bar I_bar M_bar W_bar c b t L_bar k h A_bar K_bar
       alpha ... aux

%% parameters
    c = 0.6; b = 1500; t = 0.2; k = 0.2; h = 1000; alpha = 0.5;
```

58 Static economic models

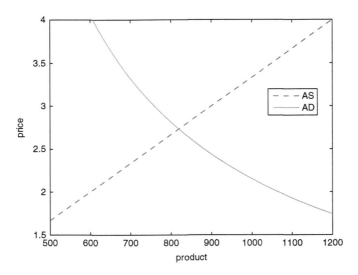

Figure 4.1 AD–AS diagram.

```
%% exogenous variables (autonomous components)
C_bar = 160;  I_bar = 100;  A_bar = 1;  K_bar = 30000;
M_bar = 1000;  W_bar = 50;  L_bar = 225;
G_bar = 200;  G_bar_new = G_bar*1.2;

%% AS–AD model solution: x=[Y P]
aux = (c*(1-t)-1)/b-k/h;  x0 = [500 5];
x = fsolve(@(x) ADAS_system(x,G_bar),x0);
R = 1/h*(L_bar-M_bar/x(2)+k*x(1));
x_new = fsolve(@(x) ADAS_system(x,G_bar_new),x0);
R_new = 1/h*(L_bar-M_bar/x_new(2)+k*x_new(1));

%% ISLM model solution: w=[Y C I R]
Q = [1 -1 -1 0; c*(t-1) 1 0 0; 0 0 1 b; k 0 0 -h];
s = [G_bar;C_bar;I_bar;M_bar/x(2)-L_bar];
w = Q\s;
s_new = [G_bar_new;C_bar;I_bar;M_bar/x_new(2)-L_bar];
w_new = Q\s_new;

%% show results
fprintf('G_bar from %6.2f to %6.2f \n',G_bar,G_bar_new);
disp('IS–LM:                    initial eq.  eq. after shock')
fprintf('   product, Y:          \t %6.2f \t %6.2f \n', ...
   w(1),w_new(1))
disp('AS–AD: ')
fprintf('   product, Y:          \t %6.2f \t %6.2f \n', ...
   x(1),x_new(1))
fprintf('   price,   P:          \t %6.2f \t %6.2f \n', ...
   x(2),x_new(2))
```

AD–AS model 59

```
fprintf('   interest rate, R (%%):    \t %6.2f \t %6.2f \n', ...
   R*100,R_new*100);

%% plot results
P = 0:0.1:1.5*x(2);
AS = A_bar*K_bar^alpha*(W_bar./P * ...
     K_bar.^(-alpha)/((1-alpha)*A_bar)).^((alpha-1)/alpha);
AD = 1/h*(L_bar-M_bar./P)/aux-1/b*(C_bar+I_bar+G_bar)/aux;
AD_new = 1/h*(L_bar-M_bar./P)/aux-1/b*(C_bar+I_bar+G_bar_new)/
         aux;

X = 0:1.5*x(1);
LM = (L_bar-M_bar./x(2)+k.*X)./h;
LM_new = (L_bar-M_bar./x_new(2)+k.*X)./h;
IS = (C_bar+X*(c*(1-t)-1)+I_bar+G_bar )/b;
IS_new = (C_bar+X*(c*(1-t)-1)+I_bar+G_bar_new)/b;

subplot(211);
plot(X,LM, '—b',X,IS, 'r'); hold on;
plot(X,LM_new, '—b',X,IS_new, 'r','LineWidth',3);
plot(w(1),w(4), 'ko'); plot(w_new(1),w_new(4),'ko');
title('equilibrium after expansion of governamental spending');
legend('LM','IS','LM_{new}','IS_{new}'); xlim([500 1200]);
xlabel('product'); ylabel('interest rate');
hold off;

subplot(212);
plot(AS,P,'—b',AD,P,'r'); hold on;
plot(AD_new,P,'r','LineWidth',3);
plot(x(1),x(2),'ko'); plot(x_new(1),x_new(2),'ko');
legend('AS','AD','AD_{new}'); xlim([500 1200]);
xlabel('product'); ylabel('price');
hold off;

%% AS–AD system
function f = ADAS_system(x, G_bar)
global C_bar I_bar M_bar W_bar L_bar b h A_bar K_bar alpha aux;
f = [
  x(1)-1/h*(L_bar-M_bar/x(2))/aux+1/b*(C_bar+I_bar+G_bar)/aux;
  x(1)-A_bar*K_bar^alpha *(W_bar/x(2)*...
    K_bar^(-alpha)/((1-alpha)*A_bar))^((alpha-1)/alpha);
  ];
```

The output is as follows (see also Figure 4.2).

```
G_bar from 200.00 to 240.00
                            initial eq.   eq. after
                                          shock
      product, Y:              819.25       846.48
      price, P:                  2.73         2.82
      interest rate, R (%):      2.27         3.99
```

60 *Static economic models*

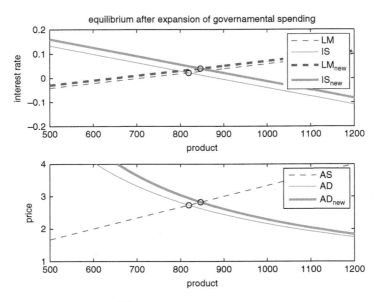

Figure 4.2 Increase in $\overline{G}$.

As expected, this shock increases the output, interest rate and prices. As a result, the consumption also increases, whereas the investment decreases due to the new higher interest rate.

2. Consider an expansion of money supply of 15 per cent. Explore both IS–LM and AD–AS diagrams.

```
M_bar from 1000 to 1150
                            initial eq.    eq. after
                                           shock
    product, Y:             819.25         872.62
    price, P:                 2.73           2.91
    interest rate, R (%):     2.27           0.42
```

If $\overline{M}$ increases, the LM curve goes to the right (see Figure 4.3). In this context, the output and prices increase, whereas the interest rate decreases. Higher output affects positively consumption and lower interest rate benefits investment.

3. Consider now a positive supply shock, by assuming that $\overline{A}$ increases 5 per cent.

```
A_bar from 1 to 1.05
                            initial eq.    eq. after
                                           shock
    product, Y:             819.25         856.11
```

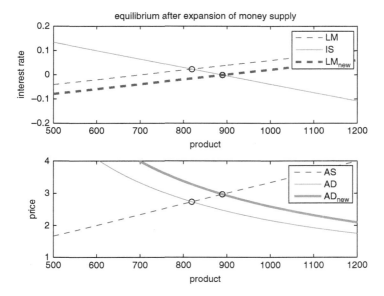

Figure 4.3 Increase in $\overline{M}$.

```
price, P:                  2.73        2.59
interest rate, R (%):      2.27        0.99
```

If $\overline{A}$ increases, the AS curve goes to the right (see Figure 4.4). As a result, the output increases and prices decrease. The interest rate also decreases since the LM curve goes to the right.

Highlights

- The AD–AS model explains price level and output considering the relationship between aggregate demand and aggregate supply.
- The AD curve is defined by the IS–LM equilibrium and the AS curve reflects the labour market.
- Iterative numerical methods for nonlinear problems are introduced.
- Newton and quasi-Newton methods for the approximate solution of nonlinear (system of) equation(s) are briefly explained.

Problems and computer exercises

1. Solve the model considering for the AS curve $P = 2.0$. Then, suppose an expansion of government spending of 30 per cent and comment on the differences with the baseline case.

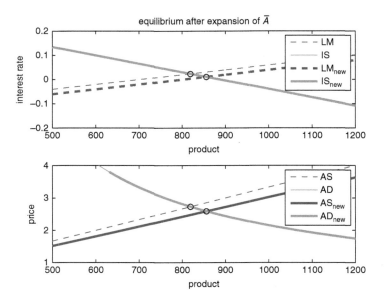

Figure 4.4 Increase in $\overline{A}$.

2. Solve the model considering for the AS curve $Y = Y^N = 700$. Then, suppose an expansion of government spending of 30 per cent and comment on the differences with the baseline case.
3. Consider the improvement in technological knowledge such that $\overline{A}$ increases, as shown in the numerical results and simulation section. What happens to the real wage, consumption, investment and demand for money?
4. Repeat exercise 3 considering:

   (a) an increase in $\overline{K}$;
   (b) an increased wealth that positively affects the autonomous consumption.

5. Consider the country 'XPTO' evaluated by the following relationships: $C = 100 + 0.6Y(1-t)$; $I = 600 - 1500R$; $\overline{G} = 425$; $t = 0.2$; $\overline{M} = 500$; $L = 225 + 0.2Y - 1000R$; $Y = F(H) = 100H - H^2$; $\overline{W} = 50$.

   (a) Find the equilibrium values for Y, P and R. Illustrate your answer.
   (b) Is it possible to increase C without penalising I? What kind of policy should be implemented? Justify.
   (c) Suppose that $\overline{M}$ increases towards 600. What happens to the level of output, interest rate and the price level? Represent graphically your answer.
   (d) What are the effects of the previous policy if the short-run AS curve is given by $P = 1$? Represent graphically your answer.

(e) Comment on the statement 'in the long run there will be only a significant increase in prices', knowing that the AS_{lr} curve is given by $Y = Y^N = 1875$.

Notes

1 The real value of a variable means that it is adjusted by price changes.
2 In the context of an open economy.
3 Menu costs are the costs of changing nominal prices in general due to information, decision and implementation costs. In the face of these costs firms do not always change their prices with every change in supply and demand.
4 The shape of the curve on a (Y, P) coordinate system is dominated by α; it is noteworthy to observe that to achieve a convex form, the usual shape in seminal textbooks, α must be higher than 0.5, which is not realistic. This is why in addressing the problem $\alpha = 0.5$ (straight line) is considered.
5 Output that keeps the inflation rate constant.
6 In practice, $\|x_k - x_{k-1}\| \leq tol$ or $\|x_k - x_{k-1}\| \leq \|x_k\| * tol$.

5 Portfolio model

Introduction

The portfolio optimisation model, originally proposed by Markowitz (1952), intends to select the proportions of various assets to be included in a portfolio which, according to certain criteria is the best solution. The criteria combine considerations of the portfolio's expected return and of the return's dispersion (and possibly other financial risk measures).

Therefore, the aim of an investor is to build a portfolio of assets that maximises a portfolio's expected return contingent on any given number of risks, usually measured by the standard deviation of the portfolio's expected return or, alternatively, that minimises risk for a given expected return. Portfolios that observe these criteria are known as efficient portfolios, such that to reach a higher (smaller) portfolio's expected return, the investor demands taking on more (less) risk. Investors are thus confronted with a trade-off between expected return and risk.

The main idea behind this model is thus the need to diversify in investing, with the aim of choosing a set of assets that has collectively the highest expected return for a defined level of risk or, alternatively, the lowest risk for a given level of expected return, resulting clearly that the investor should 'not put all eggs in one basket'.

The expected return-risk relationship of efficient portfolios is represented by an efficient frontier curve, which represents a set of portfolios offering the lowest risk for a defined level of return. Portfolios included in the efficient frontier tend to have a higher degree of diversification than the inefficient ones.

Although this model is widely used in practice in investment decisions, it has recently been extended to other fields, such as behavioural economics.

Solving this problem requires the use of optimisation knowledge and techniques. Optimisation is a broad and complex field in mathematics and this chapter only briefly introduces the topic. The focus will be on a Monte Carlo optimisation as well as on exploring some of the advanced numerical algorithms provided by the software.

MATLAB/Octave is used to gain important insights on how to develop an effective computational procedure to determine efficient portfolios. The exposition is based on seminal books[1] and papers, such as Markowitz (1952), Merton (1972), Haugen and Baker (1991), Nocedal and Wright (2006, ch. 2–7, 12–19) and Pachamanova and Fabozzi (2010, ch. 8–9).

Economic model

Mathematically, the aim is to maximise the expected return constrained to a given risk

$$\max_x c^T x, \quad \text{s.t.} \ x^T H x = \overline{\sigma}^2, \ \sum_{i=1}^n x_i = 1 \ \text{and} \ x_i \geq 0, \tag{5.1}$$

where n is the number of assets in the portfolio, x, $n \times 1$, is the column vector of the shares of the portfolio invested in each asset i, c, $n \times 1$ is the vector of the average benefit of each asset, H, $n \times n$, is the covariance matrix, and $\overline{\sigma}^2$ is the expected risk goal. The sum of all shares must equal 1 and no short selling is allowed (all $x_i \geq 0$). Problem (5.1) is known as a *quadratic programming* problem.

Alternatively, one can minimise the risk subject to an expected return goal, $\overline{c}$,

$$\min_x x^T H x, \quad \text{s.t.} \ c^T x = \overline{c}, \ \sum_{i=1}^n x_i = 1 \ \text{and} \ x_i \geq 0. \tag{5.2}$$

The concepts of global minimum variance portfolio and efficient frontier are crucial to understanding and performing portfolio selection computations.

The *global minimum variance portfolio* is the one satisfying

$$\min_x x^T H x, \quad \text{s.t.} \ \sum_{i=1}^n x_i = 1 \ \text{and} \ x_i \geq 0. \tag{5.3}$$

The *efficient frontier* is the set of pairs (risk, return) for which the returns are greater than the return provided by the minimum variance portfolio.

Numerical solution

Optimisation is critical in many areas of knowledge and economics is not an exception. The aim is to find the values of variables that optimise an objective, conditional or not on constraints. Analytical solutions are limited to small problem sizes and even these are sometimes impractical to perform. Numerical methods overcome limitations of size, but there is no universal algorithm to solve optimisation problems. Indeed, depending on the type of optimisation problem, there is an algorithm or a collection of algorithms able to solve it.

Due to the complexity of numerical optimisation, the topic is addressed only in a cursory manner, exploiting the MATLAB/Octave optimisation potentialities.

Let us consider the minimisation[2] problem

$$\min_{x \in \mathbb{R}^n} \quad f(x)$$
$$\text{s.t.} \quad c_i(x) = 0, \quad i \in E \qquad (5.4)$$
$$\phantom{\text{s.t.}} \quad c_i(x) \geq 0, \quad i \in I$$

where $f: \mathbb{R}^n \to \mathbb{R}$, $c_E: \mathbb{R}^n \to \mathbb{R}^{n_E}$ and $c_I: \mathbb{R}^n \to \mathbb{R}^{n_I}$, respectively, are the equality and inequality constraints. A feasible region is the set of points satisfying the constraints $S = \{x: c_i(x) = 0, \ i \in I \text{ and } c_i(x) \geq 0, \ i \in D\}$. Problems without restrictions $I = D = \emptyset$ emerge in many applications and also as a recast of constraint problems where restrictions are replaced by penalty terms added to the objective function in order to discourage violation of these restrictions.

Optimisation problems can be classified in various ways, according to, for example: (i) the functions involved (in the objective function and in the constraints: linear, nonlinear, convex); (ii) the type of variables used (integer, binary, discrete and continuous); (iii) the type of restrictions considered (equality, inequality); (iv) the type of solution to be obtained (local, global); and (v) differentiability of the functions involved (optimisation with or without derivatives).

Among the countless optimisation problems, linear, quadratic and nonlinear programming are the most usual. Many algorithms for nonlinear programming problems only seek local solutions: minimum in a neighbourhood. It is not always possible to find a global solution: minimum in all domains. However, in particular, for convex linear programming, local solutions are also global.

Numerical methods seek points in the feasible region of the problem generating a sequence of approximations convergent to the solution. The distinction between algorithms can be divided into two broad approaches: linesearch and trust region methods (see Nocedal and Wright 2006 for an overview).

For unconstrained optimisation problems, methods such as steepest descent, Newton and quasi-Newton are the most used approaches (Nocedal and Wright 2006, ch. 2–7); indeed, solving nonlinear systems are a closely related problem. For the software used, the functions `fminunc` and `fminsearch` perform these computations; the former using a derivative-free method.

Linear, quadratic and nonlinear programming accommodate optimisation problems with constraints. In a *linear programming* problem both the objective and constraints are linear

$$\min_{x} \ c^T x$$
$$\text{s.t.} \ Ax = b, \quad x \geq 0$$

where c and x are vectors (Nocedal and Wright 2006, ch. 13–14). A quadratic programming problem, as stated for the portfolio problem, involves a quadratic objective function and linear constraints

$$\min_{x} \frac{1}{2} x^T H x + x^T c$$

$$\text{s.t.} \quad a_i^T x = b_i, \quad i \in E$$

$$a_i^T x \geq b_i, \quad i \in I$$

where c, x and a_i are vectors, and H is a symmetric (Hessian) matrix (Nocedal and Wright 2006, ch. 16). Nonlinear constraint optimisation consists in solving (5.4) nonlinear objective functions and/or constraints. In general, numerical methods to solve a penalty function, a combination of objective function and constraints, are used to tackle this problem (Nocedal and Wright 2006, ch. 15, 17–18). For the software used, linprog solves linear programming problems, quadprog quadratic programming ones and fmincon general minimisation problems with restrictions.

A more computational approach to solve problems numerically, particularly optimisation, is based on Monte Carlo methods. These are experiments anchored on repeated random sampling to obtain numerical approximations of the solution; in general, the quality of the approximations grows as the number of simulations increases. They generate a set of possible inputs, following certain statistical properties, perform a deterministic computation with this set and analyse the results. However, numerical approximations may result in getting stuck in a local minimum.

For the portfolio problem two numerical approaches are considered, one using Monte Carlo and another quadratic programming. The latter exploits MATLAB/Octave functions.

Computational implementation

Consider the following data, respectively, for the returns vector and covariance matrix

$$c = \begin{bmatrix} 0.100 \\ 0.200 \\ 0.150 \end{bmatrix} \quad \text{and} \quad H = \begin{bmatrix} 0.005 & -0.010 & 0.004 \\ -0.010 & 0.040 & -0.002 \\ 0.004 & -0.002 & 0.023 \end{bmatrix}.$$

MATLAB/Octave code

Let us first consider the global minimum portfolio computation (5.2).

68 *Static economic models*

Portfolio with a Monte Carlo approach

A Monte Carlo procedure for the problem on hand can be schematised in the following algorithm.

1. Set an initial set of portfolios
2. For a certain number of times:

    (a) generate, for the set, variance costs according to the criterion function
    (b) select the best portfolio among the set
    (c) generate (randomly) a new set of portfolios from the best one available

The following function `portfolio_mcarlo_fun` computes the portfolio with minimum variance using a Monte Carlo approach. It is inspired by Kendrick *et al.* (2006, ch. 7).

```
function [x,x_hist] = portfolio_mcarlo_fun(H,nruns,const)
% Monte Carlo solution approach
% Implemented by: P.B. Vasconcelos and O. Afonso
% based on: Computational Economics,
% D. A. Kendrick, P. R. Mercado and H. M. Amman
% Princeton University Press, 2006
% input:
%    H, covariance matrix
%    nruns, number of Monte Carlo runs
%    const, constant to increase/reduce the magnitude of the random
%           numbers generated
% output:
%    x, best found portfolio
%    x_hist, search history for best portfolio

% initialization parameters and weights;
popsize = 10;
n = size(H,1);
pwm = (1/n)*ones(n,popsize);
crit = zeros(1,popsize);
x_hist = zeros(n,1);

% compute nruns x popsize portfolios
for k = 1:nruns
   for j = 1:popsize;
      crit(j) = pwm(:,j)'*H*pwm(:,j);
   end

   % selection of the best portfolio
   [~, top_index] = min(crit);
   x = pwm(:,top_index);

   % store the best portfolio
   x_hist(:,k) = x;
```

Portfolio model 69

```
  if k == nruns, break, end
  pwm(:,1) = x;
  for i = 2:popsize;
    x = x+randn(n,1)*const;
    pwm(:,i) = abs(x/sum(abs(x)));
  end
end
```

To execute the function just do the following.

```
nruns = 40;
const = 0.1;
[x,x_hist] = portfolio_mcarlo_fun(H,nruns,const);
disp('best portfolio:');
for i=1:length(x)
   fprintf('Asset %d \t %5.4f \n',i,x(i));
end
fprintf('expected return: %g \n',c'*x);
fprintf('risk             : %g \n',sqrt(x'*H*x));
```

Portfolio with a quadratic programming approach

Another possibility is to invoke directly a function able to solve quadratic programming problems.

```
Aeq = ones(1,length(c)); beq = 1;
     lb = zeros(1,length(c));
x = quadprog(2*H,[],[],[],Aeq,beq,lb);
disp('best portfolio:');
for i=1:length(x)
   fprintf('Asset %d \t %5.4f \n',i,x(i));
end
fprintf('expected return: %g \n',c'*x);
fprintf('risk             : %g \n',sqrt(x'*H*x));
```

To compute the portfolio which minimises the risk subject to an expected return goal (5.3), a different set of restrictions is required. This change will be embodied in the next code, where both problems will be tackled.

Efficient frontier

A procedure to compute and draw the efficient frontier consists of the following steps.

1. Compute P_1:
   (a) find the minimum variance portfolio, according to (5.3);
   (b) compute the risk and return for P_1.

Static economic models

2. Compute P_2:
   (a) find the portfolio that minimises the risk for an expected return goal equal to the return provided by the asset with maximum return, according to (5.2);
   (b) compute the risk and return for P_2.
3. Compute P_j, $j = 3, \ldots$ varying $\bar{c}$ between the returns provided by P_1 and P_2:
   (a) compute P_j according to (5.2);
   (b) compute the risk and return for the efficient P_j;
   (c) iterate on j.

The code under function ef implements the algorithm.

```
function ef(c,H)
% Efficient frontier portfolio
% Implemented by: P.B. Vasconcelos and O. Afonso
%   input:
%       c, asset returns
%       H, assets covariance matrix
clf; hold on;

% global minimum variance portfolio
Aeq = ones(1,length(c)); beq = 1;
lb = zeros(length(c),1);
xmin = quadprog(H,[],[],[],Aeq,beq,lb);
retmin = c'*xmin; riskmin = sqrt(xmin'*H*xmin);
plot(riskmin, retmin,'*')

% portfolio with the same expected return as the maximum asset
Aeq = [ones(1,length(c)); c']; beq = [1; max(c)];
xmax = quadprog(H,[],[],[],Aeq,beq,lb);
retmax = c'*xmax; riskmax = sqrt(xmax'*H*xmax);
plot(riskmax, retmax,'s')

% find other efficient portfolios
rr = linspace(retmin,retmax,10); l_rr = length(rr);
ret = zeros(l_rr,1); risk = ret;
for i = 1:l_rr
    Aeq = [ones(1,length(c)); c']; beq = [1; rr(i)];
    x = quadprog(H,[],[],[],Aeq,beq,lb);
    ret(i) = c'*x; risk(i) = sqrt(x'*H*x);
end
scatter(risk, ret);

% plot assets
plot(sqrt(diag(H)),c,'r+')
xlabel('risk (standard deviation)'); ylabel('return');
ylim([0.95*min(retmin,min(c)),1.05*max(retmax,max(c))]);
hold off

end
```

Some short comments on the codes

Portfolio with a Monte Carlo approach

For Monte Carlo, the m-file follows the algorithm provided. An initial tentative portfolio with equally distributed assets is taken and a matrix to store the convergence history of the optimisation procedure is pre-allocated with zeros. Then, the Monte Carlo loop is powered by taking `popsize` portfolios; the variance of all of them is computed and the best selected. From this (partial) best, using a random number generator (normally distributed), other `popsize-1` portfolios are generated. This new set of `popsize` portfolios are subject to a new loop. The process ends after `nruns` have been completed. It is important to note that the new generated portfolios must comply with the restrictions: this is ensured by the absolute value `abs` and the normalisation (division of `x` by `sum(x)`). In this process the `randn` function was used together with a `const` parameter to control the order of magnitude of the values generated.

Portfolio with a quadratic programming approach

With regard to the quadratic programming approach, both pieces of software have functions to perform

$$\min c^T x + \frac{1}{2} x^T H x$$

subject to a set of linear constraints: inequality, $Ax \leq b$; equality $Aeq \times x = beq$; and bounds on x, $lb \leq x \leq ub$. Yet, the syntax is not the same:

- MATLAB: `x = quadprog(H,c,A,b,Aeq,beq,lb,ub,x0)`.
- octave: `x = qp(x0,H,c,A,b,lb,ub,A_lb,A_in,A_ub)`

where x_0 is an initial approximation. For Octave, $A_{lb} \leq A_{in} \leq A_{ub}$. If some of the parameters do not exist, set them to an empty matrix [ ].

The use of this function is straightforward. The commands `Aeq = ones(1,length(c))` and `beq = 1` ensure the condition $\sum_{i=1}^{n} c_i = 1$, while `lb = zeros(length(c),1)` imposes $x_i \geq 0$ for $i = 1, \ldots, n$. Furthermore, one needs to multiply H by 2 since the solver is built to minimise $\frac{1}{2} x^T H x$ and not $x^T H x$ (the minimum is different but the minimiser is the same).

Efficient frontier

This code begins by computing the global minimum variance portfolio. Then it computes the portfolio with the same return as that of the asset with greater return. After that, it computes a set of efficient portfolios for expected returns between the one corresponding to the global minimum and the one associated

72 *Static economic models*

with the asset with greater return. Finally, the efficient frontier is plotted along with the assets.

Numerical results and simulation

For the solution obtained with Monte Carlo the result is as follows.

```
------------------------------------------------------
Portfolio optimization: global minimum variance
                        Monte Carlo solution approach
------------------------------------------------------
best portfolio:
Asset 1    0.7649
Asset 2    0.2355
Asset 3    0.0004
expected return: 0.123644
risk            : 0.0392812
```

Figure 5.1 illustrates the history of the successive best portfolios. Each execution delivers slightly different results, although with similar interpretation, since the set of portfolios is being generated making use of a random function. For this simulation, 40 runs were sufficient to provide a quite good approximation of the sought solution. Other combinations of assets can require a large number of runs.

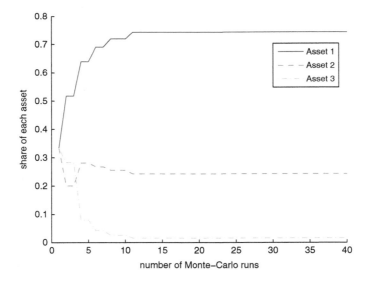

Figure 5.1 Monte Carlo convergence path for the portfolio with minimum variance.

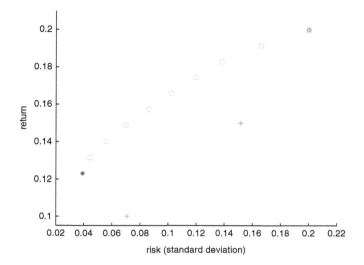

Figure 5.2 Efficient frontier (o), minimum variance portfolio (∗), portfolio with return equal to the asset with greater return (□) and the assets (+).

Similar results can be obtained via the quadratic programming with much less effort for the user.

```
------------------------------------------------------
Portfolio optimization: global minimum variance
                        quadratic programming approach
------------------------------------------------------
best portfolio:
Asset 1    0.7692
Asset 2    0.2308
Asset 3    0.0000
expected return: 0.123077
risk           : 0.0392232
```

The result of both approaches is the portfolio with minimum variance, and the two results are similar.

Finally, Figure 5.2, as a result of function ef, depicts the efficient frontier for the three assets, as well as the position on the (risk, return) axis of each one of the assets.

Highlights

- The portfolio optimisation model selects the optimal proportions of various assets to be included in a portfolio, according to certain criteria.

74 *Static economic models*

- A rational investor aims at choosing a set of assets (diversification) delivering collectively the lowest risk for a target expected return.
- A portfolio is considered efficient if it is not possible to obtain a higher return without increasing the risk.
- The expected return-risk relationship of efficient portfolios is represented by an efficient frontier curve.
- The model is a quadratic programming problem. It is solved by using a simple Monte Carlo approach that only requires the notion of a minimum conditioned to a set of restrictions, and by a more sophisticated method deployed by MATLAB/Octave.

Problems and computer exercises

Assume the data c and H used in this chapter.

1. For the Monte Carlo code, do the following.
   (a) Build a function to produce Figure 5.1.
   (b) Change the normally distributed pseudo-random number generator `randn` to the uniformly distributed `rand`. Verify that the method is not able to well approximate the solution, since an efficient portfolio without one asset (zero share) is almost impossible to approximate.
   (c) To solve the previous problem use the same generator but within the interval $[-1, 1]$.

2. Compute the portfolio that assures the same return as Asset 2. Do the same for Asset 3. Comment on the results.

3. Consider the problem with short selling (possibility).
   (a) Compute P_1, the global minimum variance portfolio
   $$\min_x x^T H x, \quad \text{s.t. } c^T x = \bar{c} \quad \text{and} \quad \sum_{i=1}^{n} x_i = 1.$$
   (b) Compute P_2, the efficient portfolio with expected return as the asset with maximum return.
   (c) Given the efficient portfolios, P_1 and P_2, other efficient ones can be easily computed through a convex combination of them:
   $$P_j = \alpha P_1 + (1 - \alpha) P_2, \quad \text{for } j = 3, \ldots.$$
   P_j is an efficient portfolio whenever the return of P_j is greater than the return corresponding to P_1 ('two-fund theorem'). Draw the efficient frontier, taking values for α between -1 and 1.
   (d) For what values of α is the portfolio not efficient? Draw the frontier of these portfolios.

(e) Combine both graphics in the same figure ('Markowitz bullet').
(f) Illustrate that the efficient frontier with short selling obtained with the procedure in the chapter or via convex combination are the same.
(g) Illustrate in the same figure the efficient frontier with and without short selling.

4. Consider the mean-variance portfolio problem

$$\max_{x} c^T x - \frac{1}{2}\beta x^T H x, \quad \text{s.t.} \quad \sum_i x_i = 1 \quad \text{and} \quad x_i \geq 0 \qquad (5.5)$$

where β is the subjective (adverse) rate to risk (adapted from Kendrick *et al.* 2006, ch. 7).

(a) Solve the problem, for $\beta = 2$, using Monte Carlo (Hint: `c'*pwm(:,j)-beta*0.5*pwm(:,j)'*H*pwm(:,j)` must be inserted in the code; also change the `min` function by the `max` function).
(b) Solve the problem, for $\beta = 2$, using quadratic linear programming (Hint: call `quadprog(beta*H,-c,[],[],Aeq,beq,lb)` since now a maximisation problem is to be solved and β should also be included).
(c) Illustrate the impact of β on the portfolio optimisation procedure.

Notes

1 Among the books of particular use was 'An Introduction to Computational Finance and Financial Econometrics' by Eric Zivot, a manuscript in preparation.
2 To maximise a function f just minimise $-f$.

Part II
Dynamic economic models

6 Supply and demand dynamics

Introduction

In 1930, Ricci, Tinbergen and Shultz published studies containing the first explicit models of a theory that, since Kaldor (1934), has come to be known as the cobweb model. For further details see Pashigian (2008).

In the basic model of supply and demand (see Chapter 1), the price adjusts so that the quantity supplied and the quantity demanded are equal. In turn, the economic cobweb model explains why prices can be subject to periodic fluctuations, bearing in mind goods whose production is not instantaneous or continuous, but needs some period of time. In this model the quantity supplied is a function not of the current price, but of the price of the preceding time period. Hence, producers believe that the price holds in the next period and thus start the new production according to the current price. For some slopes of the demand and supply curves, the equilibrium can be reached. Thus, the dynamic behaviour by economic agents may not always converge with supply equal to demand.

The assumption that supply must equal demand can be relaxed, as in the case of the market model with inventory. Since supply reacts with a one period lag to market prices, because it takes one period to complete the production process, it is natural for producers to hold an inventory to meet unexpected demand.

These models are presented to illustrate the use of first-order difference equations in economic analysis. Discrete-time problems can be easily solved numerically.

The analysis in this chapter follows Gandolfo (2010, ch. 2–7), Chiang and Wainwright (2005, ch. 17–18) and Pashigian (2008).

Cobweb model

The cobweb model is based on a time lag between supply and demand decisions. To have an idea about the model, consider a situation in which the producer's output decision must be made one period in advance; for example, suppose that, as a result of an unexpectedly bad productive year of good G, producers go to market with an unusually small production. This shortage, equivalent to a leftward shift in the market's supply curve, results in high prices.

If producers expect these high price conditions to continue in the following year, they will raise the production of G, and when they go to market the supply will be high, resulting in low prices. Then if low prices are expected to continue, producers will decrease the production of G, resulting again in higher prices. As this process repeats itself, oscillating between periods of low supply with high prices and high supply with low prices, the set price-quantity traces out a spiral.

This set may spiral inwards and the economy converge to the equilibrium or it may spiral outwards and the economy diverges since the fluctuations increase in magnitude. Therefore, there is convergence if the supply curve is steeper than the demand curve (fluctuations decrease in magnitude in each cycle) and divergence otherwise. It is noteworthy to mention that divergence also includes the case where fluctuations remain of constant magnitude (supply and demand curves have the same slope in absolute value).

Variables, parameters and functional forms

Assume that the output decisions in time t are based on the current price, P_t. Since this output will not be available for the sale until the next period time $t+1$, P_t determines $Q_{s,t+1}$ or, equivalently, P_{t-1} affects $Q_{s,t}$, which interacting with a demand function, imposes dynamic price patterns. The standard equations that characterise the market are:

- demand, $Q_{d,t} = \overline{Q}_d - aP_t$;
- supply, $Q_{s,t} = \overline{Q}_s + bP_{t-1}$;
- equilibrium, $Q_{d,t} = Q_{s,t}$,

where linear versions of the lagged supply and unlagged demand functions, respectively $Q_{s,t}$ and $Q_{d,t}$, are considered. It is assumed that in each time t the price is set at a level which clears the market, i.e. no producer is left with unsold output and no consumer with unsatisfied demand (there is no inventory).

The endogenous variables are: quantity demanded, $Q_{d,t}$; quantity offered, $Q_{s,t}$; and price of the good, P_t. The exogenous variables are: independent/autonomous quantity demanded, $\overline{Q}_d$; independent/autonomous quantity offered, $\overline{Q}_s$; and the price of the good in the previous period, P_{t-1}. Parameters are: a, $b > 0$, respectively, the sensitivity of the demand to price at time t and the sensitivity of the supply to price at time $t-1$.

Demand

As in Chapter 1, quantity demanded at time t, $Q_{d,t}$, is the total amount of a good that buyers would choose to purchase under given conditions, which include the price of the good, P_t, as well as other variables, represented by the exogenous variable $\overline{Q}_d$, such as income and wealth, prices of substitutes and complements, population, preferences (tastes) and expectations of future prices. The Law of Demand states that, *ceteris paribus*, when the price of a good rises, the quantity of the good demanded falls. A demand curve (or line) is a graphical representation of the relationship between price and quantity demanded, assuming that everything else remains constant. Changes in demand occur when one of the determinants of demand other than price changes; i.e. 'when the *ceteris* are not *paribus*'.[1]

Supply

Again, like in Chapter 1, the quantity supplied, $Q_{s,t}$, is the total amount of a good that sellers would choose to produce and sell under given conditions, which include the price of the good at the previous time period, P_{t-1}, as well as other variables, represented by the exogenous variable $\overline{Q}_s$, such as prices of factors of production, prices of alternative products the firm could produce, technology, productive capacity and expectations of future prices. The Law of Supply states that, *ceteris paribus*, when the price of a good at the previous time period rises, the quantity of the good supplied also rises. A supply curve (or line) is a graphical representation of the relationship between the price in the previous period and quantity supplied (*ceteris paribus*). Changes in supply occur when one of the determinants of supply other than the price of the previous period changes.[2]

Putting the demand and the supply curves together

By substituting $Q_{d,t}$ and $Q_{s,t}$ in $Q_{d,t} = Q_{s,t}$, the model can be reduced to a single first-order difference equation,

$$a P_t + b P_{t-1} = \overline{Q}_d - \overline{Q}_s,$$

which, since $a \neq 0$, can be rewritten as

$$P_{t+1} = -\frac{b}{a} P_t + \frac{\overline{Q}_d - \overline{Q}_s}{a}. \tag{6.1}$$

Now, (6.1) can be rewritten in terms of P_0, by replacing P_t by $-(b/a)P_{t-1} + (\overline{Q}_d - \overline{Q}_s)/a$ and then P_{t-1} by $-(b/a)P_{t-2} + (\overline{Q}_d - \overline{Q}_s)/a$ and so on:

$$P_{t+1} = -\frac{b}{a}\left(-\frac{b}{a}P_{t-1} + \frac{\overline{Q}_d - \overline{Q}_s}{a}\right) + \frac{\overline{Q}_d - \overline{Q}_s}{a}$$

$$= \left(-\frac{b}{a}\right)^2 P_{t-1} + \frac{\overline{Q}_d - \overline{Q}_s}{a}\left(1 - \frac{b}{a}\right)$$

82 Dynamic economic models

$$= \left(-\frac{b}{a}\right)^2 \left(-\frac{b}{a}P_{t-2} + \frac{\overline{Q}_d - \overline{Q}_s}{a}\right) + \frac{\overline{Q}_d - \overline{Q}_s}{a}\left(1 - \frac{b}{a}\right)$$

$$= \left(-\frac{b}{a}\right)^3 P_{t-2} + \frac{\overline{Q}_d - \overline{Q}_s}{a}\left(1 - \frac{b}{a} + \left(-\frac{b}{a}\right)^2\right)$$

$$= \ldots$$

$$= \left(-\frac{b}{a}\right)^{t+1} P_0 + \frac{\overline{Q}_d - \overline{Q}_s}{a}\left(1 - \frac{b}{a} + \left(-\frac{b}{a}\right)^2 + \cdots + \left(-\frac{b}{a}\right)^t\right).$$

The last term is the sum of the first $t+1$ terms of a geometric series, and thus

$$P_{t+1} = \left(-\frac{b}{a}\right)^{t+1} P_0 + \frac{\overline{Q}_d - \overline{Q}_s}{a}\left(\frac{1 - \left(-\frac{b}{a}\right)^{t+1}}{1 + b/a}\right)$$

$$= \left(-\frac{b}{a}\right)^{t+1} P_0 + (\overline{Q}_d - \overline{Q}_s)\frac{1 - \left(-\frac{b}{a}\right)^{t+1}}{a + b},$$

and, rewriting for t instead of $t+1$, we have

$$P_t = \left(P_0 - \frac{\overline{Q}_d - \overline{Q}_s}{a+b}\right)\left(-\frac{b}{a}\right)^t + \frac{\overline{Q}_d - \overline{Q}_s}{a+b}.$$

Three points are crucial in regard to this time path. First, the expression $(\overline{Q}_d - \overline{Q}_s)/(a+b)$ can be interpreted as the inter-temporal equilibrium price, which, being constant, is the stationary equilibrium. Second, the sign of $P_0 - (\overline{Q}_d - \overline{Q}_s)/(a+b)$ bears on the question of whether the time path starts above or below the equilibrium (mirror effect), whereas its magnitude decides how far above or below (scale effect). Third, the expression $-b/a$ generates an oscillatory time path and, consequently, gives rise to the cobweb phenomenon, showing three possible varieties of oscillation patterns: explosive, uniform or damped if, respectively, b is higher, equal or smaller than a. Indeed, it is easy to understand that P_t will converge to $(\overline{Q}_d - \overline{Q}_s)/(a+b)$ as t tends to ∞ if $|-(b/a)| < 1$.

Market model with inventory

The market model with inventory permits that sellers do keep an inventory of the good, assuming that the quantity demanded, $Q_{d,t}$, and the quantity currently produced, $Q_{s,t}$, are unlagged (linear) functions of P_t. Moreover, the adjustment of P_t is affected through a process of price-setting by the sellers and not through market clearance in every period. It is considered that sellers, at the beginning of each period, set a price for that period bearing in mind the inventory situation. Thus, the price adjustment made from period to period is inversely proportional to the observed change in the inventory (stock). The model is summarised by:

- demand, $Q_{d,t} = \overline{Q}_d - aP_t$;
- supply, $Q_{s,t} = \overline{Q}_s + bP_t$;
- price-setting, $P_{t+1} = P_t - \sigma(Q_{s,t} - Q_{d,t})$,

where $\sigma > 0$ is the (inventory) price-adjustment parameter.

By substituting the demand and supply equations in the price-setting equation, the model can be condensed into a single first-order difference equation,

$$P_{t+1} = (1 - \sigma(a+b))P_t + \sigma(\overline{Q}_d - \overline{Q}_s), \qquad (6.2)$$

and the solution is given by (following a similar procedure to that used previously)

$$P_t = \left(P_0 - \frac{\overline{Q}_d - \overline{Q}_s}{a+b}\right)(1 - \sigma(a+b))^t + \frac{\overline{Q}_d - \overline{Q}_s}{a+b}.$$

The dynamic stability of the model will hinge on the expression $1 - \sigma(a+b)$. The method converges whenever $|1 - \sigma(a+b)| < 1$, that is, for $0 < \sigma < 2/(a+b)$.

Numerical solution: difference equations

Dynamical systems describe the evolution of certain quantities over time. In this section time is considered to be discrete; that is, it evolves in periods from an integer to the next.

A first-order discrete dynamic system is a sequence of numbers given by a relation (*first-order difference equation*) $y_{t+1} = f(y_t)$, where $f(y_t)$ can be linear or nonlinear, giving rise to *linear* and *nonlinear difference equations*, respectively. In other words, it involves a one-period time lag only. If the system depends also on t itself, then it is said to be *nonautonomous* and *autonomous* otherwise.

Equations (6.1) and (6.2) are of the form $y_{t+1} = f(y_t) + g(t)$, with $g(t)$ a constant function, both examples of autonomous first-order difference equations; they are also *nonhomogeneous* since $g(t) \neq 0$, otherwise they would be *homogeneous*.

An nth-order difference equation involves a time lag of more than one period, $y_{t+n} = f(y_{t+n-1}, \ldots, y_t)$. The solution of a nonhomogeneous linear equation,

$$y_{t+n} + \sum_{i=1,\ldots,n} c_{n-i} y_{t+n-i} = g(t)$$

84 Dynamic economic models

with constant coefficients, $c_{n-1}, \ldots, c_0$, can be obtained from the sum of a *complementary function*, y_c, solution of the homogeneous part, and with a *particular solution*, y_p, any solution of the nonhomogeneous part.

For a first-order problem a complementary solution can be obtained by trying a solution of the form $k\lambda^t$, giving rise to the solution

$$y_t = k\lambda^t + y_p,$$

where k is specified provided that an initial condition at $t=0$ is given. The particular solution can be interpreted as the equilibrium state and $y_t - y_p = k\lambda^t$ gives the deviation from the equilibrium. Thus, the stability of the solution depends on the complementarity solution, that is, on the absolute value of λ: when $t \to \infty$ the solution is convergent (divergent) if $|\lambda| < 1$ ($|\lambda| > 1$). Furthermore, the cases $|\lambda| = 1$ are also divergent (the homogeneous part is constant for $\lambda = 1$ and oscillates for $\lambda = -1$). If $\lambda < 0$ ($\lambda > 0$) the time path of λ^t is oscillatory (nonoscillatory). For the cobweb model, $\lambda = -b/a$ and since both a and b are positive, oscillatory behaviour is shown.

For a second-order problem, the solution of the complementarity problem is obtained trying a solution of the form λ^t in $y_{t+2} + c_1 y_{t+1} + c_0 y_t = 0$:

$$\begin{aligned}\lambda^{t+2} + c_1 \lambda^{t+1} + c_0 \lambda^t &= 0 \\ \lambda^t(\lambda^2 + c_1 \lambda + c_0) &= 0 \\ \lambda^2 + c_1 \lambda + c_0 &= 0\end{aligned} \tag{6.3}$$

for $\lambda \neq 0$. The two sought roots of the second-order (characteristic) polynomial are the solution of (6.3), the *characteristic equation*:

- if λ_i, $i = 1, 2$, are distinct real roots, $y_t = k_1 \lambda_1^t + k_2 \lambda_2^t$, for two constants k_1 and k_2;
- if $\lambda = \lambda_1 = \lambda_2$, $y_t = k_1 \lambda^t + k_2 t \lambda^t$, for two constants k_1 and k_2;
- if $\lambda_1 = a - ib$ and $\lambda_2 = a + ib$ are complex (conjugate), $y_t = \rho^t (k_1 \cos(wt) + k_2 \sin(wt))$, with $\rho = \sqrt{a^2 + b^2}$ and $w = tg^{-1}(b/a)$.

With respect to stability, convergence will occur: for real distinct roots whenever $|\lambda_1| < 1$ and $|\lambda_2| < 1$; for a real root of multiplicity 2 whenever $|\lambda| < 1$; for conjugate complex roots when $\rho < 1$ (with a trigonometric oscillation).

For an nth-order difference linear equation, solutions are combinations of those presented for the second-order and the path towards the equilibrium is governed by the n roots of an nth-order polynomial.

Linear difference equations, with constant coefficients, play an important role in scientific problems, particularly in economics: the convergence behaviour of the time path can be well understood. Nonlinear equations are far more difficult to solve (analytically) than the linear counterpart since many of them are not solvable in terms of elementary functions; nevertheless, solutions can be obtained by iterating the equation numerically on a computer easily.

Roots of polynomials

Finding roots of high-degree polynomials can be a difficult problem.

Analytically there is no general algebraic solution to polynomial equations of degree five or higher with arbitrary coefficients (Abel-Ruffini theorem). On the other hand, root-finding algorithms are numerically unstable.

The solution is to resort to eigenvalue computations, which will be discussed in Chapter 7. Notice that the characteristic polynomial of A is the polynomial $p_A(\lambda) = \det(A - \lambda I)$. In particular, for 2×2 matrices A, $p_A(\lambda) = \lambda^2 - \text{trace}(A)\lambda + \det(A)$.

Roots of polynomials in practice

The MATLAB/Octave command roots(p) returns the roots of the polynomial p (stored as a vector of polynomial coefficients). For example, the roots of polynomial $p = \lambda^2 + 2*\lambda - 1$ can be obtained from the following commands: p=[1 2 -3], roots(p).

There is an important relation between the roots of a polynomial and the eigenvalues of the associated companion matrix. The *companion matrix* to a monic polynomial $\lambda^n + c_1\lambda^{n-1} + \cdots + c_1\lambda + c_0$ is the $n \times n$ matrix

$$\begin{bmatrix} -c_{n-1} & -c_{n-2} & \cdots & -c_1 & -c_0 \\ 1 & 0 & \cdots & 0 & 0 \\ 0 & 1 & \cdots & 0 & 0 \\ \vdots & \vdots & \ddots & \vdots & \vdots \\ 0 & 0 & \cdots & 1 & 0 \end{bmatrix}$$

and it is the result of the command compan(p), where p is the vector of polynomial coefficients. The eigenvalues are the polynomial roots eig(compan(p)). The function eig will be explained in the next chapter.

Computational implementation

The same baseline model from Chapter 1 is considered: $\overline{Q}_d = 1000$, $\overline{Q}_s = 250$, $a = 10$ and $b = 5$.

MATLAB/Octave code

The cobweb model (6.1) can be implemented with the cobweb.m script

```
%% Cobweb model
% Implemented by: P.B. Vasconcelos and O. Afonso
```

86 Dynamic economic models

```
clear; clc;
disp('————————————————————————————————————');
disp('Cobweb model                                          ');
disp('————————————————————————————————————');

%% parameters
a = 10; % sensitivity of the demand to price
b =  5; % sensitivity of the supply to price

%% exogenous variables
Qd_bar = 1000; % independent/autonomous quantity demanded
Qs_bar =  250; % independent/autonomous quantity offered

%% model
fprintf('Qd,t = %g - %g*Pt \n',Qd_bar,a) % demand
fprintf('Qs,t = %g + %g*Pt-1 \n',Qs_bar,b) % supply
fprintf('Qd,t = Qs,t \n')

%% compute the endogenous variables
tmax = 100; tol = 1e-5; % maximum nb of periods and tolerance
t = 1; P(t) = 25; Qs(t) = NaN; % initial price; no value for Q
disp('   t        Qt       Pt')
fprintf('  %d \t  \t %5.2f \n',t-1,P(t))

t = 2;
Qs(t) = Qs_bar+b*P(t-1);
P(t) = -b/a*P(t-1)+(Qd_bar-Qs_bar)/a;
fprintf('  %d \t %5.2f \t %5.2f \n',t-1,Qs(t),P(t))

while t<tmax && abs(P(t)-P(t-1))>tol*P(t)
    t = t+1;
    Qs(t) = Qs_bar+b*P(t-1);
    P(t) = -b/a*P(t-1)+(Qd_bar-Qs_bar)/a;
    fprintf('  %d \t %5.2f \t %5.2f \n',t-1,Qs(t),P(t))
end

%% cobweb plots
Qd(2:length(Qs)) = Qd_bar-a*P(1:length(Qs)-1); Qd(1) = NaN;
cobweb_plots(Qd_bar,Qs_bar,a,b,P,Qs,Qd)
```

with the function `cobweb_plots.m` for the plots.

```
function cobweb_plots(Qd_bar,Qs_bar,a,b,P,Qs,Qd)
% Cobweb plots: price, quantity cobweb plot, price phase diagram

% plot axis limits
ymin = min(P)*.95; ymax = max(P)*1.05;
yy = [ymin, ymax];

% prices
subplot(2,2,1)
t = 0:length(Qs)-1;
plot(t,P); xlabel('t'); ylabel('P'); ylim(yy);
```

```
% cobweb plot
subplot(2,2,2)
Pt = linspace(ymin,ymax,length(P))';
plot([Qd_bar-a*Pt Qs_bar+b*Pt],Pt,'—');
xlabel('Q'); ylabel('P'); ylim(yy);
hold on;
for t = 1:length(P)-1
    plot([Qs_bar+b*P(t),Qd_bar-a*P(t)],[P(t),P(t)],'r');
    plot([Qd_bar-a*P(t),Qs_bar+b*P(t+1)],[P(t),P(t+1)],'r');
end
hold off

% phase diagram (price)
subplot(2,2,3)
plot([0,ymax],[0,ymax]);
yy = [P(1)*0.95,ymax];
hold on;
for t = 1:length(P)-1
    plot([P(t),P(t)],[P(t),P(t+1)],'r');
    plot([P(t),P(t+1)],[P(t+1),P(t+1)],'r');
end
xlabel('P_{t}'); ylabel('P_{t+1}');
xlim(yy); ylim(yy);
hold off

% quantities demanded and supplied
subplot(2,2,4)
t = 0:length(Qs)-1;
plot(Qs,t,'-',Qd,t,'—');
xlabel('Q'); ylabel('t'); legend('Q_s','Q_d');

end
```

For the market model with inventory (6.2), a similar implementation, inventory.m, is prepared.

```
%% Market model with inventory
% Implemented by: P.B. Vasconcelos and O. Afonso
clear; clc;
disp('——————————————————————————————————');
disp('Market model with inventory         ');
disp('——————————————————————————————————');

%% parameters
a = 10; % sensitivity of the demand to price
b = 5;  % sensitivity of the supply to price
sigma = 0.05; % price-adjustment

%% exogenous variables
Qd_bar = 1000; % independent/autonomous quantity demanded
Qs_bar = 250;  % independent/autonomous quantity offered

%% model
fprintf('Qd,t = %g - %g*Pt \n',Qd_bar,a); % demand
```

88   Dynamic economic models

```
fprintf('Qs,t = %g + %g*Pt \n',Qs_bar,b); % supply
fprintf('Pt+1 = Pt-%g*(Qs,t-Qd,t) \n',sigma); % price adjustment
fprintf('Qd,t = Qs,t \n')

%% compute the endogenous variables
tmax = 100; tol = 1e-5; % maximum nb of periods
t = 1; P(t) = 25; Q(t) = Qs_bar+b*P(t);
disp('     t              Pt')
fprintf('   %d \t \t %5.2f \n',t-1,P(t))

t = t+1;
P(t) = (1-sigma*(a+b))*P(t-1)+sigma*(Qd_bar-Qs_bar);
Q(t) = Qs_bar+b*P(t-1);
fprintf('   %d \t %5.2f \t %5.2f \n',t-1,Q(t),P(t))

while t<tmax && abs(P(t)-P(t-1))>tol*P(t)
    t = t+1;
    P(t) = (1-sigma*(a+b))*P(t-1)+sigma*(Qd_bar-Qs_bar);
    Q(t) = Qs_bar+b*P(t-1);
    fprintf('   %d \t %5.2f \t %5.2f \n',t-1,Q(t),P(t))
end

inventory_plot(P)
```

Some short comments on the code

The script `cobweb.m` does not reveal new features, except the NaN that is used to explicitly express that there is no initial value for the quantity (vectors Q_s and Q_d could well be set to zero at the first component, but this would complicate the code since exceptions would be required to avoid the first component). A dual mechanism to control the iterative process is used, controlling both the number of iterations and the error of the approximation.

The function `cobweb_plot.m`, along with the two curves for the demand and supply, plots a segment connecting the iterates. The `linspace` function generates a row vector of dimension given by the third argument, equally spaced between the first and second arguments.

Numerical results and simulation

The iterative process along (discrete) time t is given by

```
--------------------------------------------------
Cobweb model
--------------------------------------------------
Qd,t = 1000 - 10*Pt
Qs,t = 250 + 5*Pt-1
Qd,t = Qs,t
   t      Qt           Pt
   0                   25.00
```

1	375.00	62.50
2	562.50	43.75
3	468.75	53.12
4	515.62	48.44
5	492.19	50.78
6	503.91	49.61
7	498.05	50.20
8	500.98	49.90
9	499.51	50.05
10	500.24	49.98
11	499.88	50.01
12	500.06	49.99
13	499.97	50.00
14	500.02	50.00
15	499.99	50.00
16	500.00	50.00
17	500.00	50.00
18	500.00	50.00

and Figure 6.1 displays a set of plots for the model.

Figures 6.1a and 6.1d show the evolution of prices and quantity along time. They can be read along with Figure 6.1b (*phase diagram*). Starting with a price $P=25$, the quantity supplied is smaller than that demanded. In the next period, price increases and, as a result, also the quantity supplied. Then, the price decreases as well as the quantity demanded. The iterative process continues until convergence. Due to the criteria established, the process was stopped when the relative error of P with respect to the previous period was smaller than 10^{-5}; if the tolerance for the relative error were smaller, the process would end either because the precision was achieved or the number of maximum iterations (100) was reached. Finally, in Figure 6.1c, prices P_{t+1} and P_t are plotted against each other (*phase diagram*), showing the dynamic of prices.

For the market model with inventory, the output, for $\sigma = 0.05$, is

---
Market model with inventory

```
Qd,t = 1000 - 10*Pt
Qs,t = 250 + 5*Pt
Pt+1 = Pt-0.05*(Qs,t-Qd,t)
Qd,t = Qs,t
time   Qt       Pt
  0             25.00
  1    375.00   43.75
  2    468.75   48.44
  3    492.19   49.61
```

90 *Dynamic economic models*

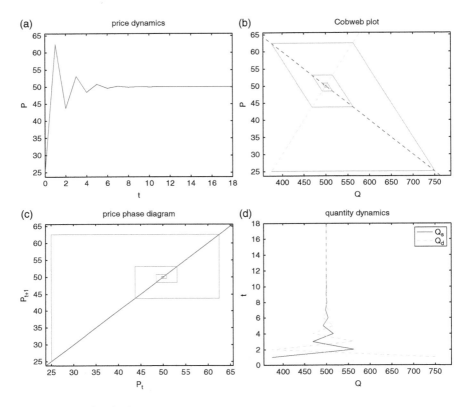

Figure 6.1 Cobweb plots.

```
4    498.05    49.90
5    499.51    49.98
6    499.88    49.99
7    499.97    50.00
8    499.99    50.00
9    500.00    50.00
```

and the phase diagram is illustrated in Figure 6.2.

The model is again convergent since $|1+\sigma(a+b)|=0.25<1$ but now with nonoscillatory behaviour because $0<1+\sigma(a+b)=0.25<1$.

Highlights

- The cobweb is a dynamic model derived from the static supply–demand model.
- It assumes that supply reacts to price with a lag of one period (or more) of time, while demand depends on current price.

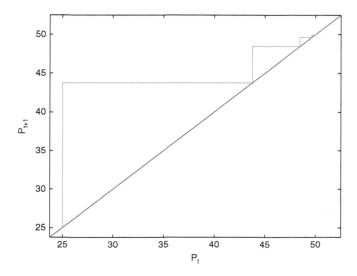

Figure 6.2 Price phase diagram for the inventory market model.

- It explains why prices might be subject to periodic fluctuations in certain types of markets.
- The market model with inventory relaxes the assumption that supply must equal demand.
- Difference equations are introduced and specifications about convergence are shown.

Problems and computer exercises

1. Consider the implemented Cobweb model.

   (a) Due to the increase in production costs, $\overline{Q}_s$ decreases to 200. What is the new equilibrium?

   (b) Suppose now that $\overline{Q}_d$ decreases towards 900 owing to a decrease in the available income. Discuss the impact on the equilibrium price and quantity.

   (c) The sensitivity of the supply to price (in the previous period), b, increased to 15. What happens to the equilibrium? And if b was 10?

2. *Cobweb with normal price expectations:* Consider that the quantity supplied at time t depends not on P_{t-1} but on an expected price, function of the price that producers would think to obtain in the market (normal price, P_N): $P_t^e = P_{t-1} + \alpha(P_N - P_{t-1})$, with $0 < \alpha < 1$. Note that if $\alpha = 0$ the original Cobweb model is recovered, while if $\alpha = 1$ then $P_t^e = P_N$ and the adjustment is immediate.

(a) Show that the recurrence relation for the price is given by

$$P_t = -\frac{b}{a}(1-\alpha)P_{t-1} - \alpha\frac{b}{a}P_N + \frac{\overline{Q}_d - \overline{Q}_s}{a},$$

and the convergence behaviour depends on $|-(b/a)(1-\alpha)|$. This version of the Cobweb can be convergent when the original diverges (the action of $1-\alpha$).

(b) Compute the equilibrium for $P_N = 50$ and $\alpha = 0.5$. Indicate the number of iterations required for convergence as well as the rate of convergence.

(c) Simulate the above exercise for $\alpha = 0, 0.2, 1$. Compare the results.

3. *Cobweb with adaptative expectations:* Consider now that expectations are adaptative: $P_t^e = P_{t-1}^e + \beta(P_{t-1} - P_{t-1}^e)$, with $0 < \beta < 1$. Note that if $\beta = 1$, the original Cobweb model is recovered, while if $\beta = 0$, then $P_t^e = P_{t-1}^e$ and the adjustment is immediate.

(a) Show that the new recurrence relation for the price is given by

$$P_t = \left(1 - \beta\left(1 + \frac{b}{a}\right)\right)P_{t-1} + \beta\frac{\overline{Q}_d - \overline{Q}_s}{a},$$

and the convergence behaviour depends on $|1 - \beta(1+b/a)|$.

(b) Compute the equilibrium for $\beta = 0.5$. Indicate the number of iterations required for convergence as well as the rate of convergence.

(c) Simulate the above exercise for $\beta = 0, 0.2, 1$. Compare the results.

Notes

1 See Chapter 1 for additional comments.
2 With the necessary adaptations, see Chapter 1 for additional comments.

7 Duopoly model

Introduction

This chapter focuses on imperfect competition, which may take the form of monopoly, oligopoly or monopolistic competition. Oligopoly markets are a case of imperfect market structure and consist of a small number of firms that dominate the market, selling differentiated or homogenous products. There are different ways of modelling oligopolies, depending on the way firms interact in the market. These approaches are as follows.

- Firms choose quantity and then price adjusts so that demand equals supply – these are the *Cournot* and *Stackelberg* models; in the former, competition among firms is simultaneous and independent, whereas in the latter the leader firm decides first and then the follower firms, sequentially, decide on their own production.
- Firms choose the prices and then consumers choose from which firm to buy – this is the *Bertrand* model.

The predictions of what the equilibrium will look like differ between these models. Cournot was the first author to address the stability of the equilibrium in a context where a learning process among firms occurs.

As it is common in industrial organisation literature, to understand the Nash equilibrium[1] of the above models, this chapter focuses on the duopoly case, in which the market has only two firms, and the aim is to analyse the market equilibria. It starts with a simple static case and then a dynamic interpretation is considered, using a discrete time formulation – simultaneous difference systems. A continuous duopoly case is considered as a project in Appendix A.

References Gandolfo (2010, ch. 9–10), Perloff (2013, ch. 14) and Varian (1992, ch. 16) are the basis for the exposition of the economic problem and Demmel (1997, ch. 4–5, 7) and Bai *et al.* (2000, ch. 2–4, 7) for the mathematical and computational support.

Cournot, Stackelberg and Bertrand models of duopoly markets

To understand the concepts, this section considers a static case with two firms in the industry – duopoly – each with a marginal cost $\overline{MC}$ and where the total

94 *Dynamic economic models*

demand is given by the (inverse) demand function:

$$P = \frac{1}{a}(\overline{Q}_d - (Q_1 + Q_2)),$$

where, in line with Chapter 1, P is the price, $\overline{Q}_d$ is the autonomous demand, $a > 0$ is the sensitivity of the demand to price and Q_i is the quantity offered by firm i, $i = 1, 2$.

The total revenue, TR_i, is

$$TR_i(Q_1, Q_2) = P \times Q_i = \frac{1}{a}(\overline{Q}_d - (Q_1 + Q_2))Q_i,$$

and thus the marginal revenue, MR_i, is

$$MR_i(Q_1, Q_2) = \frac{1}{a}(\overline{Q}_d - (Q_1 + Q_2 + Q_i)).$$

Then, firm i maximises profits by setting marginal revenue equal to marginal cost, $MR_i = \overline{MC}$.

Cournot

The Cournot equilibrium (P^*, Q^*), $Q^* = Q_1^* + Q_2^*$ is computed as follows.

- First, the best response of firm 1 to firm 2's decisions should be obtained; from $MR_1 = \overline{MC}$ and given Q_2, it results that $Q_1^*(Q_2) = \frac{1}{2}(\overline{Q}_d - a\overline{MC}) - \frac{1}{2}Q_2$.
- Second, the best response of firm 2 to firm 1's decision is computed; similarly, to firm 2, it results that $Q_2^*(Q_1) = \frac{1}{2}(\overline{Q}_d - a\overline{MC}) - \frac{1}{2}Q_1$.
- Finally, the Cournot equilibrium occurs when Q_1^* is replaced in Q_2^* (and vice versa): $Q_1^* = Q_2^* = \frac{1}{3}(\overline{Q}_d - a\overline{MC})$.

Stackelberg

To compute the Stackelberg equilibrium (P^*, Q^*), suppose that firm 1 is the leader (it decides first) and firm 2 is the follower; the sequential mechanism is as follows.

- First, similarly to step 2 in Cournot, the best response of firm 2 to leader firm 1 decision is computed; $Q_2^*(Q_1) = \frac{1}{2}(\overline{Q}_d - a\overline{MC}) - \frac{1}{2}Q_1$.
- Second, firm 1's total revenue, given firm 2's best response, is obtained:

    (i) $TR_1(Q_1, Q_2^*) = \frac{1}{2}(\overline{Q}_d + a\overline{MC}) - \frac{1}{2}Q_1$;
    (ii) $MR_1(Q_1, Q_2^*) = -(1/a)Q_1 + (\overline{Q}_d + a\overline{MC})/(2a)$;

(iii) from $MR_1 = \overline{MC}$, $Q_1^* = (\overline{Q}_d - a\overline{MC})/2$.

- Finally, given firm 1's optimal decision, Q_2^* is obtained using firm 2's best response function $Q_2^*(Q_1^*) = \frac{1}{4}(\overline{Q}_d - a\overline{MC})$.

The firm leader produces more in the Stackelberg equilibrium than the follower due to the first-mover advantage.

Bertrand model

In this case firms compete by setting prices, and thus the (Nash) equilibrium is such that the prices are equal to the marginal costs of the firms; that is, (P_1^*, P_2^*) has to be such that $P_1^* = \overline{MC}$ and $P_2^* = \overline{MC}$. To understand why such an equilibrium emerges, consider all possible prices that are different from $P_1^* = \overline{MC}$ and $P_2^* = \overline{MC}$, and show that they cannot be an equilibrium.

1. $P < \overline{MC}$ cannot be an equilibrium because at least one firm will earn negative profits and thus the firms have an incentive to deviate.
2. $\overline{MC} = P_1 < P_2$ is not an equilibrium because firm 1 can deviate by setting prices so that $\overline{MC} < P_1' < P_2$ and make higher profits; at this new price P_1', firm 1 does not lose any customers, but is selling at a higher price (i.e. it obtains higher profits).
3. $\overline{MC} < P_1 < P_2$ is not an equilibrium because firm 1 has an incentive to deviate by setting $P_1 < P_1' < P_2$, so that it does not lose any customers, but sells at a higher price (i.e. it gets more profits); moreover, firm 2 can also deviate by setting $\overline{MC} < P_2' < P_1$ in order to grab the whole market and sell at a price above the marginal cost.
4. $\overline{MC} < P_1 = P_2$ is not an equilibrium; firm 1, for example, has an incentive to deviate by setting $\overline{MC} < P_1' < P_1$ in order to capture the whole market by charging a lower price.

Discrete dynamics Cournot duopoly game

Under a duopolistic market consider two firms producing a homogeneous good. Each firm i, at any time period t, observes the other firm's output and assumes that this quantity stays unchanged in the next time period, $t+1$. Thus, given the linear market demand curve

$$P_t = \frac{\overline{Q}_d}{a} - \frac{1}{a} Q_{d,t},$$

firm i chooses its profit-maximising output. As in Chapter 1, P is the price of the good, $\overline{Q}_d > 0$ is the independent/autonomous quantity demanded, Q_d is the quantity demanded, which is also the quantity produced, $Q_{1,t} + Q_{2,t}$,

96 Dynamic economic models

and $a > 0$ is the sensitivity of the demand to price. Linear total cost curves $TC = TC_1 = TC_2$ are considered for each firm, and thus the marginal cost $\overline{MC}$ is constant.

Thus, each firm has an *ex ante* market price based on the belief that the other firm's output remains fixed:

$$P_{i,t+1} = \frac{\overline{Q}_d}{a} - \frac{1}{a}(Q_{i,t+1} + Q_{j,t}), \quad j \neq i.$$

Then, firm i determines $Q_{i,t+1}$ in order to maximise its expected profits:

$$\pi_{i,t+1} = P_{i,t+1} Q_{i,t+1} - TC$$

$$= \frac{\overline{Q}_d}{a} Q_{i,t+1} - \frac{1}{a}(Q_{i,t+1}^2 + Q_{i,t+1} Q_{j,t}) - TC.$$

The first-order conditions for an interior maximum are:[2]

$$\frac{\partial \pi_{i,t+1}}{\partial Q_{i,t+1}} = 0 \;\Rightarrow\; Q_{i,t+1} = -\frac{1}{2} Q_{j,t} + \frac{\overline{Q}_d - a\overline{MC}}{2}, \quad i,j = 1,2,\; i \neq j,$$

which is a nonhomogeneous first-order difference system. In matrical form,

$$Q_{t+1} = AQ_t + g \tag{7.1}$$

where $A = \begin{bmatrix} 0 & -\frac{1}{2} \\ -\frac{1}{2} & 0 \end{bmatrix}$, $Q_t = \begin{bmatrix} Q_{1,t} \\ Q_{2,t} \end{bmatrix}$ and $g = \begin{bmatrix} \frac{\overline{Q}_d - a\overline{MC}}{2} \\ \frac{\overline{Q}_d - a\overline{MC}}{2} \end{bmatrix}$.

The study of the homogeneous system, $Q_{t+1} = AQ_t$, will provide insight on the convergence of the process (as illustrated in Chapter 6). The fact that convergence is ruled by the eigenvalues of A, which is equivalent to obtaining the roots of the characteristic equation $\det(A - \lambda I) = 0$, is explained in the next section. For the case in analysis, $\lambda_1, \lambda_2 = \pm\frac{1}{2}$, and hence, the movement is convergent towards the equilibrium solution: $Q_1^* = Q_2^* = (\overline{Q}_d - \overline{MC})/3a$ (given for the static Cournot equilibrium in the previous section).

Numerical solution: systems of difference equations

Beginning with the simplest case, let us consider a first-order 2×2 system

$$Y_{t+1} = AY_t + g(t)$$

where $Y_t = [y_{1,t}, y_{2,t}]^T$, A is a 2×2 (transition) matrix of constants and $g(t) = [g_1(t), y_2(t)]^T$ a vector of two known functions. To access the convergence characteristics of the solution, the focus is on the homogeneous part, $g_1(t) = g_2(t) = 0$. As for difference linear equations, let us suppose that $Y_t = \begin{bmatrix} k_1 \\ k_2 \end{bmatrix} \lambda^t$ with k_1 and k_2 constants is a solution; then

$$\begin{bmatrix} k_1 \\ k_2 \end{bmatrix} \lambda^{t+1} = A \begin{bmatrix} k_1 \\ k_2 \end{bmatrix} \lambda^t$$

$$\lambda^t \left(\begin{bmatrix} k_1 \\ k_2 \end{bmatrix} \lambda - A \begin{bmatrix} k_1 \\ k_2 \end{bmatrix} \right) = 0$$

which, for $\lambda \neq 0$, leads to the following homogeneous system of linear equations:

$$(A - \lambda I) \begin{bmatrix} k_1 \\ k_2 \end{bmatrix} = 0.$$

Since the nontrivial solution $k_1 = k_2 = 0$ is sought, then matrix $A - \lambda I$ must have a null determinant, leading to the characteristic equation $\lambda^2 - \text{trace}(A) + \det(A) = 0$. The roots of this equations, λ_1 and λ_2, are the eigenvalues of matrix A.

The generalisation for $n \times n$ systems is immediate although the presence of more than two eigenvalues can lead to more complex behaviour over time.

As already explained in Chapter 6, depending on the eigenvalues, different types of solution result, and thus different stability conditions. In particular, the system is convergent if and only if all eigenvalues have absolute value less than 1.

Eigenvalue problem

An eigenvalue problem consists in computing solutions, scalars λ and nonzero x, of the matrix equation

$$Ax = \lambda x, \tag{7.2}$$

where A is a matrix of dimension $n \times n$. The scalar λ is an *eigenvalue*, $x \neq 0$ is the corresponding (right) *eigenvector* and (λ, x) is an *eigenpair*. The set of all eigenvalues of A is called the *spectrum* of A.

Eigenvectors are invariant directions under multiplication by A. Eigenvalues can be interpreted as the n roots of the characteristic polynomial $p(\lambda) = \det(A - \lambda I)$, and a particular λ_i as the representation of A in the subspace spanned by the corresponding x_i, $i = 1, \ldots, n$.

Note that real matrices can have complex eigenvalues, in which case they occur in conjugate pairs.

Numerical algorithms for computing eigenvalues (and eigenvectors) can be divided between transformation methods and in iterative methods. The former are based on similarity transformations to reduce the original matrix A to a form from which the eigenvalues are easier to compute while the latter first reduce matrix A into one of much smaller order and then use techniques to extract the eigenpairs from the smaller subspace where the problem was projected.

QR algorithm

The most well-known transformation method is the QR algorithm, which is based on two important concepts:

- *Schur form*: $A = UTU^*$, for U unitary ($U^* = U^{-1}$) and T triangular, where U^* is the conjugate transpose of U (there exists a real Schur Form);
- *QR factorisation*: $A = QR$, where Q is unitary and R is upper triangular.

The *QR algorithm* reduces A to the Schur form via an iterative process: perform a QR factorisation of A followed by the computation of the product of $R \times Q$; this new matrix is again subjected to the previous process that, under certain conditions, will converge to the Schur form.

In practice, the algorithm is much more complex in order to ensure stability and speed of convergence.

Iterative methods

While transformation methods are suited for small-dimension matrices and computing all eigenpairs, iterative methods, on the other hand, are good for large-dimensional problems and computing a subset of the spectrum. In this class of methods, the simplest are the *power method*, the *inverse iteration* and the *Rayleigh quotient iteration* (RQI), and the more powerful and sophisticated projection methods, for large-dimensional matrices, such as the *Arnoldi* method (Sorensen 1997), based on Krylov subpaces, and *Jacobi–Davidson* (Sleijpen and van der Vorst 2000) type methods. For an excellent overview of all these methods see Bai *et al.* (2000). Details on parallel implementations of these two methods can be consulted in Sorensen (1997) and Romero *et al.* (2011).

Eigenvalue computations in practice

Using MATLAB/Octave to factorise A as the product of Q and R only requires the command [Q,R]=qr(A). To use the QR algorithm to compute all eigenpairs of a small/moderate size matrix A just do [V,D]=eig(A), where D is a diagonal matrix of eigenvalues and V a matrix whose columns are the corresponding eigenvectors.

MATLAB/Octave command [V,D] = eigs(A) implements the Arnoldi method, an implicit version, for a sparse matrix A.

Computational implementation

Consider, along with the marginal cost $\overline{MC}$, the same baseline model from Chapter 6: $\overline{Q}_d = 1000$, $a = 10$ and $\overline{MC} = 10$.

MATLAB/Octave code

The Cournot dynamic duopoly game in equation (7.1) is implemented in the script cournot.m.

```
%% Discrete dynamic Cournot duopoly game
% Implemented by: P.B. Vasconcelos and O. Afonso
clear; clc;
disp('———————————————————————————————————————');
disp('Discrete dynamic Cournot duopoly game              ');
disp('———————————————————————————————————————');

%% parameters
a = 10; % sensitivity of the demand to price
MC_bar = 10; % marginal cost common to both firms

%% exogenous variables
Qd_bar = 1000; % independent/autonomous quantity demanded

%% model
A = [0 −0.5; −0.5 0];
g = [(Qd_bar−a*MC_bar)/2; (Qd_bar−a*MC_bar)/2];
fprintf('Qt+1 = AQt + g \n')
disp('A = '), disp(A);
disp('g = '), disp(g);

%% compute the endogenous variables
tmax = 100; tol = 1e−4; % maximum nb of periods
t = 1; Q(:,t) = [25; 25];
disp('   t       Q1,t       Q2,t')
fprintf('  %d \t %5.2f    %5.2f \n',t−1,Q(1,t),Q(2,t))

t = 2;
Q(:,t) = A*Q(:,t−1)+g;
fprintf('  %d \t %5.2f    %5.2f \n',t−1,Q(1,t),Q(2,t))

while t<tmax && norm(Q(:,t)−Q(:,t−1))>tol*norm(Q(:,t))
    t = t+1;
    Q(:,t) = A*Q(:,t−1)+g;
    fprintf('  %d \t %5.2f    %5.2f \n',t−1,Q(1,t),Q(2,t))
end

%% phase diagram
cournot_plot(Q)
```

The function cournot_plot.m is used to plot the phase diagram.

```
function cournot_plot(Q)
% Cournot phase diagram
```

```
q = Q(1,:); % for Cournot Q1=Q2

xmin = min(q)*0.8; xmax = max(q)*1.1;
xx = [xmin,xmax];
plot([0,xmax],[0,xmax]);

hold on;
for t = 1:length(q)-1
    plot([q(t),q(t)],[q(t),q(t+1)],'r');
    plot([q(t),q(t+1)],[q(t+1),q(t+1)],'r');
end
xlabel('Q_{t}'); ylabel('Q_{t+1}');
xlim(xx); ylim(xx);
hold off

end
```

Some short comments on the code

The codes in this chapter are very similar to those of Chapter 6, the main difference being the fact that to control the error, the norm function must be used instead of abs since now for each time period $Q_t = [Q_{1,t} Q_{2,t}]^T$ is a vector.

Numerical results and simulation

The iterative process along time t is given by the following.

```
------------------------------------------------------------
Discrete dynamic Cournot duopoly game
------------------------------------------------------------
Qt+1 = AQt + g
A =       0    -0.5000
    -0.5000         0
g =  450
     450

     t      Q1,t      Q2,t
     0      25.00     25.00
     1     437.50    437.50
     2     231.25    231.25
     3     334.38    334.38
     4     282.81    282.81
     5     308.59    308.59
     6     295.70    295.70
     7     302.15    302.15
     8     298.93    298.93
     9     300.54    300.54
    10     299.73    299.73
```

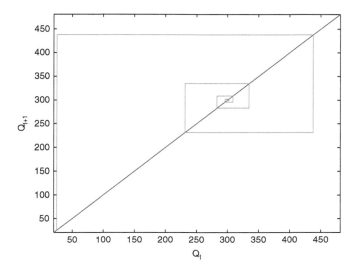

Figure 7.1 Quantity phase diagram for the dynamic duopoly Cournot game.

```
11     300.13    300.13
12     299.93    299.93
13     300.03    300.03
14     299.98    299.98
15     300.01    300.01
```

Figure 7.1 displays the quantity phase diagram.

The model is convergent since both eigenvalues of A are real and less than one in magnitude, that is, $|\lambda_1| = |\lambda_2| = 0.5 < 1$. The eigenvalues can be easily computed from `eig(A)`.

Highlights

- Oligopoly markets are characterised by a small number of firms and the focus in this chapter is on the duopoly case in which there are only two firms.
- The dynamic learning process through which each firm refines its own belief of the market behaviour is explored.
- Stability of systems of difference linear equations is analysed through the eigenvalues of the matrix that represents the linear autonomous system (with constant coefficients); the duopoly equilibrium for the Cournot game with a linear demand and cost functions is stable.
- Systems of difference equations are exposed and numerical algorithms to compute eigenvalues, such as the QR or Arnoldi algorithm are briefly

Problems and computer exercises

1. Compute the equilibrium for the Cournot $(Q_1^* = Q_2^* = (\overline{Q}_d - a\overline{MC})/3)$ and Stackelberg $(Q_1^* = (\overline{Q}_d - a\overline{MC})/2, Q_2^* = (\overline{Q}_d - a\overline{MC})/4)$ models, considering $\overline{Q}_d = 1000$, $a = 10$ and $\overline{MC} = 10$. Comment on the results.
2. Consider the dynamic discrete Cournot game implemented in cournot.m. Redo the problem, considering $P_0 = 100$ for initial price.
3. With linear demand and marginal constant costs, the discrete Cournot model for two firms (duopoly), $n = 2$, is stable.

   (a) Illustrate that for $n = 3$ the oligopoly shows constant oscillations.
   (b) Illustrate that for $n = 4$ the oligopoly is unstable (oscillations are explosive).
   (c) Illustrate that for $n > 3$ the oligopoly is unstable since the largest eigenvalue in magnitude are always equal to $-(n-1)/2$ and is thus greater than 1.

4. Consider that $P(Q) = Q^{-1/\eta}$ and that the two firms that produce the product, $i = 1, 2$, have cost function $C_i(Q_i) = 0.5 c_i Q_i^2$, Q_i and P_i being respectively, the quantity produced and the price. The profit of firm i is $\pi_i(Q_1, Q_2) = P(Q_1 + Q_2)Q_i - C(Q_i)$. Firm i takes the output of the other firm as given and chooses its production level such that $\partial \pi_i / \partial Q_i = 0$ (Miranda and Fackler 2002, ch. 3).

   (a) Show that the equilibria are the solutions of

   $$(Q_1 + Q_2)^{\frac{-1}{\eta}} - \frac{1}{\eta}(Q_1 + Q_2)^{\frac{-1}{\eta}-1} Q_i - c_i Q_i = 0, \quad i = 1, 2.$$

   (b) Assume $\eta = 1.6$, $c_1 = 0.8$ and $c_2 = 0.6$. Compute the equilibrium. Hint:
   (i) define the function $f(Q, c, \eta)$ as

   ```
   sum(Q)^(-1/eta)+(-1/eta)*sum(Q)^(-1/eta-1)
       *Q-diag(c)*Q
   ```

   (ii) for an initial guess, say [0.2; 0.2], find the zeros by calling

   ```
   x = fsolve(@(Q) f(Q,c,eta),[0.2;0.2]).
   ```

Notes

1 In simple words, in a Nash equilibrium players know the equilibrium strategies of the others and no one benefits by changing their own strategy.
2 It is easy to show that the second-order conditions are satisfied.

8 SP–DG model

Introduction

The *SP–DG model, Short-run expectations augmented Phillips–Demand Growth*, is a macroeconomic framework used to analyse the dynamics of inflation and output gap in three different cases: disinflation strategies, permanent demand shocks and temporary supply shocks. For disinflation strategies, both an aggressive strategy and a more gradual one are illustrated. In the case of a permanent demand shock, the dynamics of the state variables, assuming different processes of expectation formation by economic agents, are studied. In the third case, three different policymaker responses – neutral, accommodating and extinguishing – are considered.

The model is built from three central equations. Two of them describe the aggregate supply, which together are the ingredients necessary to construct the SP curve: the short-run supply curve that depends on the expected inflation rate. The third equation sets the demand growth curve, DG. The general equilibrium corresponds to the intersection of the curves.

The presentation of the SP–DG model in this chapter is based on the exposition in Gordon (2011, ch. 9) and takes also into consideration Andrade *et al.* (2007).

Economic model

The set-up of the model starts by specifying relationships among variables through the three central equations: the expectation formation process of the inflation rate, the SP and the DG curves.

Variables, parameters and functional forms

In this model the economy is characterised by:

- the expectation formation process, $\pi_t^e = \lambda \pi_{t-1} + (1-\lambda)\pi_{t-1}^e$;
- the short-run aggregate supply, $\pi_t = \pi_t^e + \alpha \hat{Y}_t + z_t^s$; and
- the demand side, $\hat{Y}_t = \hat{x}_t - \pi_t + \hat{Y}_{t-1} - z_t^d$.

104 *Dynamic economic models*

The main endogenous variables at time t are the inflation rate, π_t, the expected inflation rate, π_t^e, and the log of the output gap, $\hat{Y}_t$; this is defined as the percentage deviation between effective output and the economy's natural output, $Y_t^N = Y^N$.

The main exogenous variables are: the impact of a supply shock on the inflation rate at time t, z_t^s; the inflation rate at time $t-1$, π_{t-1}; the expected inflation rate at time $t-1$, π_{t-1}^e; and the demand shock, z_t^d.

The main parameters are the speed of the adjustment process of inflation rate expectations, λ, and the sensitivity of π_t to $\hat{Y}_t$, α.

Furthermore, the real output, Y_t, the nominal output, X_t, the actual nominal output growth rate, $\hat{x}_t$, and the general level of prices, P_t, at time t, are also required.

Expected inflation rate curve

An equation to describe the expectation formation process of the inflation rate is provided. Following Gordon (2011, ch. 9), one of a backward-looking type is assumed:

$$\pi_t^e = \lambda \pi_{t-1} + (1-\lambda)\pi_{t-1}^e. \tag{8.1}$$

Two extreme scenarios arise when $\lambda = 0$ and $\lambda = 1$. The former implies that economic agents do not adjust their expectations ($\pi_t^e = \pi_{t-1}^e$), whereas in the latter, expectations are adaptive and the speed of their adjustment is at maximum ($\pi_t^e = \pi_{t-1}$).

SP curve: short-run expectations augmented Phillips

The SP curve characterises the short-run aggregate supply and considers that the inflation rate depends positively on the expected inflation rate, on the output gap, and on a supply shock

$$\pi_t = \pi_t^e + \alpha \hat{Y}_t + z_t^s. \tag{8.2}$$

When there are no supply shocks, i.e. $z_t^s = 0$, and the output is at its natural level, i.e. $\hat{Y}_t = 0$, the economy is at long-run equilibrium. In this situation, the aggregate supply is graphically represented by a vertical line in the space $(\hat{Y}_t, \pi_t)$, with $\hat{Y}_t = 0$; thus, depending on the case, the value of the inflation rate π_t is equal to the expected one π_t^e.

The adjustment process induces changes in the SP curve towards the steady state. Bearing in mind (8.1), (8.2) can be rewritten as

$$\pi_t = \lambda \pi_{t-1} + (1-\lambda)\pi_{t-1}^e + \alpha \hat{Y}_t + z_t^s. \tag{8.3}$$

However, at time t and for a given π_t^e, what is the exact point $(\hat{Y}_t, \pi_t)$ that characterises the economy? In order to answer this question, an additional expression is required.

DG curve: demand growth

Finally, a DG curve, which accommodates the IS–LM model behaviour, should be derived to find the equilibrium values of the endogenous variables.

The nominal output, $X_t = P_t Y_t$, is given by the product of the general level of prices and the real output. Taking the logarithms and differentiating with respect to time yields

$$x_t = \pi_t + y_t, \tag{8.4}$$

where $x_t = \log(X_t) - \log(X_{t-1})$ and $y_t = \log(Y_t) - \log(Y_{t-1})$ represent, respectively, the effective nominal and real output growth rates. By subtracting the growth rate of natural real output, $y_t^N = \log(Y_t^N) - \log(Y_{t-1}^N)$, from each side of (8.4), it follows that

$$x_t - y_t^N = \pi_t + y_t - y_t^N, \tag{8.5}$$

where $\hat{x}_t = x_t - y_t^N$ represents the excess nominal output growth, and $y_t - y_t^N$ is the excess of actual over natural real output growth. Thus, (8.5) can be reflected in the usual DG curve

$$\hat{Y}_t = \hat{x}_t - \pi_t + \hat{Y}_{t-1} - z_t^d, \tag{8.6}$$

which represents the set of combinations $(\hat{Y}_t, \pi_t)$ for a given demand growth rate. Noteworthy is the inclusion of the variable z_t^d that represents an exogenous demand shock.

Global equilibrium

The equilibrium corresponds to the intersection of the curves SP in (8.3) and DG in (8.6), which can be analytically obtained by

$$\pi_t = \left(\frac{1}{1+\alpha}\right)\left[\lambda \pi_{t-1} + (1-\lambda)\pi_{t-1}^e + \alpha\left(\hat{x}_t + \hat{Y}_{t-1} - z_t^d\right) + z_t^s\right]. \tag{8.7}$$

In particular, when $\hat{Y}_t < 0$ ($\hat{Y}_t > 0$) the expected and observed inflation rate decreases (increases) until $\hat{Y}_t = 0$ and $\pi_t = \pi_t^e$. The model can be easily solved using numerical techniques.

Numerical solution

It is assumed that the economy is initially in long-run equilibrium, i.e. the output gap is zero, $\hat{Y}_0 = 0$, and $\pi_0 = \pi_0^e$. Regardless of the shock that affects the economy, either from the supply or demand side, π_t and $\hat{Y}_t$ will follow a convergence path towards a new steady state, in which $\hat{Y}_t$ will again be zero and $\pi_t = \pi_t^e$.

In order to introduce this feature one must consider an iterative process, which from an initial approximation tries to improve the successive solutions being computed. During each iteration a linear system based on (8.1), (8.2) and (8.6) is solved. Alternatively, since for this model an explicit solution was derived, one could implement directly the aggregate equation (8.7) (left as an exercise). A stopping criterium must be imposed to end the iterative process (if not, an endless process can happen). Usually a dual mechanism to accomplish this mission is used: both a predefined maximum number of iterations and a prescribed tolerance that a certain quantity must satisfy.

Algorithm

1. *parameter initialisation*: α, SP curve slope; λ, expectations formation; tol, tolerance for stopping criterion; $maxit$, the maximum number of iterations allowed;
2. *exogenous variables initialisation*: π_{t-1}, $\hat{x}_t$, $\hat{Y}_{t-1}$, z_t^d, z_t^s;
3. *endogenous variables*: π_t, π_t^e, $\hat{Y}_t$;
4. *provide shocks*, at $t = 0$;
5. while $abs(\hat{Y}_t) > tol$ and $t \le maxit$
   (a) $t = t + 1$;
   (b) (possibly) provide shocks at time t;
   (c) solve $((8.1) + (8.2) + (8.6))$ or (8.7) to obtain new values for π_t, π_t^e, $\hat{Y}_t$;
6. *solution history*: show the endogenous variables along with plots at the state variables space.

Computational implementation

Although the model can be used to study the effects of a permanent demand shock, a temporary supply shock and disinflation strategies, only the last of these is going to be implemented; that is, how a policymaker can achieve disinflation. The others are left as an exercise.

There are several economic motives for a policymaker to pursue a quantitative goal for the inflation rate; for example, a participation in a Monetary Union usually requires a specified set of formal economic convergence criteria.

The most straightforward way of reducing inflation is by decreasing demand growth. The policymaker can follow two different disinflation strategies: (i) a 'cold turkey' strategy, where there is a sudden reduction in demand growth;

SP–DG model 107

or (ii) a gradual strategy, where the policymaker gradually reduces demand growth. Assuming that the economy is initially in long-run equilibrium (output gap is zero, and observed and expected are equal), consider as a possible scenario an initial inflation rate of 12 per cent and that the policymaker's objective is to achieve 3 per cent.

MATLAB/Octave code

The code `spdg_disinflation.m` to solve the disinflation problem with both strategies is presented.

```
%% SP-DG Model
% Disinflation (cold turkey and gradual) versions
% Implemented by: P.B. Vasconcelos and O. Afonso
clear; clc;
disp('------------------------------------------------------------');
disp('SP-DG Model: Disinflation                                   ');
disp('------------------------------------------------------------');

%% parameters
alpha = 0.5;   % SP slope curve
lambda = 0.5;  % expectations speed of adjustment
tol = 1e-3;    % tolerance for stopping criterium
itmax = 100;   % maximum number of iterations allowed
disp('execution with: ');
fprintf(' precision     : %6.1e  \n',tol);
fprintf(' maximum iter. : %g      \n',itmax);
fprintf(' lambda        : %4.2f \n',lambda);
fprintf(' alpha         : %4.2f\n\n',alpha);
disp('policy adjustment process:');

%% Cold Turkey strategy
zd = [12,3]; zs = 0;
[sol,t] = spdg(alpha,lambda,zd,zs,itmax,tol);
fprintf(' Cold Turkey   : %d periods\n',t);
disp('  inflation      e.inflation    output gap');
fprintf('%12.8f  %12.8f  %12.8f\n',[sol(1,1:t);sol(2,1:t);
    sol(3,1:t)]);

% show the solution
subplot(1,2,1); hold on;
plot(sol(3,1:t),sol(1,1:t),'rx-');
xlabel('Output gap'); ylabel('Inflation rate');
legend('Cold Turkey'); legend('boxoff')
subplot(1,2,2); hold on;
plot(linspace(1,t,t),sol(3,1:t),'rx-')
plot(linspace(1,t,t),sol(1,1:t),'rx-.');
xlim([0 t]); xlabel('Time'); ylabel('Output gap and
    Inflation rate');
legend('Output gap (Cold Turkey)','Inflation rate (Cold Turkey)');
legend('boxoff')
```

108 *Dynamic economic models*

```
%% Gradual strategy
zd = [12,11,10,9,8,7,6,5,4,3]; zs = 0;
[sol,t] = spdg(alpha,lambda,zd,zs,itmax,tol);
fprintf(' Gradual      : %d periods\n',t);
disp(' inflation    e.inflation    output gap');
fprintf('%12.8f  %12.8f  %12.8f\n',[sol(1,1:t);sol(2,1:t);sol(3,1:t)]);

% show the solution
subplot(1,2,1);
plot(sol(3,1:t),sol(1,1:t),'b.-');
legend('Cold Turkey','Gradual','location','NorthWest');
legend('boxoff')
subplot(1,2,2);
plot(linspace(1,t,t),sol(3,1:t),'b.-')
plot(linspace(1,t,t),sol(1,1:t),'b.-.')
plot([0 t],[sol(3,t) sol(3,t)],'k:',...
     [0 t],[sol(1,t) sol(1,t)],'k:');
legend('Output gap (Cold Turkey)','Inflation rate (Cold Turkey)',...
       'Output gap (Gradual)','Inflation rate (Gradual)' );
legend('boxoff')
```

Some short comments on the code

The convergence process of the state variables in both strategies is studied. The considered initial inflation rate is 12 per cent, the output gap is 0 and the policymaker's objective is to achieve a 3 per cent inflation rate. Moreover, parameters α and λ are both equal to 0.5. With the "cold turkey" strategy, the demand growth suddenly shifts from 12 per cent to 3 per cent, whereas with a gradual strategy the demand growth slowly decreases (1 per cent a year) until it reaches a rate of 3 per cent.

The code begins by defining the parameters of the model along with other variables to control the iterative process. The matrix of the coefficients of the linear system that characterises the model is defined. The exogenous variables are the endogenous ones computed in the previous time iteration. Initial values to begin the iterative process are mandatory.

In order to implement the iterative process, spdg function, convergent to the new long-run equilibrium level after a shock, a while loop is considered. Inside the loop, the Gauss elimination method with partial pivoting can be used to compute the next iterate. As already known, only the right-hand side changes between iterations. The iterative process will continue until the maximum number of iterations (chosen as 100) is achieved or the output gap, $\hat{Y}$, is less than a prescribed tolerance. It is worth mentioning that since $\hat{Y}$ is a real number, one should not use a criterion like $\hat{Y}=0$. The criterion can never be satisfied; one requires that $\hat{Y}$, in absolute value, is less than 10^{-3} (or a more stringent tolerance).

Once the iteration process has finished, the program plots the results for $(\hat{Y}_t, \pi_t)$.

A separate function for the iterative process (called spdg) is provided, allowing its reuse to tackle other economic scenarios (the reader can easily do the proposed exercises by simply changing the type of shocks and calling this `spdg` function). A concise description of input and output variables is provided for this function, which can be easily accessed via the command line `help spdg`.

```
function [sol,t] = spdg(alpha,lambda,demand,supply,itmax,tol)
%SP-DG function model
% Input (parameters and exogeneous variables):
%     alpha  = SP slope curve
%     lambda = expectations speed of adjustment
%     demand = permanent demand shock: first value = initial condition,
%              replicate the last value
%     supply = temporary supply shock: (similar to demand)
%     itmax  = maximum number of iterations allowed
%     tol    = tolerance for stopping criterium
% Output (endogenous variables):
%     sol    = solution history
%              [inflation, expected_inflation, output_gap]'
% Implemented by: P.B. Vasconcelos and O. Afonso

% test data and set default parameters
if isempty(demand) || isempty(supply)
  disp('vector(s) of shocks empty'); return;
end
if nargin<6, tol = 1e-3; end
if nargin<5, itmax = 100; end

A = [1 -1 -alpha; 0 1 0; 1 0 1]; % coef. endogenous variables
[L,U] = lu(A);                   % LU factorization
sol = zeros(3,itmax);            % initializations
zd = zeros(1,itmax); zs = zd;

% set demand side of the shock
i_zd = length(demand);
if (i_zd >1), zd(1:i_zd-1) = demand(1:i_zd-1); end
zd(i_zd:itmax) = demand(i_zd);

% set supply side of the shock
i_zs = length(supply);
if (i_zs >1), zs(1:i_zs-1) = supply(1:i_zs-1); end
zs(i_zs:itmax) = supply(i_zs);

% initial solution inflation=expected_inflaton and output_gap=0
t = 1; sol(:,t) = [zd(t); zd(t); 0];

% loop for the iterative solution
while (abs(sol(1,t)-zd(end))>tol || abs(sol(3,t))>tol || t<=2) && t<itmax
  t = t+1;
  d = [zs(t-1);lambda*sol(1,t-1)+(1-lambda)*sol(2,t-1);...
       sol(3,t-1)+zd(t-1)];
  sol(:,t) = U\(L\d);
end
end
```

Numerical results and simulation

The output is presented here, omitting most of the intermediate iterations.

```
----------------------------------------------------
SP-DG Model: Disinflation
----------------------------------------------------
execution with:
 precision     : 1.0e-03
 maximum iter. : 100
 lambda        : 0.50
 alpha         : 0.50

policy adjustment process:
 Cold Turkey   : 48 periods
 inflation      e.inflation    output gap
 12.00000000   12.00000000    0.00000000
 12.00000000   12.00000000    0.00000000
  9.00000000   12.00000000   -6.00000000
  6.00000000   10.50000000   -9.00000000
  3.50000000    8.25000000   -9.50000000
  1.75000000    5.87500000   -8.25000000
  0.79166667    3.81250000   -6.04166667
  0.52083333    2.30208333   -3.56250000
     ...           ...            ...
  3.00093708    2.99991302    0.00204812
  3.00096607    3.00042505    0.00108205
  3.00082439    3.00069556    0.00025766
 Gradual       : 52 periods
 inflation      e.inflation    output gap
 12.00000000   12.00000000    0.00000000
 12.00000000   12.00000000    0.00000000
 11.66666667   12.00000000   -0.66666667
 11.00000000   11.83333333   -1.66666667
 10.05555556   11.41666667   -2.72222222
  8.91666667   10.73611111   -3.63888889
  7.67129630    9.82638889   -4.31018519
  6.39583333    8.74884259   -4.70601852
     ...           ...            ...
  3.00018164    2.99931278    0.00173772
  3.00041071    2.99974721    0.00132701
  3.00049498    3.00007896    0.00083203
```

Figure 8.1 shows the convergence process. In both cases the inflation rate converges to the desired value; however, the process differs greatly during the transitional dynamics phase, mainly during the first periods of the process. The

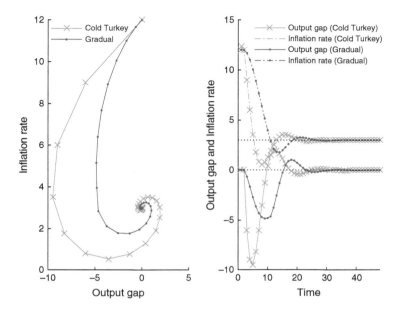

Figure 8.1 SP-DG disinflation process.

'cold turkey' strategy shows a more severe disinflation process of the economy; that is, it implies a higher negative output gap and, therefore, recession is more severe under this strategy. However, the adjustment process is faster.

To sum up, the disinflation process is associated with some losses in terms of both output and employment, and the choice between strategies depends on the policymaker's preferences and objectives.

Highlights

- The SP–DG model was first proposed by Robert J. Gordon (see Gordon (2011)).
- The present version is able to analyse the dynamics of the inflation and output gap under disinflation strategies, as well as permanent demand shocks and temporary supply shocks.
- Computational implementation provides insights on iterative processes: the dual stopping criterion mechanism and data structures to store the convergence history.

Problems and computer exercises

1. Redo the example, considering the aggregate equation (8.7).
2. Consider a steady-state situation where $\hat{Y} = 0$, $\pi = \pi^e = 6$. Analyse the effect on the dynamics of inflation and output gap due to a permanent

demand shock of 3 per cent, with no supply shocks ($z_s = 0$) and $\alpha = 0.3$, considering:

(a) $\lambda = 0$ (no adjustment of expectation);
(b) $\lambda = 1$ (pure adaptive expectations); and
(c) $\lambda \in \,]0, 1[$.

3. Illustrate the dynamics of inflation and output gap taking into account permanent demand shocks equal to 3 per cent and -3 per cent, considering several values of λ.
4. Show the effect of a negative temporary supply shock equal to 3 per cent for two temporal periods, for $\alpha = 0.5$ and $\lambda = 0.5$, considering:

(a) neutral ($\hat{x}$ constant);
(b) extinguishing ($\hat{x}$ decreases); and
(c) accommodating ($\hat{x}$ increases)

policy strategies.

9 Solow model

Introduction

In 1956, Robert Solow published a seminal paper on economic growth and development titled 'A Contribution to the Theory of Economic Growth', which is explored in this chapter. The Solow model of economic growth, also known as the Solow–Swan model, ignores some important aspects of macroeconomics, such as short-run fluctuations in employment and savings rates, and makes several assumptions that may seem to be heroic in order to describe the long-run evolution of the economy. The resulting model remains highly influential even today and despite its relative simplicity conveys a number of very useful insights about the dynamics of the growth process. In particular, it provides an important cornerstone for understanding why some countries flourish while others are impoverished.

The Solow model is also worth teaching from a methodological perspective because it provides a simple example of the type of dynamic model that is commonly used in today's more advanced macroeconomic theory.

In this chapter numerical methods for solving differential equations will be introduced and the Euler method implemented to solve initial value problems (Dahlquist and Björck 2008, ch. 1 and Süli and Mayers 2003, ch. 12).

Economic model

This is a model of capital accumulation in a pure production economy: the world considered in this chapter consists of countries that produce and consume only a single, homogeneous good (output, GDP or real income), there are no prices because there is no need for money. Everyone works all the time, saves a fixed portion of income, hence invests, and owns the representative firm; i.e. collects all 'wage' income and profit in the form of all output. As a result, the 'consumer side' is not modelled. Moreover, there is no government, thus no taxation nor subsidies, and it is a closed economy model.

This model then captures the pure impact that savings (investment) has on the long-run standard of living (per capita income).

114 *Dynamic economic models*

Solow model ingredients

The model is built around two equations: a production function and a capital accumulation equation.

Most of the key results for Solow's model can be obtained using any of the standard production functions. However, for concreteness, the production function is assumed to have the Cobb–Douglas form:

$$Y(t) = F(K(t), L(t)) = K(t)^\alpha L(t)^{1-\alpha} \tag{9.1}$$

where $K(t)$ is capital input, $L(t)$ is labour input and α, between 0 and 1, is the capital share in production. This production function is neoclassic since it exhibits constant returns to scale, presents positive and diminishing marginal returns to factor accumulation, and satisfies the *Inada conditions*.[1] Moreover, when zero units of input is used for either K or L, then nothing is produced. Exogenous technological progress $A(t)$, here omitted, is often considered.[2]

In per capita terms, the production function (9.1) is given by

$$\frac{Y(t)}{L(t)} = \frac{K(t)^\alpha L(t)^{1-\alpha}}{L(t)} \Leftrightarrow y(t) = k(t)^\alpha, \tag{9.2}$$

where $y = f(k(t)) = Y(t)/L(t)$ and $k(t) = K(t)/L(t)$. With more per capita capital, firms produce more per capita output; however, there are diminishing returns to per capita capital: each additional unit of per capita capital increases the per capita output by less and less.

From (9.1), taking logs and differentiating with respect to time on both sides, denoting by $\dot{Y}(t)$ and $\dot{L}(t)$ the derivatives of Y and L with respect to t, the result is

$$\frac{\dot{Y}(t)}{Y(t)} = \alpha \frac{\dot{K}(t)}{K(t)} + (1-\alpha)\frac{\dot{L}(t)}{L(t)},$$

which converts the Cobb–Douglas production function involving levels to a simple formula involving growth rates. The growth rate of per capita output is then simply (or, alternatively, taking logs and differentiating with respect to time on both sides of (9.2)):

$$\frac{\dot{Y}(t)}{Y(t)} - \frac{\dot{L}(t)}{L(t)} = \alpha \left(\frac{\dot{K}(t)}{K(t)} - \frac{\dot{L}(t)}{L(t)} \right),$$

i.e.

$$\frac{\dot{y}(t)}{y(t)} = \alpha \frac{\dot{k}(t)}{k(t)}.$$

Thus, there is just one source of increase in per capita output: the capital deepening (i.e. increases in per capita capital). Indeed, the model provides a useful framework for understanding how capital deepening determines the growth rate of per capita output.

The second key equation of the model is an equation that describes the path of capital accumulation (9.3), which accumulates according to

$$\dot{K}(t) = Y(t) - C(t) - \delta K(t), \tag{9.3}$$

i.e. the addition to the capital stock each period, $\dot{K}(t)$, depends positively on savings (this is a closed-economy model so savings, $Y(t) - C(t)$, equals gross investment) and negatively on depreciation, which is assumed to take place at rate δ. Since a fraction s of output is saved each period, $Y(t) - C(t) = sY(t)$, the labour input grows at rate n, $\dot{L}(t)/L(t) = n$, the path of per capita capital accumulation is given by

$$\dot{k}(t) = sy(t) - (\delta + n)k(t) \tag{9.4}$$

since $\dot{K}(t)/L(t) = \dot{k}(t) + (K(t)/L(t))n$.

Therefore, the change in per capita capital each period is determined by three terms: per capita investment, $sy(t)$, increases $k(t)$, while per capita depreciation, $\delta k(t)$, reduces $k(t)$. The term that is new in this equation is a reduction in k because of population growth, $nk(t)$. Each period there are $nL(t)$ new workers around who were not there during the last period. If there were no new investment and no depreciation, per capita capital would decline because of the increase in the labour force. The amount by which it would decline is exactly $nk(t)$.

Equation (9.4) is a differential equation and, for an initial stock of capital k_0, it defines an initial value problem. The numerical solution to this type of mathematical problems will be tackled in this chapter as well as in the following two.

Transitional dynamics: the Solow diagram

From (9.2) and (9.4) the denominated Solow diagram can be depicted (Figure 9.1). This diagram can be used to understand how per capita output evolves over time, taking into account an economy that starts out with a given stock of capital per worker, k_0, and a given population growth rate, depreciation rate and investment. The Solow diagram consists of two curves, plotted as functions of $k(t)$.

The first curve, $y(t) = f(k(t)) = k(t)^\alpha$, is the production function. The second curve is the amount of per capita investment, $sy(t) = sk(t)^\alpha$, which has the same shape as the production function, but is shifted down by the factor s. The third curve is the line $(\delta + n)k(t)$, which represents the amount of new per capita investment required to keep the amount of per capita capital constant.

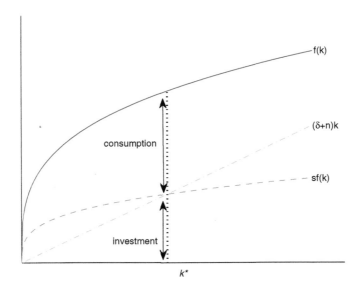

Figure 9.1 Solow diagram.

Indeed, both depreciation and the growing labour force tend to reduce the amount of per capita capital. The difference between these two curves is the change in the amount of per capita capital. When this change is positive and the economy is increasing its per capita capital, it is said that capital deepening is occurring. When the difference is zero, the per capita change is zero, but the capital stock, K, is growing (due to population growth), and it is said that only capital widening is occurring.

As an example, suppose an economy with capital equal to the amount k_0, which is smaller than the steady-state level. At k_0 the amount of per capita investment exceeds the amount needed to keep per capita capital constant, so that capital deepening occurs; i.e. $k(t)$ increases over time. This capital deepening will continue until the point $sy(t) = (n+\delta)k(t)$, so that $\dot{k}(t) = 0$. At this point, the amount of per capita capital remains constant, and such a point is a steady state.

If, instead, the economy begins with a per capita capital larger than the steady-state level, the amount of per capita investment provided by the economy is less than the amount needed to keep k constant. Therefore, the amount of per capita capital begins to decline, which occurs until the amount of per capita capital falls to the steady-state level.

The Solow diagram determines the steady-state value of per capita capital. In turn, the production function then determines the steady-state value of output per worker, as a function of the steady-state value of per capita capital. The production function is included in the Solow diagram itself to make this point clear. Moreover, notice that steady-state per capita consumption is then given by the difference between steady-state per capita output and steady-state per capita investment.

Steady state

The Solow-model economy tends to converge over time towards the steady state in which the output growth is constant (and the per capita output level is constant). First note that all variations in output growth are due to variations in the growth rate of capital input: $\dot{Y}(t)/Y(t) = \alpha(\dot{K}(t)/K(t)) + (1-\alpha)n$.

Hence, for output growth to be constant, capital growth should also be constant. That is, the growth rates for capital and output must be the same, and the capital–output ratio is constant along with constant growth. To see this, note that from (9.3) dividing by $K(t)$ on both sides gives $\dot{K}(t)/K(t) = s(Y(t)/K(t)) - \delta$. The growth rate of capital stock depends negatively on the capital–output ratio $K(t)/Y(t)$. Thus, for the capital stock to be growing at a constant rate, then $K(t)/Y(t)$ must be constant. But, $K(t)/Y(t)$ can only be constant if the growth rate of $K(t)$ is the same as the growth rate of $Y(t)$.

With this result in mind, the steady-state growth rate must satisfy $\dot{Y}(t)/Y(t) = \alpha(\dot{Y}(t)/Y(t)) + (1-\alpha)n$, and thus $(1-\alpha)(\dot{Y}(t)/Y(t)) = (1-\alpha)n$. The steady-state output (and capital) growth rate is then $\dot{Y}(t)/Y(t) = \dot{K}(t)/K(t) = n$ and the growth rate of per capita output (and capital) is $\dot{y}(t)/y(t) = \dot{k}(t)/k(t) = 0$. Thus, for example, economies with higher saving rates do not have faster steady-state growth rates. This is because an increase in, for instance, the saving rate can raise the growth rate initially by boosting capital accumulation. But diminishing marginal returns imply that during this period capital growth will outstrip output growth. Hence, higher saving rates can produce temporary increases of the growth rate of output, but cannot bring the economy to a path involving a faster steady-state growth rate.

Since, in steady state, $\dot{k}(t) = 0$, (9.4) and (9.2) can be used to solve the steady-state values of per capita capital and per capita output; thus,

$$\dot{k}(t) = sk(t)^\alpha - (\delta+n)k(t) \implies 0 = sk^{*\alpha} - (\delta+n)k^*$$

and so the steady-state values are

$$k^* = \left(\frac{s}{\delta+n}\right)^{\frac{1}{1-\alpha}} \tag{9.5}$$

$$y^* = \left(\frac{s}{\delta+n}\right)^{\frac{\alpha}{1-\alpha}}. \tag{9.6}$$

Notice that the endogenous variables k^* and y^* are now written in terms of the parameters of the model. Consequently, it can be stated that the model has a solution. *Ceteris paribus*, countries that have high savings/investment rates will

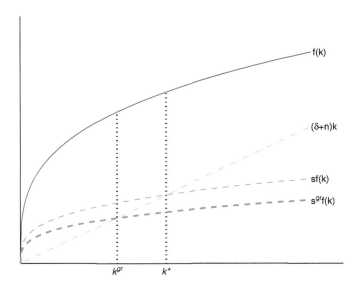

Figure 9.2 Golden rule savings rate.

tend to be richer. Such countries accumulate more per capita capital and, as a result, have more per capita output. In turn, countries that have high population growth rates will tend to be poorer.

The golden rule

The optimal capital accumulation leads to the *golden rule* savings rate that maximises the steady-state level of consumption. The per-capita consumption $c(t)$ is given by $c(t) = (1-s)y(t)$ and s can be written as $s = (y(t) - c(t))/y(t)$. At the steady state, $\dot{k}(t) = 0$, that is, $sy^* = (\delta + n)k^*$. The latter can be written in terms of $c(t)$, as $c^* = y^* - (\delta + n)k^*$. To find k that maximises c, the first-order condition, $dc/dk = 0$, produces

$$k^{gr} = \left(\frac{\alpha}{\delta + n}\right)^{\frac{1}{1-\alpha}}, \tag{9.7}$$

considering $A = 1$ (see Figure 9.2). Note that $k^* > k^{gr}$ whenever $s > \alpha$.

Linear approximation

The Solow model is one of the few growth models that has a closed solution. It can also be demonstrated that the convergence process is (globally) stable. For most part of the growth models the stability is studied from a linear approximation around the steady state.

Taking (9.4), considering $\dot{k}(t) = \phi(k(t))$, a first-order Taylor approximation for $\dot{k}(t)$, being $\phi(k(t))$ at least twice differentiable, is given by

$$\dot{k}(t) \simeq \phi(k^*) + \left.\frac{d\phi(k(t))}{dk(t)}\right|_{k^*} (k(t) - k^*)$$

$$\simeq \left(sf'(k^*) - (n+\delta)\right)(k(t) - k^*)$$

since $\phi(k^*) = 0$. Thus, whenever $k(t) < k^*$ ($k(t) > k^*$) then $\dot{k}(t) > 0$ ($\dot{k}(t) < 0$) and physical capital will accumulate (diminish) towards the steady state.

Numerical solution: initial value problems

Wide varieties of economic problems are modelled through differential equations. Since most differential equations are not analytically soluble, numerical solution of ordinary differential equations is a fundamental technique in continuous time dynamics to obtain information about the model's behaviour.

A differential equation is an equation involving an unknown function, $y(t)$, and its derivatives. A first-order *ordinary differential equation*, ODE, has the form

$$\dot{y}(t) = \frac{dy}{dt}(t) = f(t, y(t)), \qquad (9.8)$$

where $f: \mathbb{R} \times \mathbb{R} \to \mathbb{R}$ and $y(t): [t_0, t_T] \subset \mathbb{R} \to \mathbb{R}$.[3] The equation (9.8) is called nonautonomous but often economic problems are time-autonomous, that is of the form

$$\dot{y}(t) = \frac{dy}{dt}(t) = f(y(t)). \qquad (9.9)$$

Thus, basically, we know the derivative of an unknown function $y(t) \in \mathbb{R}$ as a (nonlinear) function f of t (the independent variable) and $y(t)$ (the dependent variable). From the resolution of (9.8) (or (9.9)) a family of solutions determined by a constant is obtained. A particular solution is computed by requiring that it goes through a specific point, the initial condition, $(t_0, y_0 = y(t_0))$. The problem specified both by (9.8) or (9.9) and the initial condition is called an *initial value problem*, IVP. Thus, solving the IVP is to predict the path that a quantity will take during a certain time interval, given the initial quantity (the condition can be at another point, rather than the initial).

Problems involving ODEs of a higher-order can be reduced to a system of first-order ODEs by introducing new variables. In Chapter 11, the study to a system of differential equations is extended. Furthermore, later on the book, in Chapter 12, *boundary value problems*, BVPs, where conditions are specified at the 'boundaries' of the independent variable, are also considered.

120   *Dynamic economic models*

Unfortunately it is seldom that these equations have solutions which can be expressed in a closed form. And if they can, the analytical form is often too cumbersome and the solution techniques are generally unable to deal with large and nonlinear systems of equations that arise in real problems. Numerical methods can often produce a solution to any degree of accuracy that the computer can represent.

To solve a continuous problem in a computer, a discretisation process is required. IVPs can be numerically solved using finite difference methods and recursive procedures.

The numerical procedures to be developed are based on approximations $y_0, y_1, \ldots, y_T$ to the exact solution $y(t_0), y(t_1), \ldots, y(t_T)$ at the grid points: $t_0 < t_1 < \cdots < t_T$. The distances $h_n = t_n - t_{n-1}$, $n = 1, \ldots, T$, are called step sizes and, for simplicity, equal step sizes, that is, uniform grids, where $h = (t_T - t_0)/T$, are considered. The aim is, starting with the initial value $y_0 = y(t_0)$, to find y_n, which approximates $y(t_n)$, by recurrence relations in such a way that the value of y_{n+1} could be stated as a function of y_n.

Euler method

A geometrically simple idea can be followed to compute the unknown function f. From (9.8), the slope of the tangent line at the initial point $(t_0, y(t_0))$ can be computed. Then, taking a small step along the computed tangent, another point (t_1, y_1) is reached, from where again a tangent can be computed. By doing this process iteratively until (t_T, y_T) a polygonal curve, $y_0, \ldots, y_T$ is computed that will approximate the sought-after solution: solution $y(t_0), \ldots, y(t_T)$ at points $t_0, \ldots, t_T$. The approximation error can be reduced by considering small step sizes, h. This is know as the *Euler method*:

$$y_{n+1} = y_n + h f(t_n, y_n), \quad n = 0, 1, \ldots, T. \tag{9.10}$$

Euler method in practice

A simple MATLAB/Octave function for the Euler method is provided.

```
function [t,y] = my_euler(f,tspan,y0,h)
%(progressive) Euler method with tspan=[t0 tf] and fixed
% step size to solve the IVP y'=f(t,y), y(t0)=y0
% input:
%   f      : function to integrate (f=@(t,y))
%   tspan  : integration interval [t0,tfinal]
%   y0     : initial condition at t0
%   h      : (constant) step size
% output:
%   t : specific times used
%   y : solution evaluated at t

t0 = tspan(1); tf = tspan(2);
t = t0:h:tf; y = zeros(1,length(t));
y(1) = y0; yn = y0; tn = t0;
```

```
for n = 1:length(t)−1
   yn     = yn+h*f(tn,yn);
   y(n+1) = yn;
   tn     = tn+h;
end
end
```

Stability of equilibrium points

It is relevant for the stability of linearised economic models to get some insight on the solution of linear differential equations.

The solution of $\dot{y}(t) = ay(t) + b$, as mentioned on Chapter 6, can be obtained from the solution of the homogeneous equations ($b = 0$) and the particular solution. The stability behaviour is ruled by the former. Since e^t satisfies $\dot{y}(t) = y(t)$, one should try $e^{\lambda t}$. Then, it results that $\lambda = a$ and thus $y(t) = ce^{-at}$, c constant (which can be determined for an IVP). The stability of the solution depends on the sign of λ: if $\lambda < 0$, then the solution converges to the steady state.

It is worth mentioning that the behaviour is different from the discrete case ($e^{\lambda t}$ vs λ^t): for discrete time both sign and modulus of λ are relevant to understand the equation's behaviour.

Additional comments

Sufficient conditions are known under which an IVP has a unique solution. For a unique continuous, differentiable function $y(t)$ to exist, f must be continuous in t and Lipschitz continuous in y ($\|f(t, y) - f(t, x)\| \leq L\|y - x\|$, where $L > 0$ is the Lipschitz constant).

The Euler method is the simplest method and it is a first-order method since the error of the final result, *global error*, is proportional to h. The error in a single step, *local error*, is proportional to h^2. High-order numerical methods will be explained in the next chapters.

Computational implementation

Here the solow m-file with the code to solve the problem, making use of the MATLAB/Octave function my_euler just built, is presented. The following baseline values are considered: $s = 0.4$, $A = 1$, $\alpha = 0.3$, $\delta = 0.1$ and $n = 0.01$.

MATLAB/Octave code

```
%% Solow model
% Neoclassical growth model (exogenous growth model)
% Implemented by: P.B. Vasconcelos and O. Afonso
disp('————————————————————————————————');
disp('Solow model: exogenous growth model           ');
disp('————————————————————————————————');
```

122 Dynamic economic models

```
%% parameters
s = 0.4; % savings rate
A = 1; % technological progress (Hicks neutral)
alpha = 0.3; % capital share in production
delta = 0.1; % depreciation rate
n = 0.01; % population growth rate
fprintf('   s      A     alpha   delta    n\n');
fprintf('%6.2f %6.2f %6.2f %6.2f %6.2f\n',s,A,alpha,delta,n);

%% steady-state and numerical solution
odesolow = @(t,k) s*A*k^alpha -(delta+n)*k;
kss = fsolve(@(k) odesolow([],k),10);
[t,y] = my_euler(odesolow,[0,100],0.5*kss,0.01);
plot(t,y);
if ~exist ('OCTAVE_VERSION', 'builtin')
  % labels for MATLAB
  xlabel('$t$','Interpreter','LaTex');
  ylabel('$k$','Interpreter','LaTex');
else
  % labels for Octave
  xlabel('t'); ylabel('k');
end
```

Some short comments on the code

The code is straightforward to follow. The `odesolow` function is defined taking the Cobb–Douglas production function, $f(k(t)) = Ak^\alpha$, considering Hicks neutral technological progress. Making $A = 1$ reproduces the baseline model presented. The `my_euler` function is invoked considering a time span from 0 to 100 and considering for initial value half of the value of k in steady state. For this particular equation an analytical expression for the steady state is known; more generally, a numerical approximation is computed making use of the `fsolve` function. In order to show t and k as variables (to mimic the text), LaTeX language at `xlabel` and `ylabel` commands are used. The tested version of Octave[4] does not yet support LaTeX, so this is accommodated by distinguishing the labels according to the software used.

Numerical results and simulation

Figure 9.3 displays the transitional dynamics towards the steady state.

Let us now access the results upon shocks on the economy.

1. Consider an increase in the depreciation rate from 0.1 to 0.15. To answer this question, the following script is provided

```
% delta increases
clf;
solow_base; % Solow baseline model (without plot)
var_exp = '\delta=';

draw_solow(t,y,s,A,alpha,delta,n,kss,var_exp,delta,1);
subplot(122)
```

Solow model   123

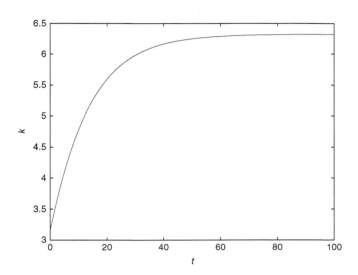

Figure 9.3 Transition dynamics to steady state.

```
hold on;
text(kss,(delta+n).*kss,'(\delta+n)*k')
hold off;

%% shock on delta
delta_new = 0.15;   % shock on delta
fprintf('delta from %6.2f to %6.2f\n',delta,delta_new);
odesolow = @(t,k) s*A*k.^alpha-(delta_new+n).*k;
[t,y] = my_euler(odesolow,[0,100],0.5*kss,0.01);
kss = (s*A/(delta_new+n))^(1/(1-alpha));

draw_solow(t,y,s,A,alpha,delta_new,n,kss,var_exp,delta_new,2);
subplot(121)
hold on;
if ~exist('OCTAVE_VERSION','builtin')
  % labels for MATLAB
  xlabel('$t$','Interpreter','LaTex');
  ylabel('$k$','Interpreter','LaTex');
  legend(strcat(var_exp, num2str(delta)), ...
         strcat('\delta_{new}=', num2str(delta_new)))
else
  % labels for Octave
  xlabel('t'); ylabel('k');
  legend(strcat('\delta=', num2str(delta)), ...
         strcat('\delta_{new}=', num2str(delta_new)))
end
hold off;
subplot(122)
hold on;
```

```
text(kss,(delta_new+n).*kss,'(\delta_{new}+n)*k')
hold off;
```

along with the function `draw_solow`

```
function draw_solow(t,y,s,A,alpha,delta,n,kss,var_exp,var,linew)
%Draws Solow diagram and transitional dynamics
% t,y: transitional dynamics provided by ODE solver
% s,A,alpha,delta,n: parameters of the Solow model
% kss: k in steady state
% var_exp, var: parameter subjet to a shock (expression, value)
% linew: line width

% transitional dynamics
subplot(121)
hold on;
plot(t,y,'LineWidth',linew);
if ~exist ('OCTAVE_VERSION', 'builtin')
  % labels for MATLAB
  xlabel('$t$','Interpreter','LaTex');
  ylabel('$k$','Interpreter','LaTex');
  legend(strcat(var_exp, num2str(var)));
else
  % labels for Octave
  xlabel('t'); ylabel('k');
end
hold off;

% Solow diagram
subplot(122)
hold on;
k = 0:0.05:1.5*kss;
plot(k,(delta+n).*k, 'm-.','LineWidth',linew);
plot(k,A*k.^alpha, 'g','LineWidth',linew);
plot(k,s*A*k.^alpha, 'r—','LineWidth',linew);
plot([kss,kss],[0,A*kss.^alpha],'k:','LineWidth',2);
if ~exist ('OCTAVE_VERSION', 'builtin')
  % labels for MATLAB
  xlabel('$k$','Interpreter','LaTex');
  ylabel('$\dot{k}$','Interpreter','LaTex');
else
  % labels for Octave
  xlabel('k'); ylabel('k^{.}/k');
end
hold off;

end
```

In this case, Figure 9.4, the $(\delta + n)k$ curve rotates up and to the left to the new curve $(\delta_{new} + n)k$. At the previous current steady-state value k^*, the per capita investment is no longer high enough to keep the capital–labour ratio constant in the face of rising δ, and therefore the capital–labour ratio begins to fall. It continues to fall until the point at which $sy = (\delta_{new} + n)k$ and k reach a smaller value for the steady state. From the

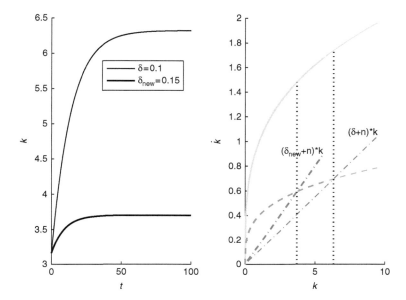

Figure 9.4 Transition dynamics and Solow diagram: variation on δ.

production function, this smaller level of k will be associated with smaller y; the economy is now poorer than before. From the figure on the left-hand side of Figure 9.4 it is evident that the convergence process is faster for increasing values of δ.

2. Next consider an increase in the technology, from $A = 1$ to $A_{\text{new}} = 1.1$.

   The increase in A from 1 to 1.1 shifts the $sy = sAk^\alpha$ curve upwards in the Solow diagram (Figure 9.5). At the previous current steady state, the per capita investment exceeds the amount required to keep k constant and hence the economy begins capital deepening again. This capital deepening continues until $A_{\text{new}}sk^\alpha = (\delta + n)k$ and k reaches a higher value. From the production function, this higher level of k will be associated with higher y. Thus, the economy is now richer than before.

3. Simulate the transition dynamics when $k_0 > k^*$ and draw on the same figure the direction field of solutions to the Solow ODE equation (suggestion: use the `quiver` MATLAB function).

   From Figure 9.6, independently of the initial value, the per capita capital goes to the steady state (the steady-state equilibrium of this model is *globally asymptotically stable*).

Highlights

- The Solow model was developed in 1956 by the Nobel Laureate of 1987, Robert Solow.

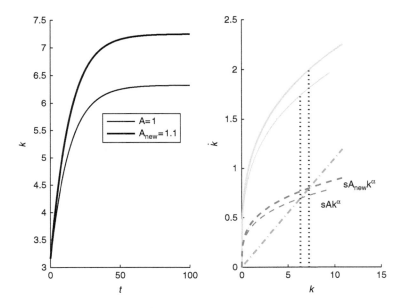

Figure 9.5 Transition dynamics and Solow diagram: variation on A.

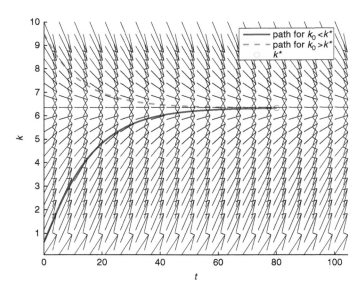

Figure 9.6 Direction field and paths to steady state.

- The Solow model shows how an economy changes over time until it gets to steady state.
- Savings rates determine the level of per capita capital (and output) level in steady state. The higher the savings rate, the higher the level of per capita capital (output) level.
- Population growth has a negative impact on capital accumulation. The higher the population growth rate, the lower level of capital (output) steady state.
- However, neither factors can explain sustained economic growth as observed in developed countries. In the current model, per capita capital (output) is invariant in steady state.
- This chapter introduces the Euler method, the simplest numerical method to solve initial value problems.

Problems and computer exercises

1. For the baseline model, build a new script that implements the analytical solution. Verify that the approximate solution for the transition dynamics is similar to the one obtained with the analytical one.
2. Consider an economy that has reached its steady-state value of per capita output.

   (a) Suppose that the consumers decide to increase the investment rate s permanently from 0.4 to 0.5. What happens to k and y?
   (b) Now suppose that it is the population growth rate n which increases, from 0.01 to 0.03. What happens to k and y?

3. With respect to economic representation, do the following.

   (a) Write an m-file to provide the Solow diagram (presented in Figure 9.1).
   (b) For the previous exercise, rewrite the code in order to produce the Solow diagram in growth rate terms.
   (c) Write an m-file to illustrate the golden rule savings rate, Figure 9.2.
   (d) Write an m-file to produce Figure 9.6.

4. What is the value of the per-capita consumption at the:

   (a) steady state (s and k^*);
   (b) moment when the savings rate changes to the golden rule (s^{gr} and k^*);
   (c) new steady state (s^{gr} and k^{gr})?

5. After exploring Chapter 11, rewrite the `solow` m-file to solve the ODE by the `ode45` function, instead of `my_euler`.

Notes

1 Inada conditions ensure stability of the growth trajectory in neoclassic models: $\lim_{K \to 0} \partial F / \partial K = \lim_{L \to 0} \partial F / \partial L = \infty$ and $\lim_{K \to \infty} \partial F / \partial K = \lim_{L \to \infty} \partial F / \partial L = 0$.

2 Three types of neutral technological progress have been discussed in the literature. The Hicks neutral occurs when technological progress augments both labour and capital, $Y(t) = A(t)F(K(t), L(t))$. The Harrod neutral recognises technological progress as being labour augmenting, $Y(t) = F(K(t), A(t)L(t))$. The Solow neutral occurs when there is capital-augmenting progress, $Y(t) = F(A(t)K(t), L(t))$.

3 The complex space can also be considered.

4 Depending on the graphing utility used for Octave, the TeX interpreter may not be present; for instance, Gnuplot provides this functionality.

10 Skill-biased technological change model

Introduction

Skill-Biased Technological Change represents a shift in the production of technological knowledge that favours high-skilled over low-skilled labour by increasing its relative productivity, and therefore its relative demand that exceeds the increase in the relative supply, thus increasing the skill premium. The analysis is based on Afonso (2006).

In Acemoglu (2002a, b, 2003) and Acemoglu and Zilibotti (2001), for example, labour endowments influence the direction of technological knowledge, which in turn drives wage inequality dynamics. In these contributions, the chain of effects is dominated by the market-size channel, by which technologies that use the more abundant type of labour are favoured.

This chapter analyses the direction of technological knowledge in a dynamic setting where the scale effects are removed (e.g. Jones 1995a, b), by considering that the difficulty in conducting R&D is proportional to the size of the market measured by the stock of labour, which results in a 'permanent-effects-on-growth' specification (e.g. Dinopoulos and Segerstrom 1999). The chain of effects is then induced by the price channel, by which there are stronger incentives to improve technologies when the goods that they produce command higher prices, i.e. technologies that use the scarcer labour are favoured.

For reasons of simplicity, it is assumed that the capacity to learn, assimilate and implement advanced technological knowledge can be different between types of labour, in line with, e.g. Nelson and Phelps (1966) and Galor and Moav (2000).

In the new context, the rise in the skill premium results from the fact that the price channel dominates the market-size channel.

In order to better understand the mechanism, a standard (in endogenous R&D-growth theory) economic structure is proposed. The production of perfectly competitive final goods uses labour together with quality-adjusted intermediate goods, which, in turn, use innovative designs under monopolistic competition. In particular, each final good is produced by one of two technologies.

130 *Dynamic economic models*

Then by solving the transitional dynamics numerically it is shown that the recent rise of the skill premium arises from the price-channel effect, complemented with a mechanism that can be called the technological-knowledge-absorption effect.

In this chapter, MATLAB/Octave is used to solve the model making use of Runge–Kutta methods (Dahlquist and Björck 2008, ch. 1 and Süli and Mayers 2003, ch. 12).

Economic model

Modelling the domestic economy

Productive (supply) side Following the contribution of Acemoglu and Zilibotti (2001), each final good $n \in [0, 1]$ is produced by one of two technologies. The L-technology uses low-skilled labour, L, complemented with a continuum of L-intermediate goods indexed by $j \in [0, J]$. The H-technology's inputs are high-skilled labour, H, complemented with a continuum of H-intermediate goods indexed by $j \in [J, 1]$. The output of n, Y_n, at time t is

$$Y_n(t) = A \left\{ \left[\int_0^J \left(q^{k(j,t)} x_n(k,j,t) \right)^{1-\alpha} dj \right] [(1-n)l L_n]^\alpha + \left[\int_J^1 \left(q^{k(j,t)} x_n(k,j,t) \right)^{1-\alpha} dj \right] [nh H_n]^\alpha \right\}. \quad (10.1)$$

The term A is the exogenous productivity dependent on the country's quality of institutions. The integrals sum up the contributions of intermediate goods to production. The quantity of each j, x, is quality-adjusted – the constant quality upgrade is $q > 1$, and k is the highest quality rung at time t. The expressions with exponent $\alpha \in (0, 1)$ represent the role of the labour inputs. An absolute productivity advantage of H over L is accounted for by $h > l \geq 1$. Also, n and $(1 - n)$ are adjustment terms such that $n \in [0, 1]$ is an ordering index meaning that H is relatively more productive in final goods indexed by higher ns, and vice versa; this implies that a threshold final good exists where a shift from one technology to another is advantageous.

The production function implying complementarity between inputs and substitutability between technologies is crucial for analysing the effects of inputs levels on the technological-knowledge bias and thus on the wage premium.

The production of quality-adjusted intermediate goods occurs under monopolistic competition; thus, there is a mark-up for the firm producing the final quality of intermediate good j. This leader firm captures the entire market by following a limit price strategy (e.g. Grossman and Helpman, 1991).

The value of the leading-edge patent depends on the profit-yields accrued by the monopolist at each time t and on the duration of the monopoly.

The duration, in turn, depends on the probability of successful R&D, which results in designs (prototypes) in order to produce a new quality of intermediate goods that creatively destroys the current leading-edge design. The determinants of the probability of success are thus at the heart of the Schumpeterian R&D models (e.g. Aghion and Howitt, 1992). Let $pb(k, j, t)$ denote the instantaneous probability at time t – a Poisson arrival rate – of successful innovation in the next quality intermediate good j, $k(j, t) + 1$, which complements m-type labour (where $m = L$ if $0 < j \leq J$ and $m = H$ if $J < j \leq 1$). Formally,

$$pb(k, j, t) = \underbrace{rs(k, j, t)}_{(i)} \underbrace{\beta q^{k(j,t)}}_{(ii)} \underbrace{\varsigma^{-1} q^{k(j,t)\left(\frac{-1}{\alpha}\right)}}_{(iii)} \underbrace{m^{-1}}_{(iv)} \underbrace{f(j)}_{(v)},$$

where:

(i) is the flow of resources (in terms of aggregate final good, Y) towards R&D in j at t;
(ii) is the positive learning effect arising from past R&D in j at t;
(iii) is the adverse effect caused by the increasing complexity of new quality improvements in j at t;
(iv) is the adverse effect induced by the market size, capturing the idea that the difficulty in introducing new quality-adjusted intermediate goods and replacing old ones is proportional to the size of the market measured by the labour employed;
(v) is the absolute advantage of H over L to learn, assimilate and implement advanced technological knowledge (the technological-knowledge-absorption effect); the specification for function $f(j)$ is

$$f(j) = \begin{cases} 1 & \text{if } 0 \leq j \leq J; \text{ i.e. } m = L \\ \left(1 + \dfrac{H}{H+L}\right)^\sigma & \text{if } J \leq j \leq 1; \text{ i.e. } m = H \end{cases},$$

$$\text{where } \sigma = 1 + \frac{H}{L}. \quad (10.2)$$

Consumption (demand) side A time-invariant number of heterogeneous individuals – continuously indexed by $a \in [0, 1]$ – decide the allocation of income, which is partly spent on consumption of the composite final good, and partly lent in return for future interest (savings). The infinite horizon lifetime utility of an individual with ability a is the integral of a discounted CIES (Constant-Intertemporal-Elasticity-of-Substitution) utility function,

$$U(a, t) = \int_0^\infty \frac{c(a, t)^{1-\theta} - 1}{1 - \theta} e^{-\rho t} \, dt, \quad (10.3)$$

where: $c(a, t)$ is the consumption (of the composite final good) by the individual with ability a, at t; ρ is the homogeneous subjective discount rate; and θ is the inverse of the inter-temporal elasticity of substitution.

Savings consists of accumulation of financial assets, with return r, in the form of ownership of the firms that produce intermediate goods in monopolistic competition.

Each individual maximises lifetime utility in (10.3), subject to budget constraint; the solution for the consumption path, which is independent of the individual, is the standard Euler equation

$$\hat{c}(a, t) = \hat{c}(t) = \frac{r(t) - \rho}{\theta}, \qquad (10.4)$$

where $\hat{c}$ is the growth rate of c, i.e. $\hat{c} = \dot{c}/c$, and r is the interest rate.

Equilibrium

Equilibrium for given factor levels Under perfect competition in final goods production, economic viability of the two technologies relies on the relative productivity, h/l, and prices of m-type labour, as well as on the relative productivity and prices of the intermediate goods, due to the complementarity between intermediate goods in production. The prices of labour rely on the quantities, H and L; in relative terms, the adjusted productivity of quantity H in production is given by $(hH)/(lL)$. As for the productivity and prices of intermediate goods, they rely on complementarity with each type of labour, H or L, on the embodied technological knowledge and on the mark-up; these determinants are summarised by the aggregate quality indexes:

$$Q_L(t) \equiv \int_0^J q^{k(j,t)(\frac{1-\alpha}{\alpha})} dj \quad \text{and} \quad Q_H(t) \equiv \int_J^1 q^{k(j,t)(\frac{1-\alpha}{\alpha})} dj.$$

The endogenous threshold final good results from the equilibrium in inputs and thus relies on determinants of the economic viability of the two technologies:

$$\bar{n}(t) = \left[1 + \left(\frac{Q_H(t)hH}{Q_L(t)lL} \right)^{1/2} \right]^{-1} \qquad (10.5)$$

which can be related with prices, since on the threshold both an L- and H-technology firm should break even; thus,

$$\frac{p_H(t)}{p_L(t)} = \left(\frac{\bar{n}(t)}{1 - \bar{n}(t)} \right)^\alpha, \quad \text{where} \quad \begin{cases} p_L = p_n(1-n)^\alpha = \exp(-\alpha)\bar{n}^{-\alpha} \\ p_H = p_n n^\alpha = \exp(-\alpha)(1-\bar{n})^{-\alpha} \end{cases}. \qquad (10.6)$$

Thus, a higher Q_H/Q_L (technological-knowledge bias measure) and/or a higher H/L imply(ies) a higher fraction of final goods using H-technology (i.e. a smaller threshold final good) – see (10.5); this in turn implies a low relative price of goods produced with H-technology (price channel affecting the technological-knowledge bias) – see (10.6).

R&D equilibrium The expected current value of the flow of profits to the monopolist producer j, $V(k, j, t)$, relies on the profits at each moment in time, $\Pi(k, j, t)$, on the given equilibrium interest rate, r, and on the expected duration of the flow, which is the expected duration of the successful researchers' technological-knowledge leadership; such duration in turn depends on the probability of a successful R&D; the expression for $V(k, j, t)$ is

$$V(k, j, t) = \frac{\Pi(k, j, t)}{r(t) + pb(k, j, t)}.$$

Under free-entry R&D equilibrium the expected returns are equal to resources spent,

$$pb(k, j, t)V(k, j, t) = rs(k, j, t)$$

and the following expression for the equilibrium m-specific growth rate is obtained:

$$\hat{Q}_m(t) = \left\{ \frac{\beta}{\zeta} \left(\frac{q-1}{q} \right) [p_m(t)A(1-\alpha)]^{\frac{1}{\alpha}} \overline{m} f(.) - r(t) \right\}$$
$$\times \left[q^{(\frac{1-\alpha}{\alpha})} - 1 \right]. \tag{10.7}$$

Steady-state equilibrium Since the aggregate output has constant returns to scale in inputs Q_H and Q_L, and macroeconomic aggregates are all multiples of Q_H and Q_L, the constant and unique steady-state endogenous growth rate, which through the Euler equation also implies a constant steady-state interest rate, is driven by an endogenous technological-knowledge progress

$$g^* = \hat{Q}^* = \hat{Y}^* = \hat{X}^* = \hat{R}^* = \hat{C}^* = \hat{c}^* = \frac{r^* - \rho}{\theta}.$$

The steady-state interest rate, r^*, is obtained by setting the growth rate of consumption in (10.4) equal to the growth rate of technological knowledge in (10.7). Having obtained the steady-state interest rate, the steady-state growth rate results from plugging r^* into the Euler equation (10.4). In particular, the steady-state wage premium, w_H/w_L, is

$$W \equiv \frac{w_H}{w_L} = \left(\frac{Q_H h L}{Q_L l H} \right)^{\frac{1}{2}} \tag{10.8}$$

which is also constant.

134   *Dynamic economic models*

Transitional dynamics At time 0, having a higher incentive to improve intermediate goods used with a particular type of labour, there will be a technological-knowledge bias, which affects wage inequality. The bias increases until the steady state, and at the steady state ends since Q_H and Q_L grow at the same rate.

The transitional dynamics is described by a differential equation and will be solved numerically. The differential equation that describes the path of the variable $D = Q_H/Q_L$ is

$$\hat{D}(t) = \frac{\beta}{\zeta}\left(\frac{q-1}{q}\right)[A(1-\alpha)]^{\frac{1}{\alpha}}\exp(-\alpha)$$

$$\times \left\{h\left(1+\frac{H}{H+L}\right)^{\sigma}\left[1+\left(D(t)\frac{hH}{lL}\right)^{\frac{-1}{2}}\right]^{\alpha}\right.$$

$$\left. - l\left[1+\left(D(t)\frac{hH}{lL}\right)^{\frac{1}{2}}\right]^{\alpha}\right\}. \tag{10.9}$$

The stability of D can be first verified and then the behaviour of other variables, namely the H-premium, W, can be characterised. The interest is to compare the baseline path with the path arising from the increase in the number of skilled workers, H, in line with recent developments in OECD economies.

Due to the increase in H, the technological-knowledge-absorption effect, $f(j)$ in (10.2), is greater than in the baseline case. This affects positively D. Such bias increases the supply of H-intermediate goods, thereby increasing the number of final goods produced with H-technology in (10.6) and lowering their relative price. Thus, relative prices of final goods produced with H-technology drop continuously towards the steady-state levels; this path of relative prices implies that D is increasing but at a decreasing rate until it reaches its new higher steady state.

Numerical solution: initial value problems

As seen in the previous chapter, a numerical procedure to solve an IVP $\dot{y}(t) = f(t, y(t))$, $y_0 = y(t_0)$, can be built by finding y_n, $n = 1, 2, \ldots$, which approximates $y(t_n)$, by recurrence relations in such a way that the value of y_{n+1} could be stated as a function of y_n, using relations of the form

$$y_{n+1} = y_n + h\Phi(t_n, y_n; h). \tag{10.10}$$

This numerical approach gives rise to the class of *one-step* (or *self-starting*) method, which uses only data gathered in the current step. For $\Phi(t_n, y_n; h) = f(t_n, y_n)$ the Euler method explained in Chapter 9 is recovered, where h stands for the integration step size.

Beyond the scope of this book are the *multistep* methods (or methods with memory) where the value of y_{n+1} is stated as a function of y_k, $k = n - r + 1, \ldots, n$ (r-step method). Relation (10.10) shows an *explicit* method as against *implicit* methods where y_{n+1} depends implicitly on itself through f: for the one-step case,

$$y_{n+1} = y_n + h\Phi(t_n, t_{n+1}, y_n, y_{n+1}; h).$$

Taylor series based methods

Assuming that f and its derivatives are well defined over the interval of interest, the truncated Taylor series expansion for $y(t)$ in t_0 can be used:

$$y(t) = y(t_0) + \sum_{k=1}^{p} \frac{1}{k!}(t - t_0)^k y^{(k)}(t_0) + O(h^{p+1}).$$

The derivatives are not known since the solution function is not known. Using the notation $f^{(j)} = d^j f/dt^j$ and $t_n = t_0 + nh$, $n \in \mathbb{Z}^+$, $y(t_1)$ can be approximated by $y(t_1) \approx y_1 = y(t_0) + \sum_{k=1}^{p}(1/k!)h^k f^{(k-1)}(t_0, y_0) + O(h^{p+1})$. Knowing the approximate value of y at time t_1, $y_2 \approx y(t_2)$ can be obtained similarly, using truncated Taylor series expansion for $y(t)$ at t_1. Now starting over, an explicit one-step method can be obtained for each p to approximate the solution $y_n \approx y(t_n)$ of the form in (10.10):

$$y_{n+1} = y_n + h\Phi(t_n, y_n; h) \quad \text{with} \quad \Phi(t_n, y_n; h) = \sum_{k=1}^{p} \frac{1}{k!} h^k f^{(k-1)}(t_n, y_n).$$

(10.11)

These are called *Taylor methods*. The simplest Taylor type method is obtained for $p = 1$, $\Phi(t_n, y_n; h) = f(t_n, y_n)$, and it is the *(explicit) Euler* method

$$y_{n+1} = y_n + hf(t_n, y_n);$$

the Euler method is a method of order 1 ($O(h)$).

Truncating the Taylor series for $p > 1$ improves the quality of the approximation, but has the disadvantage of requiring the evaluation of derivatives.

Runge–Kutta methods

The family of *Runge–Kutta* methods (RK) retain the desirable feature of Taylor methods but with the advantage of not requiring explicit evaluations of the derivatives of f. The idea is to consider time steps and to assume that the exact value of the slope of the step can be written as a linear combination of the function evaluated at certain points within that particular step.

136 *Dynamic economic models*

RK methods compute approximations y_n with initial values $y_0 = y(t_0)$ using the Taylor series expansion (10.11). Runge in 1875, based on the knowledge of $y(t_n)$, took $y(t_n + h) \approx y(t_n) + hf(t_n + h/2, y(t_n + h/2))$ and computed $y(t_n + h/2)$ using the Euler method with step $h/2$:

$$y_{n+1} = y_n + hk_2 \tag{10.12}$$
$$k_1 = f(t_n, y_n)$$
$$k_2 = f\left(t_n + \frac{h}{2}, y_n + \frac{h}{2}k_1\right).$$

This method does not need to evaluate the derivatives of f and it is more accurate than the Euler method. The explicit s-stage RK methods are a generalisation of this idea.

Explicit s-stage Runge–Kutta methods A *Runge–Kutta s-stage* (RKs) method is obtained by doing s function evaluations per step, giving rise to

$$y_{n+1} = y_n + h\Phi(t_n, y_n; h), \quad \Phi(t_n, y_n; h) = \sum_{i=1}^{s} w_i k_i, \tag{10.13}$$

where

$$k_i = f\left(t_n + hc_i, y_n + h\sum_{j=1}^{i-1} a_{i,j} k_j\right), \quad c_1 = 0,$$

for an *explicit method* and

$$k_i = f\left(t_n + hc_i, y_n + h\sum_{j=1}^{s} a_{i,j} k_j\right)$$

for an implicit one.

Explicit two-stage and second-order Runge–Kutta methods To build a two-stage and second-order method, $s = p = 2$, from (10.13), the result is

$$y_{n+1} = y_n + hw_1 k_1 + hw_2 k_2 \tag{10.14}$$
$$k_1 = f(t_n, y_n)$$
$$k_2 = f(t_n + hc_2, y_n + ha_{2,1} k_1).$$

Several solutions can be obtained that specify w_1, w_2, c_1 and $a_{2,1}$. Among them are the following.

- Modified Euler method: ($c_2 = \frac{1}{2}$, $w_1 = 0$, $w_2 = 1$ and $a_{2,1} = \frac{1}{2}$ – see (10.12))

$$y_{n+1} = y_n + hf\left[t_n + \frac{1}{2}h, y_n + \frac{1}{2}hf(t_n, y_n)\right]. \tag{10.15}$$

- Improved Euler method:[1] ($c_2 = 1$, $w_1 = \frac{1}{2}$, $w_2 = \frac{1}{2}$ and $a_{2,1} = 1$)

$$y_{n+1} = y_n + \frac{1}{2}h[f(t_n, y_n) + f(t_n + h, y_n + hf(t_n, y_n))]. \tag{10.16}$$

Explicit four-stage and fourth-order Runge–Kutta methods Proceeding similarly, higher-order methods can be developed. One of the most frequently used methods of the RK family is the (classical) fourth-order method:

$$y_{n+1} = y_n + \frac{1}{6}h(k_1 + 2k_2 + 2k_3 + k_4) \tag{10.17}$$

$$k_1 = f(t_n, y_n)$$

$$k_2 = f\left(t_n + \frac{1}{2}h, y_n + \frac{1}{2}hk_1\right)$$

$$k_3 = f\left(t_n + \frac{1}{2}h, y_n + \frac{1}{2}hk_2\right)$$

$$k_4 = f(t_n + h, y_n + hk_3).$$

The values of k_2 and k_3 represent approximations to the derivative $\dot{y}$ at intermediate points, and the value of $\Phi(t_n, y_n; h)$ is the weighted average of the k_i, $i = 1, \ldots, 4$.

Runge–Kutta methods in practice

A simple MATLAB/Octave function for the RK4 method is provided.

```
function [t,y] = my_rk4(f,tspan,y0,h)
%Runge-Kutta order 4 method with tspan=[t0 tf] and fixed
% step size to solvebthe IVP y'=f(t,y), y(t0)=y0
% input:
%   f      : function to integrate (f=@(t,y))
%   tspan  : integration interval [t0,tfinal]
%   y0     : initial condition at t0
%   h      : (constant) step size
% output:
%   t : specific times used
%   y : solution evaluated at t
```

138 *Dynamic economic models*

```
t0  = tspan(1);  tf = tspan(2);
t = t0:h:tf;  y = zeros(1,length(t));
y(1) = y0;   yn = y0;  tn = t0;
for n = 1:length(t)-1
   k1      = f(tn,yn);
   k2      = f(tn+h/2,yn+h*k1/2);
   k3      = f(tn+h/2,yn+h*k2/2);
   k4      = f(tn+h,yn+h*k3);
   yn      = yn+h*(k1+2*k2+2*k3+k4)/6;
   y(n+1)  = yn;
   tn      = tn+h;
end
end
```

Some additional comments

A p-order method has a local error of $O(h^{p+1})$ and a global error of $O(h^p)$ (Süli and Mayers 2003, ch. 12). In the next chapter a brief comment on how the step size can be automatically controlled to achieve a prescribed error is made.

Computational implementation

MATLAB/Octave code

Here, two m-files, a script and a function, are presented to solve the problem: a script with the main program and a function specifying the differential equation. The following baseline values are considered: $\beta = 1.6$, $\zeta = 4.0$, $q = 3.33$, $\alpha = 0.7$, $l = 1.0$, $h = 1.2$, $A = 1.5$, $L = 1.0$, $H = 0.7$ and $\sigma = H/L + 1$.

```
%% SBTC model
%    Skill  Biased  Technological  Change  without  scale  effects
%    based on: Oscar Afonso, Applied Economics, 38: 13-21 (2006)
%    implemented by: P.B. Vasconcelos and O. Afonso
disp('------------------------------------------------------------');
disp('SBTC without scale effects model                             ');
disp('------------------------------------------------------------');
% parameters
global beta zeta q alpha l h A L H sigma
beta = 1.6; zeta = 4.0; q = 3.33; alpha = 0.7; l = 1.0;
h = 1.2; A = 1.5; L = 1.0; H = 0.7; sigma = H/L+1;

% solve the ode
y0 = 1.0; tspan = [0 150]; step = 0.01;
[t,y] = my_rk4(@ode_sbtc,tspan,y0,step);

% plot the solution of the ODE
[ax,h1,h2] = plotyy(t,y,t,(h*L/(l*H).*y).^0.5);
if ~exist('OCTAVE_VERSION','builtin')
    xlabel('$t$','Interpreter','LaTex');
    legend('$D$','$W$'); set(legend,'Interpreter','latex');
```

```
else
  xlabel('t'); legend('D');
  legend('D','W');
end
set(get(ax(1),'Ylabel'),'String','Technological-knowledge bias')
set(get(ax(2),'Ylabel'),'String','Wage inequality')
set(h2,'LineStyle','—')

function dydt = ode_sbtc(~,y)
% ode equation for sbtc model
global beta zeta q alpha l h A L H sigma
dydt = y(1)* ...
  (beta/zeta*((q-1)/q)*(A*(1-alpha))^(1/alpha)*exp(-alpha)*...
  ((1+(H/(H+L)))^sigma*h*(1+((h/l)*(H/L)*y(1))^(-0.5))^alpha -...
  l*(1+((h/l)*(H/L)*y(1))^0.5)^alpha));
```

Some short comments on the code

At this stage, the codes should be easy to read. We just want to draw the attention of the reader to a more complicated `legend` command to incorporate special characters. The expression inside `ode_sbtc` is the one in (10.9). Furthermore the `plotyy` function is used to graph with y tick labels on the left and right.

Numerical results and simulation

The output of the code is displayed in Figure 10.1.

Let us now evaluate the result of some shocks. What happens when:

1. H increases from 0.9 to 1.1;
2. H decreases from 0.9 to 0.7?

To see the effects, the following m-file is provided.

```
% H from 0.9 to 1.1 and H from 0.9 to 0.7
global beta zeta q alpha l h A L H sigma
beta = 1.6; zeta = 4.0; q = 3.33; alpha = 0.7;
l = 1.0; h = 1.2; A = 1.5; L = 1.0;

H_values = [0.9, 1.1, 0.7]; line = {'b','r-.','—m'};
y0 = 1.0; tspan = [0 150]; step = 0.01;
for i = 1:length(H_values)
    H = H_values(i); sigma = H/L+1;
    [t,y] = my_rk4(@ode_sbtc,tspan,y0,step);
    plot(t,y,line{i});
    hold on;
end
if ~exist('OCTAVE_VERSION','builtin')
    xlabel('$t$','Interpreter','LaTex');
    legend('$D$ for $H=0.9$', '$D$ for $H=1.1$', ...
           '$D$ for $H=0.7$', 'location', 'SouthEast');
```

140 *Dynamic economic models*

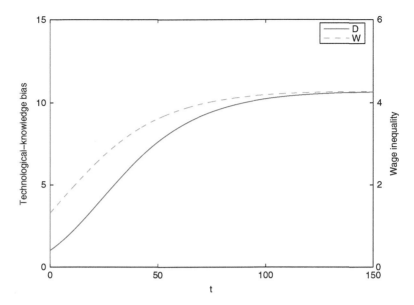

Figure 10.1 Path of variables *D* and *W*.

```
  set(legend,'Interpreter','latex');
else
  xlabel('t');
  legend('D for H=0.9', 'D for H=1.1', ...
         'D for H=0.7', 'location', 'SouthEast');
end
hold off;
```

The output of the code is displayed in Figure 10.2.

Due to the increase in high-skilled labour, the technological-knowledge-absorption effect is greater than in the baseline scenario and as a result $f(j)$ jumps immediately. This heightens the technological-knowledge bias in favour of H-intermediate goods. Such bias increases the supply of H-intermediate goods, thereby increasing the number of final goods produced with H-technology and lowering their relative price. Thus, relative prices of final goods produced with H-technology drop continuously towards the constant steady-state levels. This path of relative prices implies that the technological-knowledge bias is increasing, but at a decreasing rate until it reaches its new higher steady state. The increase of high-skilled labour causes an immediate drop in the H-premium due to the rise in the supply of high-skilled labour without any endogenous change in technological-knowledge bias. By reason of complementarity between inputs in (10.1), the increase in the supply of high-skilled labour induces technological-knowledge bias: after the immediate effect on the H-premium, there is a transition dynamics towards the new steady state,

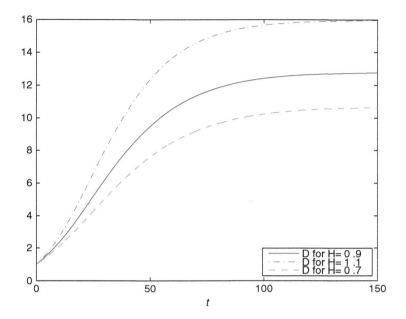

Figure 10.2 Path of variable $D = Q_H/Q_L$ for several values of H.

which is increasing at decreasing rates. Once in steady state, with a constant technological-knowledge bias, the H-premium remains constant. Moreover, it should be highlighted that with a sufficiently strong technological-knowledge-absorption effect, the steady-state H-premium is greater than that which has prevailed under the baseline case.

Highlights

- In the skill-biased technological change literature, labour levels affect the direction of technological knowledge, which in turn drives the wage inequality dynamics through the market-size channel.
- In the proposed model, the direction of technological knowledge is analysed in a dynamic setting where the scale effects are removed; the chain of effects is then induced by the price channel.
- It is assumed that the capacity to learn, assimilate and implement advanced technological knowledge is different between types of labour.
- In the proposed context, the rise in the skill premium results from the fact that the price channel dominates the market-size channel.
- This chapter continues to introduce numerical methods for the solution of initial value problems, namely, the Runge–Kutta family of methods with emphasis on the RK4 method.

Problems and computer exercises

1. By providing a graphical representation of the following shocks:

    (a) l, advantage of low-skilled labour in production, from 1 to 1.1;
    (b) A, exogenous productivity, from 1.5 to 1.7; and
    (c) q, size of a quality improvement, from 3.33 to 2.5,

    compare with the baseline model and explain the economic intuition.

2. Build two new functions: `my_meuler` – modified Euler method – and `my_ieuler` – improved Euler method.

3. After exploring Chapter 11, rewrite the `sbtc` m-file to solve the ODE by the `ode45` function.

4. For the baseline specifications, do the following.

    (a) Solve the model using the functions `my_euler` (provided in Chapter 9), `my_meuler`, `my_ieuler` and `my_rk4`.
    (b) Compare and contrast the numerical solutions, exploring the value for the integration step size h.
    (c) Build a table where values for the error between the analytical solution at certain points and the approximations at the same points are registered; take the integration step size between 1.0 and 0.001. Comment on the order of convergence (global error) in each one of the methods.

Note

1 This is also known as Heun's method or the explicit trapezoidal rule.

11 Technological-knowledge diffusion model

Introduction

In this chapter, the international technological-knowledge diffusion from developed to developing countries is analysed. The analysis is based on the model proposed in 'Technological Diffusion, Convergence, and Growth', by Barro and Sala-i-Martin (1997), published in the *Journal of Economic Growth* (see also Barro and Sala-i-Martin 2004, ch. 8).

The objective is to build a model that combines elements of endogenous growth with the proposal of the neoclassical theory concerning inter-country convergence. As a result, the analysis is based on a dynamic general equilibrium model, in which endogenous growth is driven by R&D, and where two countries are considered: an innovative (leader or North) country and an imitator (follower or South) country. Countries are different because: (i) they have different domestic institutions, which are better in the North and thus countries have different exogenous productivity; (ii) the technological-knowledge level is higher in the North. However, it is considered that countries have the same technology of production of goods as well as the same utility function. Moreover, imitation is the vehicle of international technological-knowledge transfer.

Until this paper (Barro and Sala-i-Martin 1997), the literature has treated: (i) the technological-knowledge progress with endogenous growth, but without endogenous diffusion of technological knowledge – e.g. Romer (1990), Aghion and Howitt (1992) and Barro and Sala-i-Martin (2004); (ii) the international diffusion of technological knowledge with endogenous growth, but just analysing the steady state and thus ignoring the dynamic transition; i.e. the convergence process – e.g. Grossman and Helpman (1991); (iii) the inter-country convergence process (through transitional dynamics); in the neoclassical model, economies grow more when they are distant of the steady state due to diminishing returns on capital, but growth rate is exogenous.

The analysis is done by considering three productive sectors: final goods production, intermediate goods production and R&D activities. Each economy has three productive factors at its disposal to produce the aggregate competitive final good: institutions, intermediate goods and labour. The aggregate final good (numeraire or resources) and designs (prototypes) arising from successful R&D activities are used in the production of intermediate goods, under monopolistic competition. The aggregate final good is also used to produce designs in the R&D sector, but here under perfect competition. In this latter sector, it is considered a catching-up specification under which the more backward is the South, the greater the advantage obtained from the delay.

In Barro and Sala-i-Martin (1997) the steady state of the model is studied as well as the transitional dynamics towards the steady state using phase diagrams. In this chapter the transitional dynamics of the model is analysed by solving the model numerically. The references Shampine *et al.* (2003, ch. 1) and Süli and Mayers (2003, ch. 12) can be followed for the solution of systems of differential equations, using state-of-the-art methods.

Economic model

Modelling the economies

Productive (supply) side The production of the competitive final good – in both countries, $i = 1$ (North, leader or innovator), $i = 2$ (South, follower or imitator) – uses institutions, intermediate goods and labour:

$$Y_i(t) = A_i \, L_i^{1-\alpha} \sum_{j=1}^{N_i(t)} X_{ij}^{\alpha}(t),$$

where: Y represents the aggregate final good – i.e. the consumption good (numeraire); A represents the quality of domestic institutions or exogenous productivity; L refers to labour; X is the amount of a certain specific intermediate good; N is the domestic technological frontier (number of different intermediate goods available); $\alpha \in (0, 1)$ is the intermediate goods share in production.

The production of differentiated intermediate goods occurs under monopolistic competition in the spirit of Dixit and Stiglitz (1977). In order to produce each intermediate good, a firm has to purchase one design from the R&D sector and afterwards employ resources (numeraire) in production. The cost of designs represents fixed costs for each firm and after an intermediate goods producer has purchased a design, it can transform one unit of numeraire into one unit of the intermediate good; thus, the maximisation of profit of firms

$$\pi_i = (p_{ij} - 1) X_{ij}$$

yields a mark-up over marginal cost 1 for the firm producing the intermediate good j

$$P_i = \frac{1}{\alpha}, \quad 0 < \alpha < 1.$$

The R&D activities result in designs to produce new intermediate goods (e.g. Aghion and Howitt 1992). The differences between the North, 1, and the South, 2, are considered. The North innovates and the South imitates, because imitation is cheaper than innovation and there is domestic protection – but not international protection – of Intellectual Property Rights.

The North has a constant cost of innovation, η_1, and thus successful R&D – new intermediate goods – does not present decreasing returns. The Northern technological knowledge is given by the number of intermediate goods, N_1. Similarly, the Southern technological knowledge is given by the number of intermediate goods, N_2, and this country has an increasing cost of imitation, v_2, which depends on the ratio

$$v_2 = v_2 \left(\frac{N_2}{N_1}\right)^\sigma, \quad \text{where } \dot{v}_2 > 0$$

that is, if $N_2/N_1 < 1$, the imitation cost (variable) is smaller than the (eventual) Southern innovation cost, η_2. Thus, the higher the technological-knowledge gap the higher the advantage of backwardness. An alternative solution is proposed in Afonso and Vasconcelos (2007).

Consumption (demand) side Individuals decide the allocation of income between consumption (of the composite final good) and savings. The utility function is

$$U_i(t) = \int_0^\infty \frac{C_i(t)^{1-\theta} - 1}{1-\theta} e^{-\rho t}\, dt,$$

where: C is the consumption (of the composite final good) in country i at time t; ρ is the homogeneous subjective discount rate; and θ is the inverse of the inter-temporal elasticity of substitution.

Savings consists of accumulation of financial assets, with return r, in the form of ownership of the firms that produce intermediate goods in monopolistic competition.

Carrying out utility maximisation subject to the budget constraint results in the standard Euler equation

$$\hat{C}_i(t) = \frac{r_i(t) - \rho}{\theta},$$

where $\hat{C}_i(t)$ is the growth rate of C_i.

Equilibrium

Steady-state equilibrium The steady-state endogenous growth rate is unique (common in both countries) and constant, $\gamma_2^* = \gamma_1$. Moreover, it is driven by a

Northern endogenous technological-knowledge progress

$$\gamma_2^* = \gamma_1 = \frac{1}{\theta}\left(\frac{\pi_1}{\eta_1} - \rho\right) = \frac{1}{\theta}\left\{\frac{1}{\eta_1}\left[(1-\alpha)L_1 A_1^{(1-\alpha)^{-1}} \alpha^{\frac{1+\alpha}{1-\alpha}}\right] - \rho\right\}.$$

Thus, the technological-knowledge progress in the North commands and it is not affected by the South. Moreover, Southern convergence ends when the imitation cost equals the innovation cost. Indeed, as it will be clear later on, during the transition phase the South is growing at a growth rate higher than the steady state of the North, because at that stage imitation is cheaper than innovation.

Southern transitional dynamics At time 0, when the imitation begins, it is cheaper than innovation, but the cost of imitation increases with the decreasing inter-country technological gap; that is, the cost of imitation increases until the steady state due to the decrease in the quantity of goods that need to be imitated, and in steady state equalises the cost of innovation.

The system of differential equations that describe the Southern transitional dynamics is described by two differential equations: a differential equation for consumption, C_2, and a differential equation for technological knowledge, N_2.

To find the required differential equations, first it is considered that the present value of profits of the imitator firm is

$$V_2 = \pi_2 \int_t^\infty \exp\left[-\int_t^s r_2(v)\,dv\right] ds$$

$$\pi_{2j} = \pi_2 = \left(\underbrace{p_{2j}}_{=p_1} - 1\right)\underbrace{X_{2j}}_{=X_2}$$

$$= \left(\frac{1}{\alpha} - 1\right) X_2 = (1-\alpha) L_2 A_2^{(1-\alpha)^{-1}} \alpha^{\frac{1+\alpha}{1-\alpha}}.$$

Assuming free entry into imitation activity, V_2 equals the cost of imitation v_2 at each time t. Thus,

$$V_2 = v_2 = v_2 \left(\frac{N_2}{N_1}\right)^\sigma, \quad \frac{N_2}{N_1} \leq 1, \sigma > 0$$

and deriving both sides

$$r_2 = \frac{\pi_2}{v_2} + \frac{\dot{v}_2}{v_2}$$

and therefore

$$\frac{\dot{C}_2}{C_2} = \frac{1}{\theta}\left(\frac{\pi_2}{v_2} + \sigma\frac{\dot{\hat{N}}}{\hat{N}} - \rho\right), \quad \hat{N} = \frac{N_2}{N_1}. \tag{11.1}$$

In turn, the variation of N_2 is determined by the budget constraint. Resources allocated for imitation are: $Y_2 - C_2 - N_2 X_2$; the variation of N_2 equals $1/v_2$ times the resources allocated for imitation, and growth rate of $\hat{N}$ equals the growth rate of N_2 less the growth rate of N_1, γ_1, resulting in one of the differential equations that describes the transitional dynamics:

$$\frac{\dot{\hat{N}}}{\hat{N}} = \frac{1}{v_2}\left[\pi_2\frac{(1-\alpha)}{\alpha} - \chi_2\right] - \gamma_1, \tag{11.2}$$

where $\chi_2 = C_2/N_2$. Substituting now $\dot{\hat{N}}/\hat{N}$ into $\dot{C}_2/C_2$ (11.1) provides the other required differential equation

$$\frac{\dot{C}_2}{C_2} = \frac{1}{\theta}\left(\frac{\pi_2}{v_2} + \sigma\frac{\dot{\hat{N}}}{\hat{N}} - \rho\right)$$

and thus

$$\frac{\dot{C}_2}{C_2} = \frac{1}{\theta}\left\{\frac{1}{v_2}\left[\pi_2\left[1 + \frac{\sigma(1-\alpha)}{\alpha}\right] - \sigma\chi_2\right] - \rho - \sigma\gamma_1\right\}$$

i.e.

$$\frac{\dot{\chi}_2}{\chi_2} = \frac{1}{\theta v_2}\left\{\pi_2 + (\theta - \sigma)\left[\chi_2 - \pi_2\frac{(1-\alpha)}{\alpha}\right]\right\} - \frac{1}{\theta}(\sigma\gamma_1 + \rho). \tag{11.3}$$

Numerical solution: initial value problems

In this section the numerical solution of a system of differential equations is tackled. The problem is stated similarly to what was presented in Chapter 9. A first-order *ordinary differential system* has the form

$$\dot{y}(t) = \frac{dy}{dt}(t) = f(t, y(t)), \tag{11.4}$$

where $f: \mathbb{R} \times \mathbb{R}^m \to \mathbb{R}^m$ and $y(t): [t_0, t_T] \subset \mathbb{R} \to \mathbb{R}^m$. For $m = 1$ a single differential equation is recovered. Using matrix notation

$$y(t) = \begin{bmatrix} y_1(t) \\ y_2(t) \\ \vdots \\ y_m(t) \end{bmatrix}, \quad f(t, y(t)) = \begin{bmatrix} f_1(t, y(t)) \\ f_2(t, y(t)) \\ \vdots \\ f_m(t, y(t)) \end{bmatrix}.$$

An IVP is characterised by (11.4) with the condition $y_0 = y(t_0)$.

All the iterative relations provided in the two previous chapters still apply, bearing in mind that y is now a vector.

A usual way to present RK methods is to use the *Butcher tableau*

$$\begin{array}{c|c} c & A \\ \hline & w \end{array},$$

where $w = [w_1, w_2, \ldots, w_s]$, $c = [c_1, c_2, \ldots, c_s]^T$ and $A = [a_{i,j}]$, $i = 2, \ldots, s$, $j = 1, \ldots, s - 1$. The components of the vector w are the weights in the combination of the intermediate values k_i (10.13), the components of vector c are the increments of t_n and the entries of the matrix A are the multipliers of the approximate slopes. Explicit methods can be viewed as a subset of implicit methods with $a_{i,j} = 0$, $j \geq i$ and $c_1 = 0$. For an *implicit* RKs method the j index goes from 1 to s and the Butcher tableau is represented by $A = [a_{i,j}]$, $i, j = 1, \ldots, s$:

- *Modified Euler method* (see (10.15)) $\quad \begin{array}{c|cc} 0 & & \\ \frac{1}{2} & \frac{1}{2} & \\ \hline & 0 & 1 \end{array}$

- *Improved Euler method* (see (10.16)) $\quad \begin{array}{c|cc} 0 & & \\ 1 & 1 & \\ \hline & \frac{1}{2} & \frac{1}{2} \end{array}$

- *Runge–Kutta fourth-order method* (see (10.17)) $\quad \begin{array}{c|cccc} 0 & & & & \\ \frac{1}{2} & \frac{1}{2} & & & \\ \frac{1}{2} & 0 & \frac{1}{2} & & \\ 1 & 0 & 0 & 1 & \\ \hline & \frac{1}{6} & \frac{2}{6} & \frac{2}{6} & \frac{1}{6} \end{array}$

Embedded Runge–Kutta methods

To implement an efficient code, one needs to have access to error estimates in order to be able to obtain valid numerical results. In the case of RK methods access to information during the computation is required to control the step length in a computationally inexpensive way. Several techniques can be used. One of them consists of embedded pairs of RK methods of orders p and $p+1$; the difference between the higher and lower-order solutions, $y_{n+1} - \hat{y}_{n+1}$, is used to control the local error.

Maybe the most famous of these methods of order 4 and 5 are the Runge–Kutta–Fehlberg and the explicit RK $(4,5)$ pair of Dormand and Price. The later is drawn in the following Butcher tableau (imagine all the hard work needed to develop such a method!).

	0						
	$\frac{1}{5}$	$\frac{1}{5}$					
	$\frac{3}{10}$	$\frac{3}{40}$	$\frac{9}{40}$				
	$\frac{4}{5}$	$\frac{44}{45}$	$-\frac{56}{15}$	$\frac{32}{9}$			
	$\frac{8}{9}$	$\frac{19372}{6561}$	$-\frac{25360}{2187}$	$\frac{64448}{6561}$	$-\frac{212}{729}$		
	1	$\frac{9017}{3168}$	$-\frac{355}{33}$	$\frac{46732}{5247}$	$\frac{49}{176}$	$-\frac{5103}{18656}$	
	1	$\frac{35}{384}$	0	$\frac{500}{1113}$	$\frac{125}{192}$	$-\frac{2187}{6784}$	$\frac{11}{84}$
$\hat{y}_{n+1}$		$\frac{5179}{57600}$	0	$\frac{7571}{16695}$	$\frac{393}{640}$	$-\frac{92097}{339200}$	$\frac{187}{2100}$	$\frac{1}{40}$
y_{n+1}		$\frac{35}{384}$	0	$\frac{500}{1113}$	$\frac{125}{192}$	$-\frac{2187}{6784}$	$\frac{11}{84}$	0
$y_{n+0.5}$		$\frac{5783653}{57600000}$	0	$\frac{466123}{1192500}$	$-\frac{41347}{1920000}$	$\frac{16122321}{339200000}$	$-\frac{7117}{20000}$	$\frac{183}{10000}$

Solving initial value problems in practice

MATLAB/Octave provide, among others, the `ode23` and `ode45` built-in functions, implementing, respectively, RK second/third-order and RK fourth/fifth-order methods.

Methods with memory are provided by MATLAB through `ode113`, via the implementation of the Adams–Bashforth–Moulton family formulas.

Some additional comments

An ODE problem is said to be *stiff* if the sought solution is varying slowly while there are nearby solutions that vary rapidly; therefore the numerical method must take small steps to obtain satisfactory results.

The `ode23` and `ode45` methods are intended for *nonstiff* problems, but they can solve, as well, stiff problems; nevertheless, they take a long time to compute the numerical solution. In these cases, more efficient answers can be obtained by using `ode23s` or `ode15s`, intended for stiff problems.

150 *Dynamic economic models*

Additional information on the above topic as well as on stability issues can be obtained from Shampine *et al.* (2003) and Moler (2004).

Computational implementation

An m-file with the code to solve the problem is presented, providing a function for the ode system. The following baseline values are considered: $\nu_2 = 100.0$, $L_2 = 1.05$, $A_2 = 2.3$, $\alpha = 0.75$, $\gamma_1 = 0.04$, $\theta = 2.5$, $\sigma = 4.5$ and $\rho = 0.02$.

MATLAB/Octave code

```
%% TKD model
%   Technological Diffusion, convergence, and Growth
%   based on: R. Barro, X. Sala-I-Martin,
%             J. Economic Growth, 2: 1-27 (1997)
%   implemented by: P.B. Vasconcelos and O. Afonso
disp('——————————————————————————————————————');
disp('TKD model                                 ');
disp('——————————————————————————————————————');
%% parameters
nu2 = 100.0; L2 = 1.05; A2 = 2.3; alpha = 0.75; gamma1 = 0.04;
theta = 2.5; sigma = 4.5; rho = 0.02;

%% initial values, time period and solution
tspan = [0 200]; t0 = [0.1; 0.2];
options=odeset('RelTol',1e-3,'AbsTol',1e-6);
[t,y] = ode45(@ode_tkd,tspan,t0,options,...
              nu2,L2,A2,alpha,gamma1,theta,sigma,rho);

%% plot the solution
plot(t,y(:,1),'b--',t,y(:,2),'r—')
if ~exist ('OCTAVE_VERSION', 'builtin')
  % labels for MATLAB
  xlabel('$t$','Interpreter','LaTex');
  legend('$\hat{N}$','$\chi_2$')
  set(legend,'Interpreter','latex');
else
  % labels for Octave
  set (gca, 'interpreter', 'tex')
  xlabel('t'); legend('\hat{N}','\chi_2')
end

function dydt = ode_tkd(~,y,...
                 nu2,L2,A2,alpha,gamma1,theta,sigma,rho)
% ode system of equations for tkd model
% parameter
Pi_2=(1-alpha)*L2*A2^(1/(1-alpha))*alpha^((1+alpha)/(1-alpha));
% ode system
dydt = [y(1)*((nu2*y(1)^sigma)^(-1)*...
          (Pi_2*(1+alpha)/alpha-y(2))-gamma1); ...
        y(2)*((theta*nu2*y(1)^sigma)^(-1)*...
          (Pi_2+(theta-sigma)*(y(2)-Pi_2*(1+alpha)/alpha)-...
          (1/theta)*(sigma*gamma1+rho)))];
```

Some short comments on the code

The system of differential equations formed by (11.2) and (11.3) is implemented in the `ode_tkd` function. Please note that the system is written inside a vector structure, and the dependent variables are stored in vector y. The `ode45` MATLAB/OCTAVE function integrates the system from 0 to 200 with initial conditions [0.1; 0.2]. The first input argument is a function handle. The fourth input argument is a structure of optional parameters, like the tolerance required to achieve the approximate solution (if empty,[1] the software will assume the default values). Only after this can we introduce in the function, as inputs, the required parameter. By doing this, the use of `global` variables is avoided; all variables are local, which means that they vanish as the function ends.

Numerical results and simulation

The output is drawn in Figure 11.1.

The transitional dynamics highlight the effects of North–South technological-knowledge diffusion through imitation for the South less developed country. Figure 11.1 shows that the South benefits from Northern R&D since it converges to the Northern technological knowledge. Therefore, technological-knowledge imitation is a window of opportunity for the South; during the transition towards the steady state it achieves higher growth rates. It can be emphasised that the decreasing probability of imitation towards the steady state is analogous to the diminishing returns on capital in the case of the

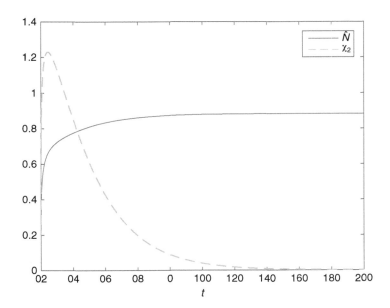

Figure 11.1 Transitional dynamics for $\hat{N}$ and χ_2.

152 Dynamic economic models

neoclassic model. It should also be stressed that the assumptions with regard to exogenous levels of productivity related to institutions and to the probabilities of successful R&D tend to keep the North as the technological-knowledge leader country. In fact, in steady state there is convergence in growth rates but not in levels.

Let us now evaluate the result of some shocks. What happens when the imitation cost v_2:

1. increases from 100 to 120;
2. decreases from 100 to 80?

To answer the previous questions, the following m-files as well as the outputs (Figures 11.2 and 11.3) are provided.

```
% nu2 from 100 to 120
nu2 = 100.0; L2 = 1.05; A2 = 2.3; alpha = 0.75;
gamma1 = 0.04; theta = 2.5; sigma = 4.5; rho = 0.02;
y0 = [0.1; 0.2]; tspan = [0 200];

options=odeset('RelTol',1e-3,'AbsTol',1e-6);
nu2_values = [100, 120];
hold on;
for i = 1:length(nu2_values)
    nu2 = nu2_values(i);
    [t,y] = ode45(@ode_tkd, tspan, y0, options,...
        nu2, L2, A2, alpha, gamma1, theta, sigma, rho);
```

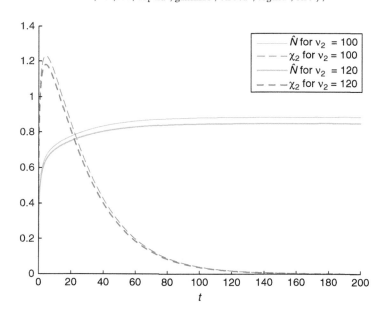

Figure 11.2 Increase in v_2.

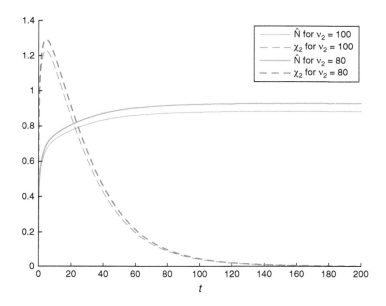

Figure 11.3 Decrease in v_2.

```
    plot(t,y(:,1),'b--','LineWidth',i);
    plot(t,y(:,2),'r—','LineWidth',i);
end
if ~exist('OCTAVE_VERSION', 'builtin')
  % labels for MATLAB
  xlabel('$t$','Interpreter','LaTex');
  legend('$\hat{N}$ for $\nu_2=100$',...
         '$\chi_2$ for $\nu_2=100$',...
         '$\hat{N}$ for $\nu_2=120$',...
         '$\chi_2$ for $\nu_2=120$')
  set(legend,'Interpreter','latex',...
      'Location','east');
else
  % labels for Octave
  xlabel('t');
  legend('\hat{N} for \nu_2=100',...
         '\chi_2 for \nu_2=100',...
         '\hat{N} for \nu_2=120',...
         '\chi_2 for \nu_2=120')
end
hold off;

% nu2 from 100 to 80
nu2 = 100.0; L2 = 1.05; A2 = 2.3; alpha = 0.75;
gamma1 = 0.04; theta = 2.5; sigma = 4.5; rho = 0.02;
y0 = [0.1; 0.2]; tspan = [0 200];
```

```
options=odeset('RelTol',1e-3,'AbsTol',1e-6);
nu2_values = [100, 80];
hold on;
for i = 1:length(nu2_values)
    nu2 = nu2_values(i);
    [t,y] = ode45(@ode_tkd,tspan,y0,options,...
             nu2,L2,A2,alpha,gamma1,theta,sigma,rho);
    plot(t,y(:,1),'b-','LineWidth',i);
    plot(t,y(:,2),'r—','LineWidth',i);
end
if ~exist ('OCTAVE_VERSION', 'builtin')
  % labels for MATLAB
  xlabel('$t$','Interpreter','LaTex');
  legend('$\hat{N}$ for $\nu_2=100$',...
         '$\chi_2$ for $\nu_2=100$',...
         '$\hat{N}$ for $\nu_2=80$',...
         '$\chi_2$ for $\nu_2=80$')
  set(legend,'Interpreter','latex',...
       'Location','east');
else
  % labels for Octave
  xlabel('t');
  legend('\hat{N}} for \nu_2=100',...
         '\chi_2 for \nu_2=100',...
         '\hat{N} for \nu_2=80',...
         '\chi_2 for \nu_2=80')
end
hold off;
```

Highlights

- Technological-knowledge progress with endogenous growth and diffusion, during the transitional dynamic towards the steady state and in the steady state, was analysed.
- The economies of less developed countries grow more due to the cheaper imitative R&D; in the neoclassical model, they grow more since they are distant from the steady state due to diminishing returns on capital, but growth rate is exogenous.
- This chapter introduces the MATLAB/Octave solver function `ode45` (and the lower-order `ode23`) for nonstiff differential (systems of) equations.
- Methods with memory and methods to tackle stiff problems are briefly mentioned.

Problems and computer exercises

1. What happens when the Southern dimension L_2:

    (a) increases from 1.05 to 1.25;
    (b) decreases from 1.05 to 0.85?

2. What happens when the Southern institutions A_2 are:

   (a) better (say A_2 increases from 2.3 to 2.5);
   (b) worse (say A_2 decreases from 2.3 to 2.1)?

3. Assume that imitation is impossible; thus, in expression $V_2 = v_2 = v_2(N_2/N_1)^\sigma$ consider that $\sigma = 0$. Solve the exercise and comment on the results, considering:

   (a) $v_2 = 100.0$ (high innovation cost in the South);
   (b) $v_2 = 45.0$ (low innovation cost in the South).

4. Consider an extension of the model by introducing government in order to analyse the effects from public investment, in line with Barro (1990).

$$Y_i = A_i L_i^\alpha G_i^\beta \sum_{j=1}^{N_i} X_{ij}^{1-\alpha-\beta},$$

where G_i stands for public investment, $0 < \alpha, \beta < 1$ and $0 < \alpha + \beta < 1$.

   (a) Develop analytically the new model and find the new expression for profits of an imitator firm.
   (b) Derive the new system of differential equations and implement the model.
   (c) Verify that for $\beta = 0$ the original system is recovered (note that all exponents in the production functions have changed).
   (d) What are the main implications for the South due to this extension (compare with the baseline model)?
   (e) For the new model, analyse the effects on Southern convergence due to an increase in G (consider $\alpha > \beta$).
   (f) For the new model, and for a fixed G, analyse the implications from considering $\beta > \alpha$.

Note

1 Octave displays a warning showing the default values that will be assumed; MATLAB does not provide this warning but these defaults can be accessed from the help page of `ode45`.

12 Ramsey–Cass–Koopmans model

Introduction

We now turn to the neoclassical growth model with an endogenous saving rate, which is often labelled the Ramsey–Cass–Koopmans model, RCK, or simply the Ramsey model (e.g. Barro and Sala-i-Martin 2004, ch. 2). Indeed, Cass (1965) and Koopmans (1965) combined the maximisation for an infinite horizon, suggested by Ramsey (1928) with Solow and Swan's capital accumulation. In the last of these the savings rate is considered exogenous (see Chapter 9), while for the RCK model it is endogenously computed through a consumer optimisation problem. It aims at studying whether the accumulation of capital accounts for the long term growth. This is accomplished by modelling the inter-temporal allocation of income, i.e, the relation between consumption and savings focusing on the dynamics. By allowing consumers to behave optimally, the analysis permits us to discuss how incentives affect the behaviour of the economy. Now, infinitely-lived households that choose consumption and savings to maximise their dynastic utility, bearing in mind the intertemporal budget constraint, are taken into account. The increase or decrease of the savings rate with economic development affects the transitional dynamics.

A very brief introduction to numerical methods to solve boundary value problems will be provided, following closely Shampine *et al.* (2003, ch. 3). For a simple symbolic and numerical computational approach to this chapter see Vasconcelos (2013).

Economic model

The model represents an economy of one sector where households and firms, with optimiser behaviours, interact in competitive markets.[1] The development of the RCK model is performed within the following market economy environment: (i) households provide labour services in exchange for wages, and consume and accumulate assets; and (ii) firms have technical know-how to turn inputs into output, rent capital from consumers and hire labour services.

Assumptions of the model

There are a large number of identical households ordered on the interval [0, 1]. This assumption bears the following implications: (i) A 'large number' is required to set up a model with perfectly competitive factor and product markets; (ii) the 'overall number' of households is 1 implying that quantities per household coincide with aggregate quantities. For simplicity, it is assumed that the number of households L (as well as their size) stays constant. Each household is endowed with one unit of labour per period of time. The household income comprises labour income (w denotes the wage rate) and capital income (the amount of capital owned by the household is K, the net real rate of return is R). The representative household is assumed to maximise the present value of an infinite utility stream. This representation of preferences applies when each generation takes the well-being of its descendants into account (Barro 1974).

Households

It is assumed that each household has the same preference parameters, faces the same wage rate, starts with the same assets per worker and has the same population growth rate. As a result, the analysis can use the usual representative-agent framework, in which the equilibrium derives from the choices of a single household. The household wishes to maximise a lifetime utility given by

$$\int_0^\infty u(c(t))e^{-(\rho-n)t}\,dt, \tag{12.1}$$

where ρ is the subjective discount rate, $\rho - n$ the effective discount rate, $c(t) = C(t)/L(t)$ is the per capita consumption at t, $C(t)$ is the aggregate consumption, and u is the instantaneous utility function.[2] This utility function must follow certain assumptions: (i) u must be concave, which means that the path of the consumption is smooth; and (ii) $\rho > n > 0$ in order to have that $\lim_{t\to\infty} u(c(t))e^{-(\rho-n)t} = 0$.

Denoting by $\mathcal{A}(t)$ the asset holdings of the representative household at time t, the following law of motion can be set

$$\dot{\mathcal{A}}(t) = r(t)\mathcal{A}(t) + (w(t) - c(t))L(t),$$

where $r(t)$ is the risk-free market flow rate of return on assets, $w(t)L(t)$ is the flow of labour income earnings of the household and $c(t)L(t)$ is the flow of consumption; furthermore, denoting by $a(t) = \mathcal{A}(t)/L(t)$, per capita assets, results in

$$\dot{a}(t) = (r(t) - n)a(t) + w(t) - c(t), \tag{12.2}$$

that is, assets per person rises with $w(t) + r(t)a(t)$, the per capita income, and falls with per capita consumption and expansion of population.

158 Dynamic economic models

The budget constraint appears by considering market clearing, $a(t) = k(t)$.[3] Additionally, a non-Ponzi condition must be imposed:

$$\lim_{t\to\infty} a(t)e^{-\int_0^t r(s)-n\,ds} = 0 \tag{12.3}$$

to ensure that households cannot have exploding debt.[4]

The problem is then to maximise (12.1) restricted by (12.2) and (12.3):

$$\max_{k(t),c(t)} \int_0^\infty u(c(t))e^{-(\rho-n)t}\,dt$$

st.

$$\dot{k}(t) = (r(t) - n)k(t) + w(t) - c(t) \tag{12.4}$$

$$k(0) > 0 \text{ given}$$

$$\lim_{t\to\infty} k(t)e^{-\int_0^t r(s)-n\,ds} = 0. \tag{12.5}$$

This problem can be solved by the current-value of the Hamiltonian:

$$\mathcal{H}(t,k(t),c(t),\lambda(t)) = u(c(t)) + \lambda(t)[(r(t)-n)k(t)+w(t)-c(t)].$$

First-order conditions give rise to

$$\frac{\partial \mathcal{H}}{\partial c}(t,k(t),c(t),\lambda(t)) = u'(c(t)) - \lambda(t) = 0 \tag{12.6}$$

$$\frac{\partial \mathcal{H}}{\partial k}(t,k(t),c(t),\lambda(t)) = \lambda(t)(r(t)-n) = (\rho-n)\lambda(t) - \dot{\lambda}(t) \tag{12.7}$$

$$\lim_{t\to\infty} e^{-(\rho-n)t}\lambda(t)k(t) = 0, \tag{12.8}$$

where (12.8) is the *transversality condition*, which states that at the end of the process the stock of assets should be 0. Equations (12.6) and (12.7) state that the marginal value of the consumption should be equal to the marginal value of the investment.

From (12.7) results $\dot{\lambda}(t)/\lambda(t) = -(r(t)-\rho)$, and by differentiating (12.6), dividing by $\lambda(t)$ and referring to the previous expression, one gets the *Euler equation*

$$\frac{\dot{c}(t)}{c(t)} = (r(t) - \rho)\sigma(t), \tag{12.9}$$

where $\sigma(t) = -(u'(c(t)))/(u''(c(t))c(t))$. Equation (12.9) can be written as $(\dot{c}(t)/c(t))(1/\sigma(t)) + \rho = r(t)$, where the left side is the benefit that arises from the consumption and the right side is the benefit due to the savings.

It can be shown that the non-Ponzi condition (12.3) is implied by the transversality condition (12.8). Indeed, noting that

$$\int \frac{\dot{\lambda}(t)}{\lambda(t)} = -\int r(t) - \rho \, dt$$

$$\log(\lambda(t)) + c_1 = -\int r(t) - \rho \, dt$$

$$\lambda(t) = c_2 e^{-\int r(t) - \rho \, dt}$$

one gets

$$\lim_{t \to \infty} k(t)\lambda(t)e^{-(\rho-n)t} = \lim_{t \to \infty} k(t)e^{-\int_0^t r(s) - n \, ds} = 0.$$

The system of differential equations to be solved is thus formed by (12.4) and (12.9).

Firms

Consider an economy with a representative firm (all firms have access to the same production function) operating in a competitive context:

$$Y(t) = F(K(t), L(t)),$$

where the product (composite final good) $Y(t)$ is a function of capital $K(t)$ and labour supply $L(t)$. Assumptions on F must be taken: (i) concavity[5] and constant returns to scale;[6] and (ii) Inada conditions (see Chapter 9).

Consider that the total population at instant t is $L(t) = e^{nt}L(0)$, $L(0) = 1$, where $n = \dot{L}(t)/L(t) \equiv (dL(t)/dt)/L(t)$ is the labour growth rate. In effective labour terms, $y(t) = (1/L(t))f(k(t))$, where $y(t) = Y(t)/L(t)$ and $f(k(t)) = (1/L(t))F(K(t)/L(t), 1)$.

Firms aim at maximising profit

$$\max_{K,L} F(K(t), L(t)) - R(t)K(t) - w(t)L(t),$$

where $R(t) = r(t) + \delta$ is the rental rate of return on capital,[7] and $w(t)$ is the wage rate of effective labour.

Competitive markets imply that

$$\frac{\partial F(K(t), L(t))}{\partial K(t)} = f'(k(t)) = R(t) \tag{12.10}$$

and $\partial F(K(t), L(t))/\partial L(t) = w(t)$. Also bearing in mind the Euler identity, F is homogeneous of degree 1, $K(t)\partial F(K(t), L(t))/\partial K(t) +$

$L(t)\partial F(K(t), L(t))/\partial L(t) = F(K(t), L(t))$; dividing both sides by $L(t)$, the result is $k(t)f'(k(t)) + \partial F(K(t), L(t))/\partial L(t) = f(k(t))$. Therefore,

$$\frac{\partial F(K(t), L(t))}{\partial L(t)} = f(k(t)) - k(t)f'(k(t)) = w(t). \tag{12.11}$$

Decentralised equilibrium

Households and firms meet in the market: wages and interest paid by firms are those received by households, and the price of the composite final good paid by households is the one received by firms (this price is normalised to 1).

Bearing in mind (12.10), (12.11) and $a = k$, in (12.2),

$$\dot{k}(t) = f(k(t)) - (\delta + n)k(t) - c(t), \tag{12.12}$$

which depicts the dynamic path of the per capita capital.

Moreover, substituting (12.10) into (12.9), which depicts the behaviour of households, results in

$$\frac{\dot{c}(t)}{c(t)} = (f'(k(t)) - \delta - \rho)\sigma(t), \tag{12.13}$$

which means that there is a positive relationship between $\dot{c}(t)/c(t)$ and $f'(k(t))$.

Equations (12.12) and (12.13), together with the transversality condition, show the dynamic behaviour of the consumption, of the capital and also of the per capita GDP. Before analysing the dynamics of the economy, it is useful to compare this decentralised scenario with the centralised one.

Centralised equilibrium

The central planner imposes the following restrictions: (i) it maximises (12.1); (ii) it supports just one restriction, the physical restriction given, in per capita terms, by (12.12); and (iii) it decides by looking at all mechanisms, externalities and information, which in the context of this model are the same in both decentralised and centralised scenarios.

The central planner problem is thus given by

$$\max_{k(t), c(t)} \int_0^\infty u(c(t)) e^{-\int_0^t r(s) - n ds} dt$$

st.

$$\dot{k}(t) = f(k(t)) - (\delta + n)k(t) - c(t)$$

$$k(0) > 0 \text{ given}$$

$$\lim_{t \to \infty} k(t) e^{-(\rho - n)t} = 0.$$

The current-value of the Hamiltonian is given by

$$\mathcal{H}(t, k(t), c(t), \lambda(t)) = u(c(t))e^{-(\rho-n)t} - \lambda(t)[f(k(t)) - (\delta + n)k(t) - c(t)]$$

and from the first-order conditions, one gets

$$\frac{\partial \mathcal{H}}{\partial c}(t, k(t), c(t), \lambda(t)) = u'(c(t)) - \lambda(t) = 0$$

$$\frac{\partial \mathcal{H}}{\partial k}(t, k(t), c(t), \lambda(t)) = (f'(k(t)) - \delta - n)\lambda(t) = (\rho - n)\lambda(t) - \dot{\lambda}(t)$$

$$\lim_{t \to \infty} e^{-(\rho-n)t} \lambda(t) k(t) = 0. \tag{12.14}$$

Bearing in mind that $f'(k(t)) = r(t) + \delta$, the two approaches are similar.

Hence, the dynamic equations that characterise the centralised solution are the same that characterise the decentralised solution; i.e. (12.12), (12.13) and the transversality condition. Before the transitional dynamics analysis, some additional considerations are provided.

Steady state

Let us consider the Cobb–Douglas production function, $f(k(t)) = k^\alpha$, where α is the capital share in production, and the Constant Intertemporal Elasticity of Substitution, CIES, utility function, $u(c(t)) = (c(t)^{(1-\theta)} - 1)/(1-\theta)\ \theta \neq 1$. Both functions comply with the required assumptions.

The latter provides a degree to which people prefer a stable rate of consumption relative to higher consumption in the future; it is also referred to as Constant Relative Risk Aversion, CRRA, since it assigns a constant ratio by which people give higher weights to downside risks than to upside ones. Also, it is easy to verify that $\sigma = 1/\theta$, that is, σ is the intertemporal elasticity of substitution (or the inverse of the elasticity of marginal utility).

The steady-state equilibrium is an equilibrium path in which the capital–labour ratio, consumption and output are constant ($\dot{c} = \dot{k} = 0$)

$$\begin{cases} f'(k^*) - (\delta + \rho) = 0 \\ f(k^*) = (\delta + n)k^* + c^* \end{cases}$$

and for the Cobb–Douglas and CIES functions

$$\begin{cases} \alpha(k^*)^{\alpha-1} - (\delta + \rho) = 0 \\ (k^*)^\alpha = (\delta + n)k^* + c^* \end{cases} \Leftrightarrow \begin{cases} k^* = \left(\dfrac{\alpha}{\delta + \rho}\right)^{\frac{1}{1-\alpha}} \\ c^* = (k^*)^\alpha - (\delta + n)k^* \end{cases}. \tag{12.15}$$

The golden rule

There is a certain level of capital that maximises consumption in the long run. The *golden rule* postulates that collectively (or by policy enforcement) the propensity to save is so that future generations can enjoy the same level of per capita consumption as initial generations. The golden rule is obtained by maximising $c(t)$ along with $\dot{k}(t) = 0$:

$$\max_{k(t)} f(k) - (\delta + n)k;$$

thus, from first-order conditions $f'(k) = \delta + n$, and for the Cobb–Douglas function,

$$k^{gr} = \left(\frac{\alpha}{\delta + n}\right)^{\frac{1}{1-\alpha}}.$$

Note that $k^* < k^{gr}$ since $\rho > n$. Figure 12.1 shows a simulation for the RCK model, illustrating the golden rule, equilibrium point, steady state and the transition dynamics.

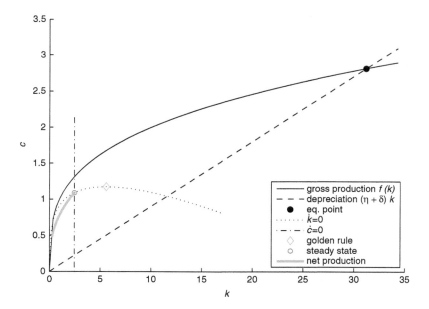

Figure 12.1 Golden rule, equilibrium point, steady state.

Connection with the Solow–Swan model

First note that taking the propensity to consume as constant, $1 - s$, and $c(t) = (1 - s) f(k(t))$, from $\dot{k}(t) = f(k(t)) - (\delta + n)k(t) - c(t)$ one recovers $\dot{k}(t) = s f(k(t)) - (\delta + n)k(t)$, which is the movement equation for the Solow–Swan model (Chapter 9).

Linear approximation

The sought solution (c^*, k^*) is a saddle point, and to understand this the local properties must be accessed. Taylor expansion of first order gives rise to

$$\begin{bmatrix} \dot{c}(t) \\ \dot{k}(t) \end{bmatrix} \approx J_{|(c^*, k^*)} \begin{bmatrix} c - c^* \\ k - k^* \end{bmatrix},$$

where the Jacobian at the equilibrium point is

$$J_{|(c^*, k^*)} = \begin{bmatrix} \dfrac{\partial \dot{c}(t)}{\partial c} & \dfrac{\partial \dot{c}(t)}{\partial k} \\ \dfrac{\partial \dot{k}(t)}{\partial c} & \dfrac{\partial \dot{k}(t)}{\partial k} \end{bmatrix}_{|(c^*, k^*)}$$

$$= \begin{bmatrix} \dfrac{f'(k(t)) - (\delta + \rho)}{\theta} & \dfrac{f''(k(t))c(t)}{\theta} \\ -1 & f'(k(t)) - (\delta + n) \end{bmatrix}_{|(c^*, k^*)}$$

$$= \begin{bmatrix} 0 & \dfrac{f''(k^*)c^*}{\theta} \\ -1 & \rho - n \end{bmatrix}$$

since in equilibrium $f'(k^*(t)) - (\delta + \rho) = 0$. This matrix has two real eigenvalues, one positive and another negative; thus the equilibrium point is a saddle point. Note that the characteristic polynomial is $\lambda^2 - (\rho - n)\lambda + \dfrac{f''(k^*)c^*}{\theta} = 0$, with $\rho - n > 0$ and $f''(k^*)c^* < 0$.

Numerical solution: boundary value problems

This section considers the numerical solution of *boundary value problems*, BVPs, that is, the solution of a system of differential equations where the conditions are specified at more than one point (previously, initial conditions where all stated at the same point). A first-order two-point boundary value problem has the form

$$y'(t) = \frac{dy}{dt}(t) = f(t, y(t))$$

164 *Dynamic economic models*

(as in (11.4)) with boundary conditions

$$g(y(t_0), y(t_T)) = 0,$$

where $f: \mathbb{R} \times \mathbb{R}^m \to \mathbb{R}^m$ and $g: \mathbb{R}^{2m} \to \mathbb{R}^m$.

Boundary value problems are more difficult to solve compared to IVPs. Mathematically, the former may have no solution or may have more than one. Numerically, the process is more challenging for BVPs since there is no single point on the integration interval where all information is available, in contrast to IVPs where that complete information allows for the existence of a local solution and to extend it to nearby points (as explained in the previous chapters).

Finite difference method

Let us consider a numerical approximation to the solution on a uniform mesh of points $t_j = t_0 + jh$, $j = 0, \ldots, n-1$, $h = (t_T - t_0)/(n-1)$. For simplicity, consider the case where f and g are linear, $f(t, y) = p(y)y + q(y)$ and $y(t_0) = y_0$, $y(t_T) = y_T$ (separated boundary conditions). Discretising using the trapezoidal rule (10.16), $y_{j+1} - y_j = (h/2)(f(t_j, y_j) + f(t_{j+1}, y_{j+1}))$, gives rise to the following system of linear equations:

$$\begin{bmatrix} 1 & & & & \\ r_0 & s_0 & & & \\ & r_1 & s_1 & & \\ & & \ddots & \ddots & \\ & & & r_{n-1} & s_{n-1} \\ & & & & 1 \end{bmatrix} \begin{bmatrix} y_0 \\ y_1 \\ y_2 \\ \vdots \\ y_{n-1} \\ y_n \end{bmatrix} = \begin{bmatrix} y(t_0) \\ u(t_1) \\ u_2 \\ \vdots \\ u_{n-1} \\ y(t_n) \end{bmatrix},$$

where $r_j = -1 - (h/2)p(y_j)$, $s_j = -1 - (h/2)p(y_{j+1})$ and $u_j = (h/2)(p(y_j) + p(y_{j+1}))$, together with the two boundary conditions. This system can be efficiently solved using Gaussian elimination (see Chapters 2 and 3) adapted for this band format (or through an iterative procedure). If the functions involved are nonlinear, a nonlinear system of equations must be solved, using the Newton method or one of its variants (see Chapter 4).

The finite difference method just developed is of order 2, due to the trapezoidal rule used. Higher-order finite difference methods can be developed considering, for instance, a RK method, usually Implicit RK formulas, leading to Gaussian quadrature rules. Since these rules do not evaluate at the end points, Implicit RK formulas leading to Lobatto quadrature rules[8] are applied.

Collocation method

In a collocation method a solution is computed according to the form

$$y(t) = \sum_{j=1}^{n} x_j \phi_j(t),$$

where ϕ_j are basis functions defined on $[t_0, t_T]$ and x is an n-dimensional vector; to determine x, a grid with n points (*collocation points*) is considered and the approximate solution is required to satisfy both the differential equation and the boundary conditions at, respectively, the interior collocation points and the endpoints. Again, a system of equations results, which is linear or nonlinear depending on f and g.

Solving boundary value problems in practice

MATLAB/Octave provide the `bvp4c` function. The implemented algorithm can be viewed either as a collocation method or as a finite difference method with a continuous extension (see Shampine *et al.* 2003). `bvp4c` is a finite difference code that implements the three-stage Lobatto IIIa formula. MATLAB also offers `bvp5c`, implementing a four-stage Lobatto IIIa formula. Both methods are based on collocation formulas and the collocation polynomials provide a C^1-continuous solution that is, respectively, fourth and fifth-order accurate (see Mathworks 2015).

Stability of equilibrium points

The solution of the matrix differential equation $\dot{Y}(t) = AY(t) + B$, where $Y(t)$ is a $n \times 1$ vector of functions, A is an $n \times n$ matrix of constants, can be obtained from the solution of the homogeneous equations ($B = 0$) and the particular solution. As already known, the stability behaviour is ruled by the former, which is given by $Y(t) = Ce^{At}$, and C can be specified for an IVP. Note that e^A is the matrix exponential, and thus $e^{At} = I + At + (1/2!)t^2 A^2 + \cdots + (1/n!)t^n A^n + \cdots$. When A results from a linearisation procedure it is known as *Jacobian* matrix (see (4.4)).

If the matrix has distinct eigenvalues, then $A = UDU^{-1}$, where $D = diag(\lambda_1, \ldots, \lambda_n)$ is the diagonal matrix of the eigenvalues of A and $U = [u_1 \ldots u_n]$ the matrix of the eigenvectors; thus, $Y(t) = \sum_{i=1}^{n} c_i e^{\lambda_i t} u_i$, where $c_i, i = 1, \ldots, n$, are constants. The clear result is that, as expected, the behaviour of the solution is ruled by the eigenvalues.

The equilibrium is asymptotically stable if all eigenvalues have negative real part and unstable if at least one has positive real part. For a 2×2 Jacobian matrix, the equilibrium point is a *node* when both eigenvalues are real, a *saddle* when eigenvalues are real but with opposite signs and a *focus* when eigenvalues are complex conjugate. The saddle point is unstable and the node (focus) point is stable when both eigenvalues are negative (have negative real part).

Some additional comments

It is the aim of this book to give some insight on the most popular numerical methods, rather than to present the whole plethora of methods or to detail one. Nevertheless, a brief comment on the well-known shooting method is provided. The idea is to solve the BVP as a sequence of IVPs, taking advantage of the numerical methods known to IVPs. The main drawback is that a well-posed BVP problem can involve unstable IVPs for its resolution. However, multiple shooting, by which the interval of integration is broken into several subintervals, can minimise this drawback. Additional information on solving BVPs can be obtained from Shampine et al. (2003).

Computational implementation

An m-file with the code to solve the problem is shown. The code is more general than the specifications above, since it incorporates an exogenous growth rate of technology, g, Harrod neutral (see exercise 4). The following baseline values are considered: $\alpha = 0.3$, $\delta = 0.05$, $\rho = 0.02$, $n = 0.01$, $g = 0.00$ (to recover the baseline model) and $\theta = (\delta + \rho)/(\alpha * (\delta + n + g) - g)$.

MATLAB/Octave code

```
%% RCK model
% The Ramsey-Cass-Koopmans model
% Implemented by: P.B. Vasconcelos and O. Afonso
function rck
disp('————————————————————');
disp('Ramsey-Cass-Koopmans model              ');
disp('————————————————————');

%% parameters
global alpha delta rho n g theta kss css k0
alpha = 0.3; % elasticity of capital in production
delta = 0.05; % depreciation rate
rho = 0.02; % time preference
n = 0.01; % population growth
g = 0.00; % exogenous growth rate of technology
theta = (delta+rho)/(alpha*(delta+n+g)-g);
        % inverse intertemporal elasticity of substitution;
        % select theta so that the saving rate is constant s=1/theta

%% Steady state values and shock
kss = ((delta+rho+g*theta)/alpha)^(1/(alpha-1));
css = kss^alpha - (n+delta+g)*kss;
k0 = 0.1*kss; % shock at k
disp('steady-state:')
fprintf('k* = %8.6f,  c* = %8.6f\n',kss,css);
disp('shock:');
fprintf('initial value for k: k0 = %8.6f \n',k0);
```

```
%% Exact solution
% for this model an analytical solution is known
k = @(t) (1./((delta+n+g).*theta)+(k0.^(1-alpha) - ...
   1./((delta+n+g).*theta))*exp(-(1-alpha) ...
   .*(delta+n+g).*t)).^(1./(1-alpha));
c = @(t) (1-1./theta).*k(t).^alpha;

%% Approximate solution using bvp4c (matlab solver)
% the RCK model is a BVP problem
nn = 100;
if ~exist('OCTAVE_VERSION','builtin')
   solinit = bvpinit(linspace(0,nn,5),[0.5 0.5]); % MATLAB
else
   solinit.x = linspace(0,nn,5);
   solinit.y = 0.5*ones(2,length(solinit.x)); % Octave
end
sol = bvp4c(@ode_bvp,@bcs,solinit);
if ~exist('OCTAVE_VERSION','builtin')
   xint = linspace(0,nn,50); Sxint = deval(sol,xint); % MATLAB
else
   xint = sol.x; Sxint = sol.y; % Octave
end

%% Plot both the analytical and numerical solution from bvp4c
subplot(2,1,1); hold on
ezplot(k,[0,nn]);            % plot analytical solution for k
plot(xint,Sxint(1,:),'r.'); % plot approx. by bvp4c for k
plot(0,k0,'go');             % plot initial value for k
if ~exist('OCTAVE_VERSION','builtin')
  legend('exact','bvp4c','$k_0$ initial value','location', ...
     'SouthEast');
  set(legend,'Interpreter','latex');
  xlabel('$t$','Interpreter','LaTex');
  ylabel('$k$','Interpreter','LaTex');
else
  legend('exact','bvp4c','k_0 initial value','location', ...
     'SouthEast');
  xlabel('t'); ylabel('k');
end

subplot(2,1,2); hold on
ezplot(c,[0,nn])             % plot analytical solution for c
plot(xint,Sxint(2,:),'r.')   % plot numerical approximation for c
if ~exist('OCTAVE_VERSION','builtin')
  legend('exact','bvp4c','location','SouthEast');
  xlabel('$t$','Interpreter','LaTex');
  ylabel('$c$','Interpreter','LaTex');
else
  legend('exact','bvp4c','location','SouthEast');
  xlabel('t'); ylabel('c');
end

%% Functions:
```

168 *Dynamic economic models*

```
% Boundary conditions
function res = bcs(ya,yb)
% Y=[k(t); c(t)], ya for initial conditions and yb for final ones
global css k0
res = [ya(1)−k0; yb(1)−kss];

% Differential system speciification
function dydt=ode_bvp(~,y)
% Y=[k(t); c(t)]
global alpha delta rho n g theta
dydt = [...
   (y(1)^alpha−y(2)−(n+delta+g)*y(1)); ...
      %ode: k
   (y(2)*(alpha*y(1)^(alpha−1)−(delta+rho+g*theta))/theta); ...
      %ode: c
   ];
```

Some short comments on the code

In order to incorporate functions inside a single file, MATLAB requires a function and not a script (a script populated with function in the same file is allowed by Octave).

The rck function is defined taking the Cobb–Douglas production function, $f(k(t)) = k^\alpha$ (see exercise 4 for an Harrod neutral technological progress). The bvp4c function is invoked considering a time span from 0 to 100 and the boundary conditions are set in the bcs function (the boundary conditions are treated as a residual function, delivering zero at the boundary values); consider $k_0 = 0.1k^*$ for initial value and $k_{100} = k^*$. A numerical approximation is used to compute (k^*, c^*), making use of the fsolve function. The system of differential equations is coded as in the previous models. Finally, to create an initial guess a call to bvpinit is required; this initial solution, as noted earlier, is the most difficult part. The *odepkg* package must be installed for Octave and since the bvpinit is not yet implemented, a slightly different code to cope with this exception is provided.

Since an analytical solution is known for this model for specific calibration values, both the analytical and numerical solutions are plotted; the good approximation provided by the collocation method is clear.

Numerical results and simulation

Figure 12.2 displays the path of variables k and c. The transitional dynamics tell how both consumption and capital increase over time. The curve c passes through the point $c = 0$ and is increasing until it reaches the steady state. The dynamics of k is similar and is induced by the law of diminishing returns, that is, k grows at a decreasing rate until the steady state and provokes a similar path for c in form, but not naturally in levels. In the long run, the economy converges towards the steady state.

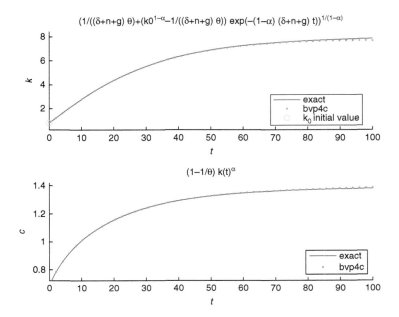

Figure 12.2 Transition dynamics to steady state.

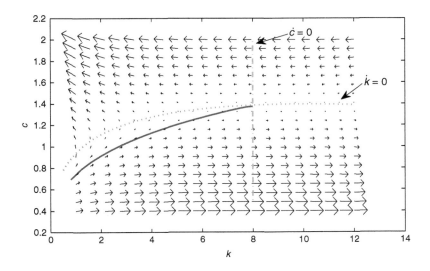

Figure 12.3 Phase diagram, RCK model.

170 *Dynamic economic models*

Figure 12.3 shows the phase diagram. To analyse the transitional dynamics it should be noted that the curves $\dot{k}=0$ and $\dot{c}=0$ divide the space into regions. The dynamics of these regions are represented by arrows. Following these arrows, it can be seen that there is one and only one stable path that converges towards the steady state (saddle-path stability).

Highlights

- The RCK model, was formulated by Ramsey (1928) followed later by Cass (1965) and Koopmans (1965). Tjalling Koopmans won the 1975 Nobel Memorial Prize in Economic Sciences.
- The model is used to analyse the performance of the economy as the rational behaviour of utility maximising individuals. It is considered a building block of dynamic general equilibrium models.
- This chapter introduces the bvp4c and bvp5c MATLAB functions to solve boundary value problems for ordinary differential equations by the collocation method.

Problems and computer exercises

1. Solve the RCK model using bvp5c solver. Contrast and compare with the solution obtained by bvp4c.
2. Write the m-file to reproduce:

    (a) Figures 12.1;
    (b) Figures 12.3.

3. Consider the following shocks in the model and comment:

    (a) increase ρ of 50 per cent;
    (b) change α of 10 per cent.

4. The differential system of equations coded in the m-file provided considers exogenous growth rate of technology at firm level – Harrod neutral type. Deduce the system and show that it is given by

$$\dot{\hat{k}}(t) = f(\hat{k}(t)) - (\delta + n + g)\hat{k}(t) - \hat{c}(t);$$

$$\frac{\dot{\hat{c}}(t)}{\hat{c}(t)} = \left(f'(\hat{k}(t)) - \delta - \rho - \frac{g}{\sigma(t)}\right)\sigma(t)$$

for $\hat{c}(t) = c(t)/A(t)$, $\hat{k}(t) = k(t)/A(t)$, $A(t) = e^{gt}A(0)$, $A(0) = 1$, where $g = \dot{A}(t)/A(t) \geq 0$. Simulate several values for g and assess their impact, regarding $g = 0$ (the code is the one provided in this chapter).

5. Write an m-file to reproduce Figure 12.4, in line with Figure 2.5 from Barro and Sala-i-Martin (2004, ch. 2, p. 117). Consider $g = 0.02$, $\theta = 3$, and simulate for $\alpha = 0.3$ and $\alpha = 0.75$.

Ramsey–Cass–Koopmans model 171

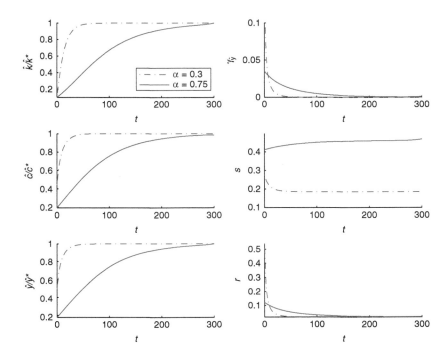

Figure 12.4 Numerical estimates of the dynamic paths in the RCK model.

6. Draw a phase diagram to illustrate the impact of θ, by considering $\theta = 3$ (high) and $\theta = 0.1$ (low), for $g = 0.02$ and $\alpha = 0.3$.

Notes

1 Each family chooses 'consumption and saving to maximise their dynastic utility, subject to an intertemporal budget constraint' (Ramsey, 1928).
2 In (12.1), the term e^{nt} is used and not $L(t)$ since $L(t) = L(0)e^{nt}$ and $L(0)$ is normalised to 1.
3 The interest adjusts to have $a = k$, and all credits are exactly the same as all debts, being the aggregate debt null and then capital is the only liquid asset.
4 This condition can be obtained from the integration of the linear first-order differential equation (12.2)
5 $\partial F/\partial K > 0$; $\partial F/\partial L > 0$; $\partial^2 F/\partial K^2 < 0$; $\partial^2 F/\partial L^2 < 0$.
6 Homogeneous function of degree one.
7 Note that the benefit rate obtained by the producer is given by $R - \delta$, where, remember, δ is the depreciation rate.
8 Lobatto methods for the numerical integration of differential equations are characterised by the use of approximations to the solution at the two end points of each subinterval of integration $[t_j, t_{j+1}]$.

Afterword

We have now reached the end of this wonderful journey.

It started with static economic models and proceeded with dynamic ones. Most of the presented models are seminal to economy, whilst a few others are new or lesser known. All models were implemented in order to be easily simulated on computers, allowing for a fresh new way to study and interpret economics. The most important numerical techniques to solve economic models were introduced and explained, conferring greater emphasis on ideas rather than on deductions.

A new journey can be undertaken. By now, you are able to pursue new challenges in computational economics, exploring both more sophisticated models and new numerical algorithms to tackle them.

It is up to you to step forward with this acquired expertise.

Part III
Appendices

Appendix A
Projects

Supply–demand model with trade: export taxes

Consider the economic model with international-trade policy in Chapter 1. As observed, at the free trade equilibrium price, the excess demand by the importing country (Home, H) equals excess supply by the exporting country (Foreign, F).

Show that when a large exporting country, F, implements an export tax, in order to reduce the quantity exported, it causes a decrease in the price of the good on the exporting country, F, and an increase in the price in the rest of the world (importing country), H. Consequently, show the following.

- Exporting country consumers experience an increase in consumption and the consumer surplus rises.
- Exporting country producers experience a decrease in production and the producer surplus decreases.
- Exporting country government receives tax revenue as a result of the export tax.
- Exporting country welfare is found by summing the gains and losses, being that the net effect consists of three components: a positive terms of trade effect, a negative consumption distortion, and a negative production distortion. Thus, the net national welfare effect can be either positive or negative. Check if, in line with the literature on international trade policy, it is confirmed that a small export tax raises national welfare and a high export tax reduces national welfare, such that there is a positive optimal export tax that maximises national welfare.
- Importing country consumers suffer a reduction in consumption and the consumer surplus decreases.
- Importing country producers experience an increase in production and the producer surplus increases.
- Importing country government is not affected as a result of the exporter's tax.

178 *Appendix A*

- Importing country welfare is also found by summing the gains and losses, being that the net effect consists of three negative components: a negative terms of trade effect, a negative production distortion, and a negative consumption distortion. Since all three components are negative, the export tax results in a reduction in national welfare for the importing country.
- Export tax effect on world welfare is found by summing the national welfare effects in the importing and exporting countries. Since the terms of trade gain to the exporting country is equal to the terms of trade loss to the importing country, the world welfare effect reduces to four components: the importer's negative production distortion, the importer's negative consumption distortion, the exporter's negative consumption distortion, and the exporter's negative production distortion. Since each of these is negative, the world welfare effect of the export tax is negative.

Product differentiation model

The first model with price competition was proposed by Bertrand, considering that the demand goes to the firm with the lowest price so that, in equilibrium, every firm sets the price equal to the marginal cost. Later, Hotelling proposed a static price competition model in which firms are located on a straight line according to specific characteristics of the produced product and consumers are also located on the line according to preferences and prices. However, product horizontal differentiation occurs in more than one characteristic and some of them cannot be ordered along a line. For an overview of product differentiation models, see, for instance, Beath and Katsoulacos (1991).

This project considers a model in which firms compete by prices and sell heterogeneous products with different unordered features and qualities (see Chapter 7 for competition by quantities). The model consists of a linear system of n equations

$$\begin{bmatrix} 2b & -\dfrac{d}{n-1} & \cdots & -\dfrac{d}{n-1} \\ -\dfrac{d}{n-1} & 2b & \cdots & -\dfrac{d}{n-1} \\ \vdots & \vdots & \ddots & \vdots \\ -\dfrac{d}{n-1} & -\dfrac{d}{n-1} & \cdots & 2b \end{bmatrix} \begin{bmatrix} P_1 \\ P_2 \\ \vdots \\ P_n \end{bmatrix} = \begin{bmatrix} n^{\alpha-1}A_1 + bC_1 \\ n^{\alpha-1}A_2 + bC_2 \\ \vdots \\ n^{\alpha-1}A_n + bC_n \end{bmatrix},$$

where b is the sensibility of the demand to the price (i.e. when a firm raises the price in one unit its demand falls b units), P_i, $i = 1, 2, \ldots, n$, is the price of product i, n is the number of firms, d, with $d < b$, represents the units lost by a firm when other similar product(s) arises (d is equally distributed among firms in the market), A_i is the demand for firm i when the price of the product is 0 and no other firm is on the market, $0 < \alpha < 1$, is a parameter such that the greater the α the greater the gain obtained by consumers due to product variety (products are perfect substitutes for $\alpha = 0$ and absolutely independent for $\alpha = 1$), and C_i is the constant marginal cost of the firm i.

Each firm produces a product with particular characteristics. The demand for each one depends on tastes and preferences of heterogeneous consumers: when all prices are equal, each group of consumers buys its favourite variety, but when the price of a particular characteristic increases, some of the respective consumers either leave the market or buy another variety.

With respect to the demand function, first consider the case where all prices are zero. If firm 1 is a monopolist that sets a null price, it is able to sell a quantity $Q_1 = A_1$, which also depends on the characteristics of the product. Suppose now that a second firm enters the market and introduces a new product variety at a zero price with the following.

- A perfect substitute product: then the total demand, A_1, remains unchanged and it is split between the two firms; i.e. $Q_1 = A_1/2$ and $Q_2 = A_1/2$.
- An independent product (its characteristics are very different): then the demand for firm 1 remains the same and total demand increases; i.e. is given by $A_1 + A_2$, and $Q_1 = A_1$ and $Q_2 = A_2$.
- An intermediate situation where goods are neither perfect substitutes nor independent: when the number of firm grows, the demand for each firm falls due to a business-stealing effect, but the total demand rises due to the increase in the number of varieties. Thus, consider that when all market prices are zero, firm i's demand function is $Q_i = A_i n^{\alpha-1}$ and total demand is $\sum_{i=1}^{n} Q_i = n^{\alpha-1} \sum_{i=1}^{n} A_i$.

Firm i's demand function is given by $Q_i = n^{\alpha-1} A_i - b P_i + \frac{d}{n-1} \sum_{j=1}^{n-1} P_j$ and total demand by $\sum_{i=1}^{n} Q_i = n^{\alpha-1} \sum_{i=1}^{n} A_i - (b-d) \sum_{i=1}^{n} P_i$. Thus, the profit of each firm is given by

$$\pi_i = Q_i(P_i - C_i) = \left(n^{\alpha-1} A_i - b P_i + \frac{d}{n-1} \sum_{j=1}^{n-1} P_j \right)(P_i - C_i).$$

Since firms compete by prices, in the Nash equilibrium each firm chooses the price that optimises profits given the prices chosen by the others. Using first-order conditions $\partial \pi_i / \partial P_i = 0$, the best reply function of firm i is obtained. The abovementioned linear system incorporates all these functions ($i = 1, \ldots, n$).

For numerical computations, consider the following parameters: $n = 5$, $A_1 = 150$, $A_2 = 100$, $A_3 = 100$, $A_4 = 100$, $A_5 = 100$, $\alpha = 0.5$, $b = 2$, $d = 1$, $C_1 = 10$, $C_2 = 20$, $C_3 = 10$, $C_4 = 10$ and $C_5 = 10$ (firm 1 has a product differentiation advantage and firm 2 has a relative disadvantage in costs).

Analyse the model.

- Plot the output matrix with all the equilibrium results: prices, marginal costs, mark-ups, quantities and profits.
- For each firm, plot the best reply function; i.e. the script should generate a figure with firm 1's optimal price as a positive function of rivals' average price.
- For each firm, plot the profit functions and observe that the profit of each firm is concave with respect to its own price and is increasing with the average price practiced by rival firms.

Show how the model reacts to changes in the economy or in the industry.

- Consider that at a certain point in time firm 2 is able to imitate the other firms' technology and becomes equally competitive; i.e. $C_2 = 10$.
    - Analyse how the price of each firm evolves between the two equilibria, and confirm that while firm 2 significantly decreases the price, the other firms only decrease the price slightly as a reaction to firm 2's behaviour.
    - Verify that in the new equilibrium the best reply function of firm 2 has moved downwards.
- Consider that at period 1 α increases to 0.6, at period 2 to 0.7, then to 0.8 and at last to 0.9. Compare the results in all these different equilibria by plotting the profits.

Some variants on the Mundell–Fleming model

This project provides a framework to analyse the short-term interactions between two economies, considering perfect and imperfect capital mobility as well as fixed and flexible exchange rates.

For the following scenarios, do the following.

- Implement the model and find the equilibrium values for the endogenous variables.
- Represent graphically the IS and LM curves for both economies.
- In order to look at the effects of some policies, find the new equilibrium values and discuss their impact in both countries, considering shocks in some of the exogenous variables.

Perfect mobility of capital and a fixed exchange rate

In this scenario external imbalances are restored by the monetary authority. Furthermore, since small differences in interest rates provoke unlimited capital flow, the interest rate must be worldwide.

- Endogenous variables: Y and Y_F are, respectively, the product of the home and foreign country (world); C, C_F the consumption; I, I_F the investment; G, G_F government expenditures; NX, NX_F the net exports; R, R_F the interest rates; T, T_F the tax rates; M, M_F the money supply; and K_F the capital balance.
- The exogenous variables and their values are: $E = 1$ the exchange rate; $P = P_F = 1$ the price levels; $\overline{C} = 20$, $\overline{C}_F = 200$ autonomous consumption; $\overline{I} = 100$, $\overline{I}_F = 150$ autonomous investment; $\overline{G} = 100$, $\overline{G}_F = 200$ autonomous government expenditures; $\overline{NX}_F = 10$ the autonomous net exports; $\overline{T} = 150$, $\overline{T}_F = 160$ autonomous tax on income; $\overline{K}_F = 5$ autonomous capital balance.
- The parameters related to the sensitivities to variables along with their values are: $c = 0.45$, $c_F = 0.4$; $b = 15$, $b_F = 20$; $k = 0.5$, $k_F = 0.6$; $h = 20$, $h_F = 25$; $g = 0.1$, $g_F = 0.15$; $t = 0.1$, $t_F = 0.1$; $n_F = 10$; $j_F = 0.1$; $l_F = 2$.

The economies are ruled by:

Home economy:
$$\begin{cases} Y - C - I - G - NX = 0 \\ C - c(Y - T) = \overline{C} \\ T - tY = \overline{T} \\ I + bR = \overline{I} \\ G - gY = \overline{G} \\ M = P(kY - hR) \end{cases}$$

Foreign economy:
$$\begin{cases} Y_F - C_F - I_F - G_F - NX_F = 0 \\ C_F - c_F(Y_F - T_F) = \overline{C}_F \\ T_F - t_F Y_F = \overline{T}_F \\ I_F + b_F R_F = \overline{I}_F \\ G_F - g_F Y_F = \overline{G}_F \\ M_F = P_F(k_F Y_F - h_F R_F) \\ K_F - n_F R_F = \overline{K}_F \\ BP_F = NX_F + K_F = 0 \end{cases}$$

182 Appendix A

$$\text{Between economies:} \begin{cases} R = R_F \\ NX = -NX_F \\ NX_F + j_F Y_F - l_F \dfrac{EP_F}{P} = \overline{NX}_F \end{cases}$$

Perfect mobility of capital and a flexible exchange rate

This scenario is characterised by a fluctuation of the exchange rate due to commercial and financial transactions, still considering perfect mobility of capitals.

- Endogenous variables: Y and Y_F are, respectively, the product of the home and foreign country (world); C, C_F the consumption; I, I_F the investment; G, G_F government expenditures; NX, NX_F the net exports; R, R_F the interest rates; T, T_F the tax rates; E the exchange rate; and K_F the capital balance.
- The exogenous variables and their values are: $M = 100$, $M_F = 200$ the money supplies; $P = P_F = 1$ the price levels; $\overline{C} = 20$, $\overline{C}_F = 200$ autonomous consumption; $\overline{I} = 100$, $\overline{I}_F = 150$ autonomous investment; $\overline{G} = 100$, $\overline{G}_F = 200$ autonomous government expenditures; $\overline{NX}_F = 2$ the autonomous net exports; $\overline{T} = 150$, $\overline{T}_F = 160$ autonomous tax on income.
- The parameters related to the sensitivities to variables along with their values are: $c = 0.45$, $c_F = 0.4$; $b = 15$, $b_F = 20$; $k = 0.5$, $k_F = 0.6$; $h = 50$, $h_F = 60$; $g = 0.1$, $g_F = 0.15$; $t = 0.1$, $t_F = 0.1$; $n_F = 5$; $j_F = 0.4$; $l_F = 20$.

The economies are ruled by:

$$\text{Home economy:} \begin{cases} Y - C - I - G - NX = 0 \\ C - c(Y - T) = \overline{C} \\ T - tY = \overline{T} \\ I + bR = \overline{I} \\ -gY + G = \overline{G} \\ M = P(kY - hR) \end{cases}$$

Foreign economy:
$$\begin{cases} Y_F - C_F - I_F - G_F - NX_F = 0 \\ C_F - c_F(Y_F - T_F) = \overline{C}_F \\ T_F - t_F Y_F = \overline{T}_F \\ I_F + b_F R_F = \overline{I}_F \\ -g_F Y_F + G_F = \overline{G}_F \\ M_F = P_F(k_F Y_F - h_F R_F) \\ BP_F = NX_F + K_F \end{cases}$$

Between economies:
$$\begin{cases} R = R_F \\ NX = -NX_F \\ NX_F - l_F \dfrac{EP_F}{P} + j_F Y_F = \overline{NX}_F \end{cases}$$

Note that equation $K_F = \overline{K}_F - n_F R_F$ is not required, and may be only used for graphical purposes. BP_F is taken as 0.

Imperfect mobility of capital and a fixed exchange rate

In an imperfect capital mobility scenario unlimited capital flow is not guaranteed. Therefore, not only the net exports matter to maintain the external equilibrium and the line BP = 0 will have a positive slope. Moreover, this case is characterised by a fixed exchange rate.

- Endogenous variables: Y and Y_F are, respectively, the product of the home and foreign country; C, C_F the consumption; I, I_F the investment; G, G_F government expenditures; NX, NX_F the net exports; R, R_F the interest rates; T, T_F the tax rates; M, M_F the money supply; and K and K_F the capital balance.
- $E = 1$ the exchange rate; $P = P_F = 1$ the price levels; $\overline{C} = 100$, $\overline{C}_F = 500$ autonomous consumption; $\overline{I} = 1000$, $\overline{I}_F = 1200$ autonomous investment; $\overline{G} = 100$, $\overline{G}_F = 200$ autonomous government expenditures; $\overline{NX}_F = 10$ the autonomous net exports; $\overline{T} = 150$, $\overline{T}_F = 160$ autonomous tax on income; $\overline{K} = -1500$, $\overline{K}_F = 50$ autonomous capital balance.
- The parameters related to the sensitivities to variables along with their values are: $c = 0.45$, $c_F = 0.4$; $b = 10$, $b_F = 30$; $k = 0.5$, $k_F = 0.6$; $h = 15$, $h_F = 20$; $g = 0.1$, $g_F = 0.15$; $t = 0.1$, $t_F = 0.1$; $n = 200$; $n_F = 20$; $j_F = 0.1$; $x = 0.05$; $l_F = 1$.

184 Appendix A

The economies are ruled by:

Home economy:
$$\begin{cases} Y = C + I + G + NX \\ C = \overline{C} + c(Y - T) \\ T = \overline{T} + tY \\ I = \overline{I} - bR \\ G = \overline{G} + gY \\ M = P(kY - hR) \\ K = \overline{K} + nR \end{cases}$$

Foreign economy:
$$\begin{cases} Y_F = C_F + I_F + G_F + NX_F \\ C_F = \overline{C}_F + c_F(Y_F - T_F) \\ T_F = \overline{T}_F + t_F Y_F \\ I_F = \overline{I}_F - b_F R_F \\ G_F = \overline{G}_F + g_F Y_F \\ M_F = P_F(k_F Y_F - h_F R_F) \\ K_F = \overline{K}_F + n_F R_F \\ BP_F = NX_F + K_F = 0 \end{cases}$$

Between economies:
$$\begin{cases} R = R_F \\ K = -K_F \\ NX_F = \overline{NX}_F + l_F \dfrac{EP_F}{P} - j_F Y_F + xY \end{cases}$$

In this scenario, the net exports of the foreign economy rely also on the output of the domestic economy. Moreover, the capital balance is independent of the interest rate of the other economy; however, since $K = -K_F$, the interest rate of one economy influences the capital balance of the other.

Imperfect mobility of capital and a flexible exchange rate

This scenario imposes a currency depreciation/appreciation due to external deficit/surplus in a context with unlimited capital flow.

- Endogenous variables: Y and Y_F are, respectively, the product of the home and foreign country; C, C_F the consumption; I, I_F the investment; G, G_F government expenditures; NX, NX_F the net exports; R, R_F the interest rates; T, T_F the tax rates; E exchange rate; K and K_F the capital balance.
- $P = P_F = 1$ the price levels; $\overline{C} = 20$, $\overline{C}_F = 200$ autonomous consumption; $\overline{I} = 500$, $\overline{I}_F = 600$ autonomous investment; $\overline{G} = 100$, $\overline{G}_F = 200$ autonomous government expenditures; $M = 300$, $M_F = 350$ the money supply; $\overline{NX}_F = 10$ the autonomous net exports; $\overline{T} = 150$, $\overline{T}_F = 160$ autonomous tax on income; $\overline{K}_F = 5$ autonomous capital balance.
- The parameters related to the sensitivities to variables along with their values are: $c = 0.45$, $c_F = 0.4$; $b = 10$, $b_F = 10$; $k = 0.5$, $k_F = 0.6$; $h = 20$, $h_F = 25$; $g = 0.1$; $g_F = 0.15$; $t = 0.1$, $t_F = 0.1$; $n_F = 10$; $j_F = 1$; $x = 0.05$; $l_F = 200$.

The economies are ruled by:

Home economy:
$$\begin{cases} Y = C + I + G + NX \\ C = \overline{C} + c(Y - T) \\ T = \overline{T} + tY \\ I = \overline{I} - bR \\ G = \overline{G} - gY \\ M = P(kY - hR) \end{cases}$$

Foreign economy:
$$\begin{cases} Y_F = C_F + I_F + G_F + NX_F \\ C_F = \overline{C}_F + c_F(Y_F - T_F) \\ T_F = \overline{T}_F + t_F Y_F \\ I_F = \overline{I}_F - b_F R_F \\ G_F = \overline{G}_F - g_F Y_F \\ M_F = P_F(k_F Y_F - h_F R_F) \\ BP_F = NX_F + K_F = 0 \end{cases}$$

Between economies:
$$\begin{cases} NX = -NX_F \\ K = -K_F \\ NX_F = \overline{NX}_F + l_F \dfrac{EP_F}{P} - j_F Y_F + xY \\ K_F = \overline{K}_F + n_F(R_F - R) \end{cases}$$

Nonlinear supply–demand model

Consider the supply–demand model in Chapter 1, but now assume that supply and demand curves are nonlinear and are given, respectively, by

$$P_s = 0.4 + 0.4 Q^{\frac{3}{2}};$$
$$P_d = (0.03 + 0.2 Q)^{\frac{-2}{7}}.$$

- Implement a script to compute the price and quantity in equilibrium (Hint: you may want to use `fsolve` and `fplot`).
- Use integral calculus to measure the consumer and producer surplus, as well as the social welfare (Hint: use `integral` for new MATLAB versions or `quad` for older versions and Octave).
- Produce a Cobweb diagram.
- Consider a shock characterised by an increase in the number of consumers, shifting the demand curve to the right, and, simultaneously, an increase in the production costs, shifting the supply curve to the left. Find the new demand and supply curves compatible with an equilibrium with the same equilibrium quantity.

Dynamic continuous duopoly game

This project, in line with Chapter 7, proposes a simple dynamic duopoly game, where two firms compete by quantities, considering that they start competing outside the steady-state equilibrium, and that each one is allowed to adjusted the quantity produced at every time period. In this case, since capacity adjustments usually take time, it is assumed that a firm can only adjust a constant fraction per unit of time of the optimal adjustment. To analyse the strategic interaction between firms, the game can be solved numerically, observing that both firms tend to the Cournot result.

The model is given by

$$\dot{Q}_1 = \frac{\overline{Q}_d - a\overline{MC}_1}{2} - \frac{Q_2}{2} - Q_1$$
$$\dot{Q}_2 = \frac{\overline{Q}_d - a\overline{MC}_2}{2} - \frac{Q_1}{2} - Q_2,$$

where, as already seen in Chapter 1, P is the price of the good, $\overline{Q}_d$ is the independent/autonomous quantity demanded, Q_d is the quantity demanded, which is also the quantity produced ($= Q_1 + Q_2$), $\dot{Q}_i = dQ_{i,t}/dt$ for $i = 1, 2$ and $a > 0$ is the sensitivity of the demand to price. It is considered that the marginal costs can be different, being $\overline{MC}_1$ the marginal cost of firm 1 and $\overline{MC}_2$ the marginal cost of firm 2.

To understand the model, assume that a linear market demand is given by

$$P = \frac{\overline{Q}_d}{a} - \frac{1}{a}Q_d.$$

Every period, each firm would like to optimise profits given the quantity produced by the other firm and thus the profit of firm 1 at time t should be expressed as a function of the quantities produced by the two firms:

$$\pi_{1,t} = Q_{1,t} \times (P - \overline{MC}_1) = Q_{1,t} \times \left(\frac{\overline{Q}_d}{a} - \frac{1}{a}Q_{1,t} - \frac{1}{a}Q_{2,t} - \overline{MC}_1 \right).$$

Using first-order conditions, we obtain the optimal quantity (firm 1's best reply function):

$$\frac{\partial \pi_{1,t}}{\partial Q_{1,t}} = 0 \;\Rightarrow\; Q^*_{1,t} = \frac{\overline{Q}_d - a\overline{MC}_1}{2} - \frac{Q_{2,t}}{2}.$$

Using the same procedure, firm 2's best reply function is

$$Q^*_{2,t} = \frac{\overline{Q}_d - a\overline{MC}_2}{2} - \frac{Q_{1,t}}{2}.$$

However, the quantity that is actually produced by each firm in time t is the quantity produced in the previous k periods plus an adjustment towards the optimal quantity. Although both firms want to adjust their capacity on $Q^*_{i,t} - Q_{i,t-k}$, they can only adjust a constant fraction v per unit of time. Since firms reset the quantities produced every k periods, they adjust a fraction $v \times k$ and the total adjustment is equal to $(Q^*_{i,t} - Q_{i,t-k})v \times k$:

$$Q_{i,t} = Q_{i,t-k} + (Q^*_{i,t} - Q_{i,t-k})v \times k, \quad i = 1, 2.$$

From now on assume that $v = 1$, and thus t is defined as the time that a firm needs to adjust the production to the optimal level. Therefore, a firm must wait k periods to adjust the quantity produced. In order to make capacity adjustments continuous, the limit of the dynamic reaction functions when k tends to zero is considered:

$$\lim_{k \to 0} \frac{Q_{i,t} - Q_{i,t-k}}{k} = Q^*_{i,t} - \lim_{k \to 0} Q_{i,t-k}$$

that is,

$$\frac{dQ_{i,t}}{dt} = Q^*_{i,t} - Q_{i,t}, \quad i = 1, 2.$$

188   *Appendix A*

Finally, the subscript t can be omitted and $Q^*_{i,t}$ can be substituted by the optimal quantity to obtain the two above differential equations that define the model.

Consider that $P = 1 - Q_d$ ($\overline{Q}_d = 1$, $a = 1$), $\overline{MC}_1 = 0.2$, $\overline{MC}_2 = 0.1$. Moreover, assume that firm 2 only participates in the market for $t > 0$; i.e. at $t = 0$ the quantity produced is 0, while firm 1 produces the monopoly quantity.

Implement the model and do the following.

- Show that after time 0, firm 2 enters the market (since it is more efficient), producing positive quantities, and that firm 1 diminishes its own production level in order to optimise profits.
- Show that after a certain period of time, industry tends to the Nash equilibrium and both firms approach the production levels of Cournot static game.
- Represent a phase diagram, mark the equilibrium and draw the saddle path.
- Represent the profits function in a three dimensional plot (use `surf`, `ezsurf` functions), for each firm, and verify that profits for firm i are concave relative to quantity Q_i.

Consider now that firm 2 enters the market under different initial conditions.

- First, assume that firm 2 enters the market producing the Cournot quantity and show that, although it produces the equilibrium quantity at $t = 0$, in the first period it reduces the amount produced and then returns to the equilibrium; indeed, when firm 1 produces the monopoly quantity, the best reply for firm 2 is to produce less than the Cournot quantity.
- Second, assume that both firms produce the Cournot quantity at $t = 0$ and show that they continue to produce the same quantity indefinitely, since they already are at the Nash equilibrium.
- Third, assume that firm 2 enters the market replying in the best possible way and show that firm 1 produces the Stackelberg quantity at time 0.
  - Additionally, if at $t = 5$ there is a marginal cost shock and firm 1 becomes as competitive as firm 2, show that until $t = 5$ the two firms are converging for their respective Cournot quantities but at $t = 5$ there is a discontinuity point and both firms start converging to the same equilibrium quantity.
  - Then, introduce a positive demand shock at $t = 7$. Show that the two firms converge for an equilibrium quantity greater than before.

Dynamic IS–LM model

Consider the following dynamic IS–LM model (see Zhang 2005, ch. 7 for additional insights):

$$\begin{cases} \dot{y}(t) = \alpha(\overline{A} + \gamma y(t) - br(t)) \\ \dot{r}(t) = \beta(\overline{L} - \overline{M} + ky(t) - hr(t)) \end{cases}$$

for $\alpha, \beta > 0$, where the endogenous variables are y, the output, and r, the interest rate. The exogenous variables and parameters are characterised as in Chapter 3 along with $\overline{A} = \overline{C} + \overline{I} + \overline{G} + \overline{NX}$ and $\gamma = c(1 - \tau) + d + g - q - 1$ where τ stands for the exogenous tax rate, d, g and q are sensitivities of the investment, public spending and imports to the output.

The model is built taking into account that:

- consumption $C(t) = \overline{C} + c(1 - \tau)y(t)$;
- investment $I(t) = \overline{I} - br(t) + dy(t)$;
- public spendings $G(t) = \overline{G} + gy(t)$;
- net exports $NX(t) = \overline{NX} - qy(t)$;
- real expenses $E(t) = C(t) + I(t) + G(t) + NX(t)$;
- real money supply, $M^s = \frac{M}{P}$; and
- real demand of money $L(t) = \overline{L} + ky(t) - hr(t)$.

Deduce analytically the model and show the following.

- The equilibrium is given by $y^* = (Ah + b(\overline{M} - \overline{L}))/(bk + h\gamma)$ and $r^* = (Ak + \gamma(\overline{M} - \overline{L}))(bk + h\gamma)$.
- The Jacobian matrix of the system is $J = \begin{bmatrix} \alpha\gamma & -\alpha b \\ \beta k & -\beta h \end{bmatrix}$.

Implement the model considering the following values for the parameters: $k = 0.25$, $b = 1.3$, $h = 0.3$, $d = 0.3$, $c = 0.7$, $g = 0.05$, $q = 0.1$, $\tau = 0.25$, $\alpha = 0.5$, $\beta = 0.4$ and for exogenous variables: $\overline{C} = 0.6$, $\overline{I} = 25$, $\overline{G} = 15$, $\overline{NX} = -3$, $\overline{L} = 3$, $\overline{M} = 30$, $\overline{P} = 1$.

- Solve the model for the initial conditions $y(0) = 75$ and $r(0) = 8$.
- Draw the phase diagram.
- Compute the eigenvalues of Jacobian matrix J and verify that they are complex-conjugate with negative real part; thus, the equilibrium is a stable focus.
- Change to $d = 0.7$, $c = 0.6$, $g = 0.0$, $q = 0.0$, $\tau = 0.3$, $\alpha = 0.81$, $\beta = 0.3$, $\overline{C} = 0.6$, $\overline{I} = 20$, and $\overline{M} = 11$.

190 *Appendix A*

- Solve the model.
- Compute the eigenvalues of J and verify that they are still complex-conjugate but now with positive real part; thus, the equilibrium is an unstable focus.

Dynamic AD–AS model

In this project a dynamic AD–AS model is considered by incorporating the expectations-augmented Phillips curve (Shone 2002, ch. 10–11) to analyse the output and inflation rate adjustment along time (Gaspar, 2015).

The dynamics AD–AS system to be considered is

$$\begin{cases} \dot{y}(t) = a(\dot{m}(t) - \alpha(1-h\beta)(y(t) - y^N) - \pi^e(t)) \\ \dot{\pi}^e(t) = \alpha\beta(y(t) - y^N) \end{cases}$$

and the effective inflation rate is obtained from the AS curve

$$\pi(t) = \alpha(y(t) - y^N) + \pi^e(t), \quad \alpha, \beta > 0$$

where the endogenous variables are $y(t)$, the output and π^e, the expected inflation rate and the exogenous variable is m, the nominal money supply. Parameters are characterised as in Chapter 4 along with

$$a = \frac{b/h}{1 - c(1-\tau) + bk/h}$$

and y^N the natural output level.

The model underlying functional forms are:

- consumption, $c(t) = \bar{c} + c(1-\tau)y(t)$, with $0 < c, \tau < 1$, where τ is the exogenous tax rate;
- investment, $i(t) = \bar{i} - b(r(t) - \pi^e(t))$, with $b > 0$, where r is the nominal interest rate;
- real output, $y(t) = c(t) + i(t) + \bar{g}$, where $\bar{g}$ is public spending;
- real money demand, $\ell(t) = ky(t) - hr(t)$; and
- real money supply, $m^s = m - p$, where p is the price level.

To derive the model, note that from the AD curve $y(t) = a((h/b)(\bar{c} + \bar{i} + \bar{g}) + m - p + h\pi^e(t))$.

Deduce analytically the model and show the following.

- In equilibrium, the real output is equal to the natural output and the inflation rate is equal to the growth rate of money supply.

- The Jacobian matrix of the system is $J = \begin{bmatrix} -\alpha(1-h\beta) & -a \\ \alpha\beta & 0 \end{bmatrix}$.

Implement the model considering the following values for the parameters: $k=0.05$, $b=0.1$, $h=0.05$, $c=0.8$, $\tau=0.3$, $\alpha=0.1$, $\beta=1.0$ and for exogenous variables: $\bar{c}=10$, $\bar{i}=5$, $\bar{g}=5$, $\overline{y^N}=1$, $\dot{m}=0.01$.

- Solve the model for the initial conditions $y(0)=0.05$ and $\pi^e(0)=0.15$.
- Draw the phase diagram.
- Compute the eigenvalues of Jacobian matrix J and verify that they are complex-conjugate with negative real part; thus, the equilibrium is a stable focus.
- Consider a fiscal policy shock: change to $\bar{g}=5.5$ and $\tau=0.25$: note that there is a level effect for the initial conditions of y ($y(0) = a((h/b)(\bar{c}+\bar{i}+\bar{g}) + m - p + h\pi^e(0)))$.
  - Verify that $y(0) \approx 2.08$.
  - Compute the eigenvalues of J and verify that they are again complex-conjugate with negative real part; thus, again, the equilibrium is a stable focus.
  - Illustrate graphically that the economy returns to the initial equilibrium.
- Consider a monetary shock: change to $\dot{m}=0.04$ and $\tau=0.25$: note that there is a level effect for the initial conditions of y ($y(0) = a((hb)(\bar{c}+\bar{i}+\bar{g}) + m - p + h\pi^e(0)))$.
  - Verify that the qualitative behaviour of the system is the same as before the shock (look at the eigenvalues).
  - Illustrate graphically that the economy converges to a new equilibrium, in which $y^*=1$ and $\pi^{e*}=0.04$.

Extensions to the neoclassic growth model

To implement the extensions below consider the usual baseline parameter values and exogenous variables; in particular, $A=1$, $s=0.15$, $\alpha=0.4$, $g=0.03$, $n=0.01$ and $\delta=0.01$, unless differently specified.

As much as possible, answer the questions by illustrating graphically the transitional dynamics.

More on Solow model

Exercise 1

Assume that the population growth, as well as technological progress, are zero and consider that the economy is described by the production function $Y = K^{0.5}L^{0.5}$. Consider $s=0.2$ and $\delta=0.1$.

Appendix A

Using the Solow model framework, answer the following questions.

- Let k denote capital per worker; y output per worker; c consumption per worker; i investment per worker. What are the steady-state values of k, y, c and i?
- What are the values of k and y if the economy operates at the golden rule level of capital accumulation?
- Imagine that you want to drive this country to the golden rule levels of k and y. What is the saving rate that you have to impose? What would be the level of c?
- Assume that you impose the new saving rate. What would be the immediate and long run effects on c, k, and y? Draw the path of these variables.

Note: The lower case letters denote per-capita variables (e.g. $y = Y/L$, $k = K/L$.)

Exercise 2

Consider the Solow growth model without population growth or technological-knowledge change. The parameters of the model are given by $s = 0.2$ and $\delta = 0.05$. Let k, y, c and i denote, respectively, the capital, output, consumption and investment per capita.

- Rewrite the production function $Y = K^{1/3}L^{2/3}$ in per capita terms.
- Find the steady-state level of the capital stock, k^*.
- What is the golden rule level of k for this economy?
- Let us consider a benevolent social planner that wishes to obtain $k = k^{gr}$ in steady state. What is the associated savings rate s^{gr} that must be imposed by the social planner to support k^{gr}?
- Plot the following functions on a single figure: $y = f(k)$, k, $sf(k)$, and $s^{gr}f(k)$. Does the savings curve pivot up or down, relative to its initial position, when the planner's s^{gr} is implemented?

Exercise 3

Consider the production function $Y = K^{\alpha}(AL)^{1-\alpha}$ where K, L, and A stand for aggregate capital, labour and technological-knowledge, respectively. Labour and technological knowledge grow at constant exogenous rates n and g. The savings rate, s, and the depreciation rate δ are both constant.

- Derive the steady-state level of capital per effective labour k and output per effective labour y as a function of the various exogenous parameters.
- Derive the golden-rule level of capital per effective labour and output per effective labour as a function of the various exogenous parameters.
- Derive the savings rate required to attain the golden-rule level of capital per effective labour.

- Now consider two countries, A and B. Both have the same production function as given above and all exogenous parameters are the same for the countries except population growth which is higher in country A. Illustrate the steady states of both economies graphically. Based on the information that you have, can you determine whether the economies will have the same steady-state stock of capital and output per effective labour or will one attain a higher steady state than the other?
- Assume that there is a one-off migration of a large number of workers from country A to country B. Discuss the impact of this event on capital and output in per capita terms, and their growth rates, both in the short term and in the long term, in both countries. Illustrate the impact of this event in the diagrams that you drew.

Exercise 4

Consider the continuous time Solow growth model with a fixed factor, which is represented by the following aggregate production function $F(K, L, Z) = K^\alpha L^\beta Z^{1-\alpha-\beta}$, where Z is land. Assume that $\alpha + \beta < 1$, capital depreciates at rate δ, and there is an exogenous savings rate of s.

- Suppose there is no population growth rate. Find the steady-state capital–labour ratio and the steady-state output level. Show that the steady state is unique and stable.
- Now suppose that population grows at rate n. What happens to capital–labour ratio and output as $t \to \infty$? What happens to the return to land and to the wage rate as $t \to \infty$?
- Do you think the results obtained change if
  - saving rate, s, is allowed to be endogenous?
  - population growth rate could be endogenous in a way that it is function of per capita output?

Neoclassic growth model with labour-augmenting technological knowledge

In this project, consider that the production function is

$$Y = F(K, AL) = K^\alpha (AhH)^{1-\alpha} \Rightarrow y = k^\alpha A^{1-\alpha}, \quad k = \frac{K}{H}, \quad y = \frac{Y}{H},$$

which incorporates the technological-knowledge labour-augmenting or Harrod-neutral, being $\dot{A}/A = g \Leftrightarrow A = A_0 e^{gt}$ where g is the technological-knowledge growth rate (i.e. $\dot{y}/y = \alpha(\dot{k}/k) + (1-\alpha)g$).

The aggregate capital accumulation function is

$$\dot{K} = sY - \delta K \Leftrightarrow \frac{\dot{K}}{K} = s\frac{Y}{K} - \delta.$$

Show the following.

- $\bar{y} = \bar{k}^\alpha$ and $\dot{\bar{k}} = s\bar{y} - (\delta + g + n)\bar{k}$ in which $\bar{y} = Y/(AL) = y/A$ and $\bar{k} \equiv K/(AL) = k/A$.
- In steady state $\bar{k}^* = (s/(\delta + g + n))^{1/(1-\alpha)}$, $\bar{y}^* = (s(\delta + g + n))^{\alpha/(1-\alpha)}$ and $y^*(t) = A^*(t)(s/(\delta + g + n))^{\alpha/(1-\alpha)}$.

AK model à la Romer

In line with the Romer (1986) model, consider the production function:

$$Y = AK^{\alpha+\beta}H^{1-\alpha}.$$

Show that by assuming $\beta = 1 - \alpha$ and $H = 1$ results in $Y = AK$. Then, assume constant population, $n = 0$, and prove that the production function can be expressed in per capita terms as

$$y = A(kH)^\beta k^\alpha = Ak^{\alpha+\beta}H^\beta, \quad \text{where } k = \frac{K}{H}.$$

Show the following in this case.

- $\dot{k} = sAk^{\alpha+\beta}H^\beta - \delta k$ or, in growth rate terms, $\dot{k}/k = sAk^{\alpha+\beta-1}H^\beta - \delta$.
- If $\alpha + \beta = 1$ the economic growth rate is $\dot{k}/k = sAH^\beta - \delta$.
- If $\alpha + \beta < 1$ the behaviour of the economy is similar to the behaviour under the Solow model: the stock of capital at the steady state is

$$k^* = \left(\frac{sAH^\beta}{\delta}\right)^{\left(\frac{1}{1-\alpha-\beta}\right)};$$

i.e. k^* depends on H.

AK model à la Lucas

Suppose now that, in line with Lucas (1988), the production function is given by

$$Y = A\left(\frac{K}{H}\right)^\kappa K^\alpha H^{1-\alpha} \Rightarrow y = Ak^{\alpha+\kappa}.$$

Show the following.

- $\dot{k} = sAk^{\alpha+\kappa} - (\delta + n)k$ or, in growth rate terms, $\dot{k}/k = sAk^{\alpha+\kappa-1} - (\delta + n)$.
- The behaviour of the economy depends on the sum $\alpha + \kappa$, such the following hold.

- $\alpha + \kappa < 1$; i.e. there are externalities, $\kappa > 0$, but insignificant; thus, the exponent of k in $\dot{k}/k$ is negative. Depict a figure with the paths of $sAk^{\alpha+\kappa-1}$ and $\delta+n$; confirm that $sAk^{\alpha+\kappa-1}$ tends to infinity when k tends to zero 0, is decreasing and goes to 0 when k tends to infinity. Since $\delta + n$ is horizontal, the stock of capital in steady state is unique and given by

$$k^* = \left(\frac{sA}{\delta+n}\right)^{\left(\frac{1}{1-\alpha-\kappa}\right)}.$$

- $\alpha + \kappa = 1$; i.e. $\kappa = 1 - \alpha$ and thus $\alpha + \kappa = 1$; therefore, the exponent of k in $\dot{k}/k$ is 0, and the economic growth rate is given by $sA - (\delta+n)$, resulting in an AK model.
- $\alpha + \kappa > 1$; i.e. $\alpha + \kappa$ is greater that 1 since the externalities are stronger, and the exponent of k in $\dot{k}/k$ is 1. Hence, depict a figure and observe that $sAk^{\alpha+\kappa-1}$ is increasing and tends to infinity when k also tends to infinity.

Unemployment and economic growth

Bearing in mind Tabellini and Daveri (1997) and Romer (1986) it is possible to discuss the mechanism through which the unemployment affects the economic growth rate. Assume that the active population is P and H is the number or workers. Thus, $P - H$ represents the number of unemployed workers and $u = (P - H)/P$ is the unemployment rate. Consider the production function:

$$Y = AK^\alpha H^{1-\alpha}\left(\frac{K}{P}\right)^{1-\alpha} \Rightarrow y = Ak^\alpha\left(\frac{KH}{HP}\right)^{1-\alpha} = Ak(1-u)^{1-\alpha}.$$

Show the following.

- $\dot{k}/k = sA(1-u)^{1-\alpha} - (\delta+n)$; i.e. the unemployment rate affects the economic growth rate.

Public expenditures and optimal taxes

Taking into account Barro (1990), consider the production function

$$Y = AK^\alpha G^{1-\alpha}.$$

In order to get resources to support G the government introduces a tax rate, τ, such that the available income is $Y^d = (1-\tau)Y = (1-\tau)AK^\alpha G^{1-\alpha}$ and in per capita terms is $y^d = (1-\tau)Ak^\alpha g^{1-\alpha}$, with $g \equiv G/H$.

Answer the following questions.

- Verify that $\dot{k} = sy^d - (\delta + n)k = s(1-\tau)Ak^\alpha g^{1-\alpha} - (\delta + n)k$; i.e. $\dot{k}/k = s(1-\tau)Ak^{\alpha-1}g^{1-\alpha} - (\delta + n)$; the economic growth rate depends positively on public expenditures g and negatively on τ.
- Since g and τ are dependent, consider $G = \tau Y$ or, in per capita terms, $g = \tau y$, and show the following, with $y = Ak^\alpha g^{1-\alpha}$:
    - $g = \tau^{(1/\alpha)} A^{(1/\alpha)} k$.
    - $y = \overline{A}k$ with $\overline{A} = A^{(1/\alpha)} \tau^{((1-\alpha)/\alpha)}$.
    - $\dot{k}/k = s(1-\tau) A^{(1/\alpha)} \tau^{((1-\alpha)/\alpha)} - (\delta + n)$; i.e. the economic growth rate depends on the savings rate, the depreciation rate, the population growth rate, and the level of technological knowledge. Confirm numerically that the steady-state economic growth rate is positive.
    - An optimal τ_{opt} is given by

$$\frac{\partial(\dot{k}/k)}{\partial \tau} = 0 \Rightarrow \tau_{opt} = 1 - \alpha.$$

Endogenous growth with diminishing returns of capital

In line with Jones and Manuelli (1990), consider the following production function:

$$Y = AK + BK^\alpha H^{1-\alpha} \Rightarrow y = Ak + Bk^\alpha.$$

Show the following:

- This production function is not neoclassic.
- $\dot{k}/k = sA + sBk^{\alpha-1} - (\delta + n)$ and then illustrate that if $sA > \delta + n$ the steady-state economic growth rate is positive.
- The determining factor for the existence of endogenous growth is the failure of one of the Inada conditions (and not the fact that the technology does not show diminishing returns on capital).
- Do you think the results obtained change (show the results graphically) if
    - the saving rate s and/or the technological-knowledge progress A increases?
    - population growth rate n and/or the depreciation rate δ increases?

AK model of Solow–Pitchford

Bearing in mind the analysis of de La Grandville (2009), consider the production function:

$$Y = (aK^\alpha + bH^\alpha)^{1/\alpha}$$

in which $a, b > 0$, and assume that $0 < \alpha < 1$ in order to reach a constant elasticity of substitution higher than 1.

Show the following:

- The elasticity of substitution is

$$\chi = -\frac{\partial(K/H)/K/H}{\partial(R/w)/R/w} = \frac{1}{1-\alpha} > 1.$$

- The production function is not neoclassic.
- $\dot{k}/k = sA - \delta - n$.

Effects of public intervention on wage inequality

Consider the paper Afonso (2008) that analyses the direction of technological knowledge in a dynamic setting where the scale effects are removed, extending the analysis in Chapter 10. By shifting to the price-channel mechanism and by taking into consideration the government policy, the project aims to analyse how the skill-biased technological change and the consequent skill-biased wage inequality can be caused by government intervention. It is assumed that each final good is produced by one of two technologies: one uses high-skilled labour together with a continuum set of high-specific intermediate goods and the other brings together low-skilled labour and a continuum set of low-specific intermediate goods. As a result of the close relationship between the production of intermediate goods and R&D, the latter can be encouraged either by a direct subsidy or through a subsidy for intermediate goods production. In any of these cases, policies also have a bearing on the demand for labour. In addition, when affecting not only the level but also the direction of R&D (through the structure of public spending), policies also have an effect on the relative demand for the different types of labour, and, thus, on wage inequality. The transitional dynamics of the technological-knowledge bias is described by the differential equation

$$\frac{\dot{D}(t)}{D(t)} = \frac{\beta}{\zeta}\left(\frac{q-1}{q}\right)[A(1-\alpha)]^{\frac{1}{\alpha}}\exp(-\alpha)$$

$$\times \left\{ h\left(\frac{1-s_{x,H}}{1-s_{r,H}}\right)\left(\frac{1}{1-s_{x,H}}\right)^{\frac{1}{\alpha}\sigma}\left[1+\left(D(t)\frac{hH}{lL}\right)^{\frac{-1}{2}}\right]^{\alpha} \right.$$

$$\left. - l\left(\frac{1-s_{x,L}}{1-s_{r,L}}\right)\left(\frac{1}{1-s_{x,L}}\right)^{\frac{1}{\alpha}}\left[1+\left(D(t)\frac{hH}{lL}\right)^{\frac{1}{2}}\right]^{\alpha} \right\},$$

where $D = Q_H/Q_L$, Q_H and Q_L are aggregate quality indexes evaluating the technological knowledge in each range of intermediate goods, $\beta > 0$ is a parameter connected with the positive learning effect of accumulated public technological knowledge from past R&D, $\zeta > 0$ is a parameter related to the adverse effect caused by the increasing complexity of quality improvements in R&D, A is a positive variable representing the level of exogenous productivity, $q > 1$ is the quality upgrade, α is the labour share in production, $h > l > 1$ represents an absolute productivity advantage of high-skilled labour, H, over low-skilled labour, L, in production, $s_{x,H}$ ($s_{x,L}$) is a governmental *ad valorem* subsidy to the production of intermediate goods belonging to the range H (L), and $s_{r,H}$ ($s_{r,L}$) is a governmental *ad valorem* subsidy to R&D belonging to the range H (L). The equilibrium H (L)-specific probability of successful R&D can be alternatively encouraged by subsidies to R&D or to intermediate-goods production.

The path of the H-premium, $W \equiv w_H/w_L = [D(t)(hL/lH)]^{1/2}$, can be computed after the path of D.

For the baseline case, consider that $\beta = 1.6$, $\zeta = 4.0$, $A = 1.5$, $q = 3.33$, $\alpha = 0.7$, $h = 1.05 > l = 1.0$, $H = 0.68$, $L = 1.0$, and $s_{x,H} = s_{x,L} = s_{r,H} = s_{r,L} = 0$.

- Compare the baseline steady-state paths of, respectively, D and W, under no government intervention with those resulting from an exogenous increase at time $t=0$ of $s_{x,H}$ and/or $s_{r,H}$ and/or H. In particular, consider six different cases:

    - both $s_{x,H}$ and $s_{r,H}$ increase to 0.2;
    - $s_{r,H}$ increases to 0.2;
    - $s_{x,H}$ increases to 0.2;
    - both $s_{x,H}$ and $s_{r,H}$ increase to 0.2 and H increases to 1.0;
    - $s_{r,H}$ increases to 0.2 and H increases to 1.0;
    - $s_{x,H}$ increases to 0.2 and H increases to 1.0.

- Illustrate the following.

    - An increase in $s_{x,H}$ and/or $s_{r,H}$ (in relation to $s_{x,L}$ and/or $s_{r,L}$, respectively) accentuates D; indeed, greater $s_{x,H}$ increases the size of profits that accrue to the producers of H-type intermediate goods, and greater $s_{r,H}$ decreases the cost of H-specific R&D. In both cases the incentives to do H-specific R&D increase, thereby raising the growth rate of the H-specific technological knowledge.
    - Such bias increases the supply of H-type intermediate goods, thereby increasing the number of final goods produced with H-technology and lowering their relative price:

$$\frac{p_H(t)}{p_L(t)} = \left(\frac{\bar{n}(t)}{1-\bar{n}(t)}\right)^\alpha, \quad \text{where } \bar{n}(t) = \left[1+\left(\frac{Q_H(t)hH}{Q_L(t)lL}\right)^{1/2}\right]^{-1}$$

is the threshold final good. As the relative price drops continuously towards the stable new steady-state level, D is increasing, but at a falling rate until it reaches its new higher steady state.

– *Ceteris paribus* the exogenous increase of H immediately decreases the skill-premium and immediately increases the price of final goods produced by low-skilled labour and, thus, the demand for R&D directed towards improvements in low-specific quality-adjusted intermediate goods.

To better understand the model, the production function considered was

$$Y_n(t) = A\left\{\left[\int_0^J \left(q^{k(j,t)} x_n(k,j,t)\right)^{1-\alpha} dj\right][(1-n)lL_n]^\alpha \right.$$
$$\left. + \left[\int_J^1 \left(q^{k(j,t)} x_n(k,j,t)\right)^{1-\alpha} dj\right][nhH_n]^\alpha \right\},$$

where: (i) the integrals sum up the contributions of intermediate goods to production, and the quantity of each j, x, is quality-adjusted – the constant quality upgrade q is affected by the highest quality rung k at time t; (ii) n and $(1-n)$ are adjustment terms such that $n \in [0, 1]$ is an ordering index meaning that H is relatively more productive in final goods indexed by higher ns, and vice versa, which implies that the threshold final good exists and indicates that a shift from one technology to another is advantageous.

Migratory movements and directed technical change

Based on Leite *et al.* (2014), this project proposes a North–South model to show how the technological-knowledge gap is hard to reverse, namely when, due to higher returns, the majority of scientists are concentrated in the North. The implications of having either perfect- or no-labour mobility between countries are studied. In addition, the project explores the effects of complementarity or substitutability of goods on scientists' incentives, allowing countries to avoid a poverty trap. The calibrated model provides consistent dynamics with the data, considering four countries around the world: the US (reference country), Mexico, Cuba, Japan and China.

Standard values are assumed for the share of capital in production, $\alpha = 0.3$, for the depreciation rate, $\delta = 0.06$, and for the increasing technology factor $\gamma = 0.1$. To calibrate the elasticity of substitution between goods, ε, is initially assumed the value of 0.8 for a convergent behaviour and the value of 1.2 for a divergent behaviour. The probability of successful innovation $Q_i \in (0, 1)$, $i = d$ and $i = u$ for a developed and a developing country, respectively, is computed by comparing the actual technological-knowledge growth rate and the growth rate in the model: $Q_d = 0.147$, for the US; $Q_u = 0.096$, for Mexico; $Q_u = 0.304$, for Cuba; $Q_u = 0.214$, for Japan; $Q_u = 0.734$, for China. The normalised quantity of scientists, s, is 1; that is $s_d + s_u = 1$. Having defined these parameters and possessing the initial value for technological knowledge, the other necessary initial values can determined from the equations in the model.

The analysis is focused on generic variable technological-knowledge gap:

$$\frac{\Pi_{u,t}}{\Pi_{d,t}} = \frac{Q_u}{Q_d}\left(\frac{p_{u,t}}{p_{d,t}}\right)^{\frac{1}{1-\alpha}} \frac{L_{u,t}}{L_{d,t}} \frac{A_{u,t-1}}{A_{d,t-1}},$$

where: $\Pi_{i,t} = Q_i(1+\gamma)(1-\alpha)\alpha p_{i,t}^{1/(1-\alpha)} L_{i,t} A_{i,t-1}$; p is the price level, A is the level of technological knowledge and L is the labour demand. From these equation and according to the country specific scenario (complementarity or substitutability vs perfect- or no-labour mobility) a particular functional form for the technological-knowledge gap is considered (see Leite et al. 2014).

Implement the model and then show that the model mimics the observed pattern of technological-knowledge gap by considering for:

- Mexico – a perfect-labour mobility of population model with substitute goods;
- Japan – a perfect-labour mobility of population model with complementary goods;
- Cuba – a no-labour mobility population model with complementary goods;
- China – a perfect-labour mobility of population model with complementary goods.

Skill-structure, high-tech sector and economic growth dynamics model

By means of an endogenous growth model of directed technical change with vertical and horizontal R&D, this project studies a transitional-dynamics mechanism that is consistent with the changes in the share of the high- versus the low-tech sectors found in recent European data. Following closely Gil et al. (forthcoming), under the hypothesis of a positive shock in the proportion of high-skilled labour, the technological-knowledge bias channel leads to nonbalanced sectoral growth with a noticeable shift of resources across sectors. The calibration exercise suggests that the model is able to account for up to 50 to about 100 per cent of the increase in the share of the high-tech sector observed in the data from 1995 to 2007. However, the model predicts that the dynamics of the share of the high-tech sector has no significant impact on the dynamics of the economic growth rate.

Given the initial conditions $Q_m(0)$ and $N_m(0)$ and the transversality condition, the equilibrium paths can be obtained from the dynamical system:

$$\dot{N}_m(t) = x_m(Q_m(t), N_m(t)) \cdot N_m(t),$$

where

$$x_m(Q_m, N_m) \equiv \left(\frac{\zeta}{\phi}\right)^{1/\gamma} \cdot Q_m^{1/\gamma} \cdot N_m^{-(\sigma+\gamma+1)/\gamma},$$

$$\dot{Q}_m(t) = (\Xi \cdot I_m(t) + x_m(Q_m(t), N_m(t))) \cdot Q_m(t),$$

and

$$\dot{C}(t) = \frac{1}{\theta} \cdot (r(t) - \rho) \cdot C(t),$$

where, in the system above: $\dot{N}_m(t)$ denotes the contribution to the instantaneous flow of new m-specific intermediate goods in which $\sigma > 0$, $\gamma > 0$ and $\phi > 0$; $m \in \{L, H\}$; $L = \int_0^{\bar{n}} L(n)\, dn$ is the low-skilled labour; $H = \int_{\bar{n}}^1 H(n)\, dn$ is the high-skilled labour; $\bar{n}(t)$ is the endogenous threshold final good, which follows from equilibrium in the inputs markets, $\bar{n}(t) = [1 + (\mathcal{H}/\mathcal{L} \cdot [Q_H(t)/Q_L(t)])^{\frac{1}{2}}]^{-1}$, which can be related to the ratio of price indices of final goods, $P_L(t)$ and $P_H(t)$, produced with L- and H-technologies, $P_L(t) = P(n, t) \cdot (1-n)^\alpha = \exp(-\alpha) \cdot \bar{n}(t)^{-\alpha}$ and $P_H(t) = P(n, t) \cdot n^\alpha = \exp(-\alpha) \cdot (1 - \bar{n}(t))^{-\alpha}$; $\omega_L \in [0, N_L]$ ($\omega_H \in [0, N_H]$) are a continuum of labour-specific intermediate goods; $Q_m(t)$ is the aggregate quality index

$$Q_m(t) = \int_0^{N_m(t)} q_m(\omega_m, t)\, d\omega, \quad q_m(\omega_m, t) \equiv \lambda^{j_m(\omega_m, t)\left(\frac{1-\alpha}{\alpha}\right)},$$

which measures technological knowledge in each m-technology sector, in which $\lambda > 1$, and thus $Q \equiv Q_H/Q_L$ measures the technological-knowledge bias; $\Xi \equiv \lambda^{\frac{1-\alpha}{\alpha}} - 1$ denotes the quality shift; $I_m(t) > 0$ denotes the Poisson arrival rate of vertical innovations in which $\zeta > 0$, and thus a successful innovation will instantaneously increase the quality index in ω_m from $q_m(\omega_m, t) = q_m(j_m)$ to $q_m(j_m + 1) = \lambda^{(1-\alpha)/\alpha} q_m(j_m)$; C is the aggregate consumption; r is the real interest rate; $\rho > 0$ is the subjective discount rate; $\theta > 0$ is the inverse of the intertemporal elasticity of substitution. By considering the growth rate of the number of varieties, x_m, the consumption rate, $z_L \equiv C/Q_L$, and the technological-knowledge bias, $Q \equiv Q_H/Q_L$, an equivalent dynamical system in de-trended variables is reached:

$$\dot{x}_L = \left[\frac{\Xi}{\gamma} \cdot I_L - \left(\frac{\sigma + \gamma}{\gamma}\right) \cdot x_L\right] \cdot x_L,$$

$$\dot{z}_L = \left[\frac{1}{\theta} \cdot (r_{0L} - \rho) - \left(\frac{1}{\theta} + \Xi\right) \cdot I_L - x_L\right] \cdot z_L,$$

$$\dot{x}_H = \left[\frac{\Xi}{\gamma} \cdot I_L - \left(\frac{\sigma + \gamma}{\gamma}\right) \cdot x_H + \frac{\Xi}{\gamma} \cdot \frac{\pi_0}{\zeta} \cdot \left(\mathcal{H} \cdot P_H^{1/\alpha} - \mathcal{L} \cdot P_L^{1/\alpha}\right)\right] \cdot x_H,$$

202 Appendix A

$$\dot{Q} = \left[\Xi \cdot \frac{\pi_0}{\zeta} \cdot (\mathcal{H} \cdot P_H^{1/\alpha} - \mathcal{L} \cdot P_L^{1/\alpha}) + x_H - x_L \right] \cdot Q,$$

where $I_L \equiv I_L(Q, x_L, x_H, z_L) = I_L(Q_L, Q_H, N_L, N_H, C)$, $I_H \equiv I_H(Q, x_L, x_H, z_L) = I_H(Q_L, Q_H, N_L, N_H, C)$, $P_L \equiv P_L(Q) = P_L(Q_L, Q_H)$, $P_H \equiv P_H(Q) = P_L(Q_L, Q_H)$, $\mathcal{L} \equiv lL$, $\mathcal{H} \equiv hH$, $\pi_0 \equiv \pi_{0L}/\mathcal{L} = \pi_{0H}/\mathcal{H}$ (see below the expressions for π_{0L} and π_{0H}). These equations, together with the transversality condition and the initial conditions $x_L(0)$, $x_H(0)$ and $Q(0)$, describe the transitional dynamics and the balanced growth path (BGP), by jointly determining $x_L(t)$, $z_L(t)$, $x_H(t)$ and $Q(t)$. Then, the level variables $N_m(t)$, $C(t)$ and $Q_L(t)$ (respectively, $Q_H(t)$), for a given $Q_H(t)$ ($Q_L(t)$) can be obtained.

As the functions in the dynamical system are homogeneous, a BGP exists only if: (i) $g_C = g_{Q_L} = g_{Q_H} = g$; (ii) $g_{N_L} = g_{N_H}$; (iii) $g_{I_L} = g_{I_H} = g_{P_L} = g_{P_H} = 0$; and (iv) $g_{Q_L}/g_{N_L} = g_{Q_H}/g_{N_H} = (\sigma + \gamma + 1)$, $g_{N_m} \neq 0$. Observe from $\dot{N}_m(t)$ that $x_m = g_{N_m}$ is always positive if $N_m > 0$. In order to characterise the interior steady state $(\tilde{x}_L, \tilde{z}_L, \tilde{x}_H, \tilde{Q})$ in terms of local stability, linearise the dynamical system in a neighbourhood of $(\tilde{x}_L, \tilde{z}_L, \tilde{x}_H, \tilde{Q})$ and obtain the following fourth-order system:

$$\begin{pmatrix} \dot{x}_L \\ \dot{z}_L \\ \dot{x}_H \\ \dot{Q} \end{pmatrix} = \begin{pmatrix} a_{11}\tilde{x}_L & a_{12}\tilde{x}_L & a_{13}\tilde{x}_L & \frac{\Xi}{\gamma}\left(\frac{\partial \tilde{I}_L}{\partial Q}\right)\tilde{x}_L \\ a_{21}\tilde{z}_L & a_{22}\tilde{z}_L & a_{23}\tilde{z}_L & a_{24}\tilde{z}_L \\ a_{31}\tilde{x}_H & a_{32}\tilde{x}_H & a_{33}\tilde{x}_H & a_{34}\tilde{x}_H \\ -\tilde{Q} & 0 & \tilde{Q} & -\Xi S_1 \tilde{Q} \end{pmatrix} \begin{pmatrix} x_L - \tilde{x}_L \\ z_L - \tilde{z}_L \\ x_H - \tilde{x}_H \\ Q - \tilde{Q} \end{pmatrix}.$$

The Jacobian matrix $J(\tilde{x}_L, \tilde{x}_H, \tilde{z}_L, \tilde{Q})$ above is evaluated at the steady state, where:

$$a_{11} \equiv -\frac{1}{\gamma}\left(\frac{\Xi}{\Xi+1}\right)S_0 - \frac{\sigma+\gamma}{\gamma};$$

$$a_{12} \equiv -\frac{1}{\zeta}\frac{1}{\gamma}\left(\frac{\Xi}{\Xi+1}\right)S_0;$$

$$a_{13} \equiv -\frac{1}{\gamma}\left(\frac{\Xi}{\Xi+1}\right)S_0\frac{\mathcal{H}}{\mathcal{L}};$$

$$a_{21} \equiv \left(\frac{1}{\theta}+\Xi\right)\frac{1}{\Xi+1}S_0 - 1;$$

$$a_{22} \equiv \left(\frac{1}{\theta}+\Xi\right)\frac{1}{\Xi+1}\frac{1}{\zeta}S_0;$$

$$a_{23} \equiv \left(\frac{1}{\theta}+\Xi\right)\frac{1}{\Xi+1}\frac{\mathcal{H}}{\mathcal{L}}S_0;$$

$$a_{24} \equiv \frac{\pi_0}{\theta \zeta} \frac{1}{2e} \mathcal{L} - \left(\frac{1}{\theta} + \Xi\right) \left(\frac{\partial \tilde{I}_L}{\partial Q}\right);$$

$$a_{31} \equiv a_{11} + \frac{\sigma + \gamma}{\gamma};$$

$$a_{32} = a_{12};$$

$$a_{33} \equiv a_{13} - \frac{\sigma + \gamma}{\gamma};$$

$$a_{34} \equiv a_{14} - \frac{\Xi}{\gamma} \mathcal{S}_1;$$

with:

$$\mathcal{S}_0 \equiv 1 / \left(1 + \frac{\mathcal{H}}{\mathcal{L}}\right);$$

$$\mathcal{S}_1 \equiv \frac{\pi_0}{\zeta} \frac{1}{2e} \mathcal{L} \frac{1}{\tilde{Q} \mathcal{S}_0};$$

$$\left(\frac{\partial \tilde{I}_L}{\partial Q}\right) = \left[\mathcal{S}_1 \tilde{Q} - \left(\frac{1}{\Xi + 1} + \frac{\sigma + \gamma}{\Xi}\right) \tilde{x}_H\right] \mathcal{S}_0 + \frac{1}{\zeta} \frac{1}{e} \mathcal{H} \frac{1}{\Xi + 1} x \frac{1}{\tilde{Q}}.$$

Since there are three predetermined variables, x_L, x_H and Q, and one jump variable, z_L, saddle-path stability in the neighbourhood of the interior equilibrium $(\tilde{x}_L, \tilde{x}_H, \tilde{z}_L, \tilde{Q})$ requires that $J(\tilde{x}_L, \tilde{x}_H, \tilde{z}_L, \tilde{Q})$ has three eigenvalues with a negative real part and one with a positive real part, hence implying $\det(J(\tilde{x}_L, \tilde{x}_H, \tilde{z}_L, \tilde{Q})) < 0$. However, as the latter condition is compatible with both one and three eigenvalues with negative real part, further conditions must be satisfied so that saddle-path stability applies. These conditions are particularly hard, if even possible, to check analytically, considering that $J(\tilde{x}_L, \tilde{x}_H, \tilde{z}_L, \tilde{Q})$ is a 4 × 4 matrix with just one zero element.

In this context, perform a numerical exercise in order to:

- check the existence of three eigenvalues with negative real part and one with a positive real part for reasonable values of the parameters, and conclude that the interior steady state is locally saddle-path stable for the typical baseline parameter values, but also over a wide range of parameter sets.

Then, consider that the economy is in the (pre-shock) steady state and that an unanticipated one-off shock in the proportion of high-skilled labour that shifts the steady state arises. The dynamical system describes the transitional dynamics after the shock, towards the new (post-shock) steady state of (x_L, x_H, Q, z_L). As a result, assess the industry dynamics, measured by the time-path of the relative number of firms,

$$N(t) = \left(\frac{x_H(t)}{x_L(t)}\right)^{-(\frac{\gamma}{\sigma+\gamma+1})} Q(t)^{\frac{1}{\sigma+\gamma+1}},$$

relative production, $X(t) = (\mathcal{H}/\mathcal{L})^{\frac{1}{2}} Q(t)^{\frac{1}{2}}$, the sectoral growth rates, $g_{Q_H}(t) = I_L(t) \cdot \Xi + x_L(t)$, $g_{Q_L}(t) = I_H(t) \cdot \Xi + x_H(t)$, and the skill premium, $W(t) = (h/l)(\mathcal{H}/\mathcal{L})^{-\frac{1}{2}} Q(t)^{\frac{1}{2}}$. At the aggregate level, the dynamics is given by the time-path of the economic growth rate, $g(t) = [\mathcal{L}^{\frac{1}{2}} \cdot g_{Q_L}(t) + (Q(t) \cdot \mathcal{H})^{\frac{1}{2}} \cdot g_{Q_H}(t)]/[\mathcal{L}^{\frac{1}{2}} + (Q(t) \cdot \mathcal{H})^{\frac{1}{2}}]$, and the real interest rate, $r(t) = \pi_0 \cdot \mathcal{L} \cdot P_L(t)^{\frac{1}{\alpha}}/\zeta - I_L(t) = \pi_0 \cdot \mathcal{H} \cdot P_H(t)^{\frac{1}{\alpha}}/\zeta - I_H(t)$. In the computational exercise consider that relatively to the baseline case, a rise in H/L occurs by considering a jump in high-skilled labour, H, from 0.1 to 0.19, while the low-skilled labour, L, is normalised to unity. As the economy evolves towards the new steady state, there is a shift of economic activity between sectors. For the baseline values of the parameters, show the following.

- Relative production, X, and the relative number of firms, N, increase a total of, respectively, 13.0 and 12.4 percentage points over the long run (i.e. variation between the initial and the final steady states), while the economic growth rate, g, and the real interest rate, r, increase a total of, respectively, 0.34 and 0.51 percentage points.
- The speed of convergence towards the new steady state is faster at the sectoral than at the aggregate level. In the first 50 years, the variable with the largest speed is relative production, and from then on it is the relative number of firms.
- There is a rising technological-knowledge bias and thus an increasing skill premium over transition.

For the structural parameters, consider the baseline values $\rho = 0.02$; $\theta = 1.5$; $A = 1$; $\phi = 1$; $\alpha = 0.6$; $\lambda = 2.5$; $\sigma = 1.2$; $\gamma = 1.2$; $l = 1.0$; $h = 1.3$.

Multiple equilibria in economic growth

Recent literature on economic growth points towards the possibility of the existence of multiple equilibria, under certain conditions. Consider a growth model to determine the conditions for the existence of long-run equilibria and to illustrate the possibility of dual equilibria: 'growth miracles' and 'poverty traps'. Numerically, the model reveals that the emergence of multiple equilibria is rare, requiring tight conditions on the parameter values (see Gaspar et al. 2014).

The dynamics is given by

$$\frac{\dot{X}}{X} = \frac{1}{\theta}[\delta\sigma\tau(1-\theta)Z^\alpha + \alpha(1-\tau)Z^{\alpha-1} - \rho] - (1-\tau)Z^{\alpha-1} + X$$

$$\frac{\dot{Z}}{Z} = (1-\tau)Z^{\alpha-1} - X - \delta\tau Z^\alpha,$$

with $X \equiv C/K$, $Z \equiv K/H$, where $H(t)$ is the level of public health infrastructure, $K(t)$ is the level of physical capital, $C(t)$ is the consumption.

The parameters stands for θ, the inverse of the intertemporal elasticity of substitution, $\delta > 0$, the technological efficiency parameter of public health creation, σ, the weight of public health in the utility function, τ, the income tax rate, α, the share of physical capital in production and ρ, the discount rate.

The model can be unfolded as

$$\frac{\dot{K}}{K} = (1-\tau)\left(\frac{K}{H}\right)^{\alpha-1} - \frac{C}{K},$$

$$\frac{\dot{H}}{H} = \delta\tau\left(\frac{K}{H}\right)^\alpha,$$

$$\frac{\dot{C}}{C} = \frac{1}{\theta}\left[\delta\sigma\tau(1-\theta)\left(\frac{K}{H}\right)^\alpha + \alpha(1-\tau)\left(\frac{K}{H}\right)^{\alpha-1} - \rho\right].$$

It is derived from a dynamic optimisation problem, where a representative agent chooses the optimal path for consumption:

$$\max_C \int_0^\infty \frac{(CH^\sigma)^{1-\theta} - 1}{1-\theta} e^{-\rho t} dt, \quad \sigma \geq 0, \theta > 0 \wedge \theta \neq 1, \rho > 0$$

s.t. $\dot{K} = (1-\tau)K^\alpha H^{1-\alpha} - C, \quad \tau, \alpha \in (0,1)$

$K(0) = K_0 > 0,$

and from the production of an homogeneous final good (productive side): $Y(t) = K(t)^\alpha [H(t)L(t)]^{1-\alpha}$, where $L(t)$ is total labour force.

Show the following:

- $Z^* = (g/(\delta\tau))^{\frac{1}{\alpha}}.$
- $\Gamma(g) \equiv \alpha(1-\tau)(g/(\delta\tau))^{\frac{\alpha-1}{\alpha}} = (\theta - \sigma(1-\theta))g + \rho \equiv \Psi(g).$
- $X^* \equiv (1-\tau)(g/(\delta\tau))^{\frac{\alpha-1}{\alpha}} - g \geq 0.$
- Balanced growth path is only relevant for $\alpha(1-\tau)(g/(\delta\tau))^{(\alpha-1)/\alpha} - g \geq 0.$

Depict the graphics for Γ, Ψ and $\alpha(1-\tau)(g/(\delta\tau))^{(\alpha-1)/\alpha} - g$ for:

- $\alpha = 0.35$, $\delta = 0.18$, $\sigma = 1.5$, $\tau = 0.04$, $\theta = 0.35$, and $\rho = 0.05$ (dual equilibrium but one without economic relevance – the low-growth equilibrium);
- $\alpha = 0.35$, $\delta = 0.18$, $\sigma = 8$, $\tau = 0.04$, $\theta = 0.35$ and $\rho = 0.17$ (dual long-run equilibria);
- $\alpha = 0.35$, $\delta = 0.18$, $\sigma = 1.5$, $\tau = 0.04$, $\theta = 1.5$, $\rho = 0.02$ (one equilibrium);
- $\alpha = 0.35$, $\delta = 0.18$, $\sigma = 3.9$, $\tau = 0.05$, $\theta = 0.8$ and $\rho = 0.01$ (no relevant long-run equilibrium).

Appendix B
Solutions

Supply and demand

Chapter 1

1. (a) new exogenous demand, Qd_bar: 1250
    new computed endogenous variables:
        (equilibrium point)
        quantity, Q: 583.33
        price, P: 66.67
        Consumer surplus, Cs: 17013.89
        Producer surplus, Ps: 27777.78
   (b) new exogenous supply, Qs_bar: 500
    new computed endogenous variables:
        (equilibrium point)
        quantity, Q: 666.67
        price, P: 33.33
        Consumer surplus, Cs: 22222.22
        Producer surplus, Ps: 19444.44
   (c) new exogenous demand, Qd_bar: 1250
    new exogenous supply, Qs_bar: 500
    new computed endogenous variables:
        (equilibrium point)
        quantity, Q: 750.00
        price, P: 50.00
        Consumer surplus, Cs: 28125.00
        Producer surplus, Ps: 31250.00
2. (a) computed quantities for P minimum = 60
        quantity, Qd: 400
        quantity, Qs: 550
        excess of supply: 150
   (b) Nothing happens.
3. (a) new exogenous demand, Qd_barH: 1250
    new computed endogenous variables (autarky):

208   *Appendix B*

```
        quantity (Home), QH:              583.33
        price (Home), PH:                  66.67
        quantity (Foreign), QF:          1000.00
        price (Foreign), PF:               20.00
        new computed endogenous variables
            (free international trade):
        quantity (World), QW:             525.00
        price (World), PW:                 31.67
        Home eq. demand at PW, QdHW:      933.33
        Home eq. supply at PW, QsHW:      408.33
        Foreign eq. demand at PW, QdFW:   766.67
        Foreign eq. supply at PW, QsFW:  1291.67
(b) new exogenous supply, Qs_barH: 500
        new computed endogenous variables (autarky):
        quantity (Home), QH:              666.67
        price (Home), PH:                  33.33
        quantity (Foreign), QF:          1000.00
        price (Foreign), PF:               20.00
        new computed endogenous variables
            (free international trade):
        quantity (World), QW:             150.00
        price (World), PW:                 23.33
        Home eq. demand at PW, QdHW:      766.67
        Home eq. supply at PW, QsHW:      616.67
        Foreign eq. demand at PW, QdFW:   933.33
        Foreign eq. supply at PW, QsFW:  1083.33
(c) new exogenous demand, Qd_barH: 1250
        new exogenous supply, Qs_barH: 500
        new computed endogenous variables (autarky):
        quantity (Home), QH:              750.00
        price (Home), PH:                  50.00
        quantity (Foreign), QF:          1000.00
        price (Foreign), PF:               20.00
        new computed endogenous variables
            (free international trade):
        quantity (World), QW:             337.50
        price (World), PW:                 27.50
        Home eq. demand at PW, QdHW:      975.00
        Home eq. supply at PW, QsHW:      637.50
        Foreign eq. demand at PW, QdFW:   850.00
        Foreign eq. supply at PW, QsFW:  1187.50
4. H limits imports to 200 units
    computed endogenous variables (tariff):
        Home price, PHt:                   36.67
        Foreign price, PFt:                24.44
```

```
              tariff:                                  12.22
              Home quantity demanded, QdHt:           633.33
              Home quantity supplied, QsHt:           433.33
              Foreign quantity demanded, QdFt:        911.11
              Foreign quantity demanded, QsFt:       1111.11
         computed welfare variation:
              Home, WH_var:                           -19.10
              Foreign, WF_var:                       -821.18
```
Comment: as suggested by the literature, high values for the tariff in H lead to negative net welfare; note that for a tariff equal to 7.78 (imports limited to 250) the net welfare at H is positive (230.90), suggesting that, indeed, there is a (small) optimal tariff.

5. ```
   F applies a subsidy to exports to trade of
   500 units computed endogenous variables
   (subsidy):
        Home price, PHs:                             16.67
        Foreign price, PFs:                          31.11
        subsidy:                                     14.44
        Home quantity demanded, QdHs:               833.33
        Home quantity supplied, QsHs:               333.33
        Foreign quantity demanded, QdFs:            777.78
        Foreign quantity demanded, QsFs:           1277.78
   computed welfare variation:
        Home, WH_var:                              1512.15
        Foreign, WF_var:                          -5710.07
   ```
   Comment: as expected, the higher the subsidy the higher the loss in the welfare of the exporting country.

IS–LM in a closed economy

Chapter 2

1.

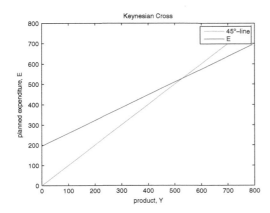
   ```

2. Budget balance is given by $T - G$.
   In this simple case, taxes are autonomous (lump-sum) and thus to cover additional public spending we need the same amount of taxes.
   Just do: G_new=G+10; g=@(x) x-G_new-(T-G); T_new=fzero(g,0); and solve the model again (for function fzero see nonlinear equations).

   ```
   Taxes required, T: 120.00 to cover the new G
   computed endogenous variables:
       product, Y:              533.90
       consumption, C:          315.76
       investment, I:             8.14
       interest rate (%), R:      4.46
   ```

3. In this case, the budget equation is given by $B = T - G - TR$.
   Since taxes are autonomous, to cover transfers to consumers the same amount of taxes is required. Note that now $C = C\_bar + c * (Y - T + TR)$ and thus this policy has no effects on neither Y nor R. Just do: TR=10; g=@(x) x-(G+TR)-(T-G); T_new=fzero(g,0); and compute the new equilibrium. (For fsolve see nonlinear equations.)

   ```
   Taxes required, T: 120.00 to cover transfers to
   consumers computed endogenous variables:
       product, Y:              528.64
       consumption, C:          318.74
       investment, I:             9.90
       interest rate (%), R:      4.34
   ```

4. (a) Two possible answers can be presented.
   (i) If consumers get public debt with resources out of the model, then the solution can be obtained by just increasing G by 10. In this case output increases.
   (ii) If consumers get public debt by decreasing autonomous consumption then the solution can be obtained by increasing G by 10 and decreasing C_bar by 10. In this case C and G are affected (the composition of the output), but Y remains unchanged. Do C_bar=C_bar-10; G=G+10; and solve the model again.

   (i) See Chapter 2, example 2, Figure 2.3.

   ```
   (ii) Shocks, C_bar and G:   45.00 and 210.00
        computed endogenous variables:
            product, Y:              528.64
            consumption, C:          308.74
            investment, I:             9.90
            interest rate (%), R:      4.34
   ```

(b) (i) As depicted in Figure 2.3 from Chapter 2, example 2, the IS curve moves to the right.
  (ii) The equilibrium remains constant (curves remain unchanged).
(c) (i) Yes, *ceteris paribus*, the higher the G the higher the Y, due to both direct and multiplier effects.
  (ii) The output is not affected, only its components.

5. New value for M: 210.00
   computed endogenous variables:
   ```
   product, Y:            536.54
   consumption, C:        323.72
   investment, I:          12.82
   interest rate (%), R:    4.15
   ```
   Mechanism: the increase in M supply requires an increase in the output Y and a decrease in R to achieve the new money market equilibrium; note that the increase in Y induces effects on consumption and so on; in turn, a decrease in R increases the investment I, and thus Y, and so on.

IS–LM in an open economy

Chapter 3

1. G_bar from 150 to 160
   computed endogenous variables in home / foreign countries
   ```
   product home/foreign             :   396.92   396.92
   consumption home/foreign         :   210.56   210.56
   investment home/foreign          :    31.36    31.36
   net exports home/foreign         :    -5.00     5.00
   interest rate home/foreign (%):       1.04     1.04
   exchange rate                    :     0.50
   ```
   As expected an increase in $\overline{G}$ implies a direct increase in Y along with an induced increase; the shift of the IS curve also generates an increase in R. Since countries are tightly connected, these effects are spread to the foreign country.

2. M_bar from 210 to 220
   G_bar from 150 to 160
   computed endogenous variables in home / foreign countries
   ```
   product home/foreign             :   409.20   392.54
   consumption home/foreign         :   218.30   207.80
   investment home/foreign          :    32.82    32.82
   net exports home/foreign         :    -1.92     1.92
   interest rate home/foreign (%):       0.95     0.95
   exchange rate                    :     0.97
   ```

212 *Appendix B*

Now the shift in the LM curve at home induces an increase at home in Y and thus in C higher than in the foreign country. Anyway, the interest rate decreases but remains equal in both countries.

3. T_bar from 150 to 140
   computed endogenous variables in home / foreign countries

product home/foreign :	394.29	394.29
consumption home/foreign :	215.20	208.90
investment home/foreign :	32.24	32.24
net exports home/foreign :	-3.15	3.15
interest rate home/foreign (%) :	0.98	0.98
exchange rate :	0.69	

   This fiscal policy, when compared with a similar increase in $\overline{G}$, has smaller impact on Y (see exercise 1.), since it acts via available income.

4. P_bar from 1 to 1.05
   Pf_bar from 1 to 1.01
   computed endogenous variables in home / foreign countries

product home/foreign :	378.44	391.64
consumption home/foreign :	198.92	207.23
investment home/foreign :	31.96	31.96
net exports home/foreign :	-2.44	2.44
interest rate home/foreign (%) :	1.00	1.00
exchange rate :	0.62	
exchange rate evaluated at PPP:	0.60	

5.  ```
    function [x,k] = gauss_seidel(A,d,x,maxit,tol)
    % Gauss-Seidel iteration to solve a linear system Ax=d
    % based on: Templates for the Solution of Linear Systems,
    % R. Barrett, M. Berry, T. F. Chan, J. Demmel, J. Donato,
    % J. Dongarra, V. Eijkhout, R. Pozo, C. Romine and
    % H. Van der Vorst. % SIAM, 1994
    %   input:
    %       A, coefficient matrix
    %       d, right-hand side
    %       x, initial vector
    %       maxit, maximum number of iterations allowed
    %       tol, tolerance to control the accuracy of the solution
    %   output:
    %       x, approximate solution (if convergent)
    %       k, number of required iterations
    if (norm(d)==0), disp('rhs should not be the zero vector');
        return, end
    M = diag(diag(A))+tril(A,-1); N = -triu(A,1);
    k = 0; r = d-A*x;
    while (k<maxit && norm(r)>tol*norm(d))
        x = M\(N*x+d); r = d-A*x; k = k+1;
    end
    ```
    ```

Solutions   213

```
function [x,k] = sor(A,d,x,w,maxit,tol)
% SOR iteration to solve a linear system A*x=b
% based on: Templates for the Solution of Linear Systems,
% R. Barrett, M. Berry, T. F. Chan, J. Demmel, J. Donato,
% J. Dongarra, V. Eijkhout, R. Pozo, C. Romine and
% H. Van der Vorst. % SIAM, 1994
%   input:
%     A, coefficient matrix
%     d, right-hand side
%     x, initial vector
%     maxit, maximum number of iterations allowed
%     tol, tolerance to control the accuracy of the solution
%   output:
%     x, approximate solution (if convergent)
%     k, number of required iterations
if (norm(d)==0), disp('rhs should not be the zero vector');
   return, end
if (w>=2 || w<=0), disp('w must be inside interval (0,2)');
   return, end
e = w*d; D = diag(diag(A));
M = w*tril(A,-1)+D; N = (1.0-w)*D-w*triu(A,1);
k = 0; r = d-A*x;
while (k<maxit && norm(r)>tol*norm(d))
   x = M\(N*x+e); r = d-A*x; k = k+1;
end
```

6. (a) Using A and d from the baseline model, perform the following.

   ```
   x0 = ones(size(A),1); maxit = 100; tol = 1e-10;
   x = jacobi(A,d,x0,maxit,tol);
   x = gauss_seidel(A,d,x0,maxit,tol);
   x = sor(A,d,x0,1.5,maxit,tol);
   ```

   The answer for all three solution algorithms is 'Matrix is singular to working precision'; these stationary iterative methods only assure convergence for diagonal dominant matrices, which is not the case here.

   (b) Using A and d from the baseline model, perform the following.

   ```
   x = gmres(A,d,[],1e-3,11); x(1)
   x = gmres(A,d,[],1e-12,11); x(1)
   x = bicgstab(A,d,1e-3,11); x(1)
   x = bicgstab(A,d,1e-10,11); x(1)
   ```

   For the first case, GMRES converged at iteration 10 to a solution with relative residual of 1.3e-05, producing $Y = 379.1556$. For the smaller tolerance, the solution is $Y = 389.8104$, and a more precise approximation to the solution is achieved.

   On the other hand, for this problem, BiCGstab, irrespectively from the required precision, was not able to produce a good approximation, computing $Y = 352.2330$ for both tolerances.

214 *Appendix B*

(c) Using *A* and *d* from the baseline model, perform

```
x1 = A\d;
x2 = gmres(A,d,[],1e-10,11);
x3 = bicgstab(A,d,1e-10,11);
fprintf('norm of the error between GE and gmres
        = %g\n',...norm(x1-x2));
fprintf('norm of the error between GE and
        bicgstab = %g\n',...norm(x1-x3));

norm of the error between GE and gmres
   = 1.92233e-10
norm of the error between GE and bicgstab
   = 74.4428
```

The Gaussian elimination, for well-conditioned matrices, provides an approximate solution within the machine precision (10^{-16}). For a required precision of 10^{-10}, GMRES fulfilled the requisites, whereas BiCGstab did not.

AD–AS

Chapter 4

1. For a fixed P=2 and G_bar=200, product is
   Y=1064.02
   For a fixed P=2 and G_bar=260, product is now
   Y=1137.20

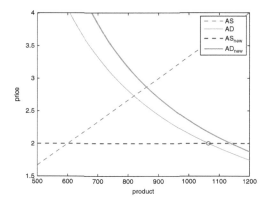

Now the aggregate supply is given by $P = 2$ (Keynesian case). The money supply in real terms is higher, affecting positively the output. As expected, due to fiscal policy, the increase in output is higher when $\overline{G}$ is also higher.

2. For a fixed Y=700 and G_bar=200, price is P=3.32
   For a fixed Y=700 and G_bar=260, price is now P=3.83

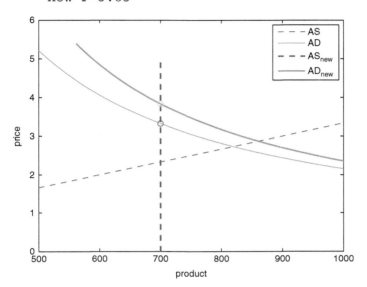

In this case the output level is defined by the AS curve (Classic case). As the (natural) output decreases, prices increase. The increase in P is higher when, due to fiscal policy, $\overline{G}$ also increases.

3. A_bar from 1 to 1.05

product, Y:	819.25	856.11
price, P:	2.73	2.59
interest rate, R (%):	2.27	0.99
consumption, C:	553.24	570.93
investment, I:	66.01	85.18
demand for money, L:	366.19	386.34
real wage, W_R:	18.31	19.32

   Due to the increase in Y and the decrease of P and R, the results are as expected: C, I, L and W_R increase.

4. (a) K_bar from 30000 to 31500

product, Y:	819.25	837.45
price, P:	2.73	2.66
interest rate, R (%):	2.27	1.63
consumption, C:	553.24	561.98
investment, I:	66.01	75.48
demand for money, L:	366.19	376.14
real wage, W_R:	18.31	18.81

216 Appendix B

Effects from increasing $\overline{K}$ are qualitatively similar to those resulting from increasing $\overline{A}$. Quantitatively, an increase of 5 per cent in $\overline{A}$ has greater effects than in $\overline{K}$ since $0 < \alpha < 1$.

(b) C_bar from 160 to 168
```
product, Y:                    819.25      824.63
price, P:                        2.73        2.75
interest rate, R (%):            2.27        2.61
consumption, C:                553.24      563.82
investment, I:                  66.01       60.81
demand for money, L:           366.19      363.80
real wage, W_R:                 18.31       18.19
```
Now the positive shock is on the AD curve: Y, P and R increase. In turn, as R increases, I is negatively affected as well as L; moreover, W_R decreases due to the increase in P.

5. (a)
```
product, Y:                   1875.00
price, P:                        1.00
interest rate, R (%):           10.00
```

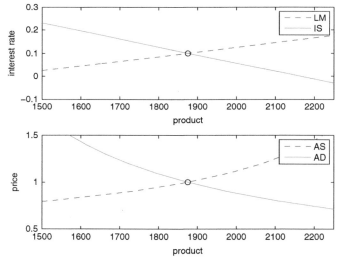

(b) In order to comply with the request, the implemented policy should be an increase in money supply. With this policy, R decreases, improving the investment, and Y increases. This will be illustrated in the following answer.

(c) M_bar from 500 to 600
```
product, Y:                   1875.00     1970.55
price, P:                        1.00        1.09
interest rate, R (%):           10.00        6.69
```

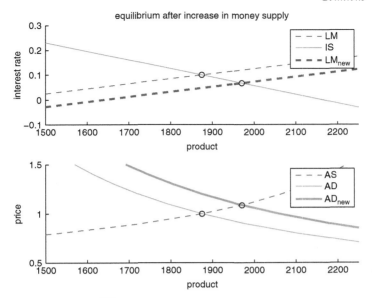

An increase in $\overline{M}$ expands the LM curve to the right, lowering R, which in turn expands the AD curve to the right, increasing P.

(d) Keynesian case: horizontal AS
```
M_bar from 500 to 600
   product, Y:           1875.00      2057.93
   interest rate, R (%):   10.00         3.66
```

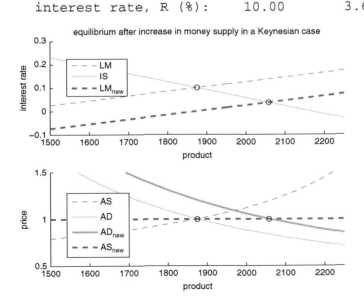

In a Keynesian case, price is fixed and, consequently, when the money supply increases the impact on the LM curve is stronger. As a result, *R* lowers more and *Y* increases more.

(e) ```
Classic case: vertical AS
M_bar from 500 to 600
    price, P: 1.00   1.20
    interest rate, R (%):   10.00   10.00
```

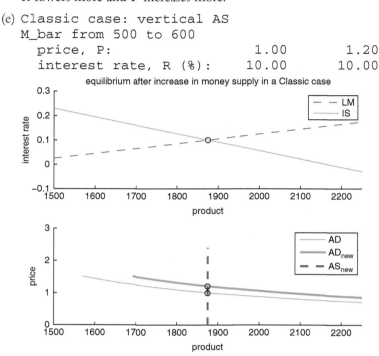

The statement is true. Now when $\overline{M}$ increases, *P* also increases (and in the same proportion). Thus the LM curve remains stable in the long run and no effects arise either in *Y* or in *R*.

## Portfolio

Chapter 5

1. (a) ```matlab
function mcarlo_plot(x_hist)
% print and graph optimal weights from Monte Carlo
line_type = {'b-','r—','g-.','m:'};
hold on;
if size(x_hist,1)<5
  for i = 1:size(x_hist,1)
    plot((1:size(x_hist,2))',x_hist(i,:),line_type{i});
  end
else
  plot((1:size(x_hist,2))',x_hist);
end
hold off;
ylabel('share of each asset');
```

```
xlabel('number of Monte-Carlo runs')
end
```

(b) One possible output is

```
best portfolio:
Asset 1    0.5248
Asset 2    0.2938
Asset 3    0.1814
expected return: 0.138451
risk             : 0.0552405
```

which is not correct (compare with the solution provided in the chapter).

(c) Change to $x = x + \text{const} * (-1 + 2 * \text{rand}(n, 1))$; $a + (b - a) * \text{rand}$ generates numbers in the interval $[a, b]$. With this change, the code is able to approximate the correct portfolio.

2.
```
best portfolio with the same return as Asset 2:
Asset 1    0.0000
Asset 2    1.0000
Asset 3    0.0000
expected return: 0.2
risk             : 0.2

best portfolio with the same return as Asset 3:
Asset 1    0.4037
Asset 2    0.4037
Asset 3    0.1927
expected return: 0.15
risk             : 0.0723777
```

The optimal portfolio with expected return equal to Asset 2 is composed of only Asset 2. Note that the return of the portfolio computed is 0.2 (equal to Asset 2) and the standard deviation is 0.2 (also the same as Asset 2, whose variance is 0.04). With respect to the second portfolio, the shares are distributed among all three assets; the expected return of the portfolio is the same as Asset 3 but with less risk (0.0724 instead of 0.1517).

3. (a)
```
Asset 1    0.8187
Asset 2    0.2387
Asset 3   -0.0574
expected return: 0.121001
risk             : 0.0384268
```
(b)
```
Asset 1   -0.3119
Asset 2    0.6881
Asset 3    0.6239
```

220 *Appendix B*

```
expected return: 0.2
risk          : 0.171448
```

(c)
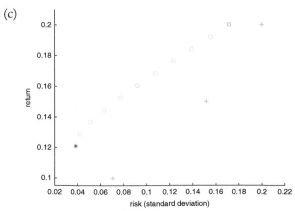

(d) All non-positive α.
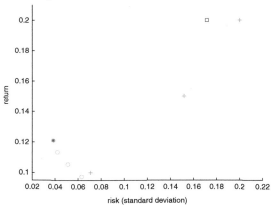

(e)
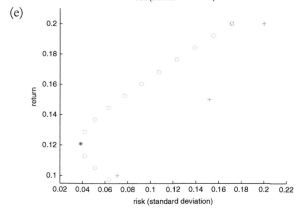

(f)

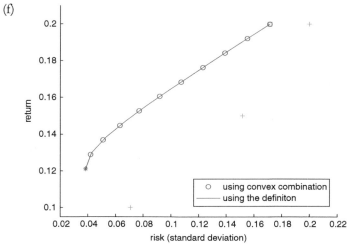

(g)

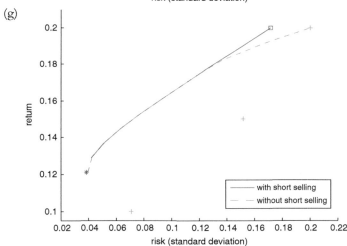

4. (a) best portfolio:
    Asset 1   0.0007
    Asset 2   0.7510
    Asset 3   0.2483
    expected return: 0.187512
    risk   : 0.152386
   (b) best portfolio:
    Asset 1   0.0000
    Asset 2   0.7463
    Asset 3   0.2537
    expected return: 0.187313
    risk   : 0.151658

(c)
beta	Asset 1	Asset 2	Asset 3	return	risk
0	0.0000	1.0000	0.0000	0.2000	0.2000
2	0.0000	0.7463	0.2537	0.1873	0.1517
4	0.0189	0.5566	0.4245	0.1769	0.1243
6	0.2855	0.4506	0.2639	0.1583	0.0877
8	0.4188	0.3977	0.1836	0.1489	0.0705

A higher β means strong risk aversion. For smaller values of β the investor is willing to take risks and so the portfolio is composed mainly of those assets delivering higher returns. As β increases, the role of risk appears in the game; for higher values of β the investor is almost looking for the risk, so the portfolio is composed of more assets with lower variance, which also induces lower expected returns. Obviously the covariance is affecting the portfolio; otherwise for high values of β, portfolios will only be composed of Asset 1, which is not the case (try for even higher values of β).

Supply and demand dynamics

Chapter 6

1. (a)
```
----------------------------------------
Cobweb model
----------------------------------------
Qd,t = 1000 - 10*Pt
Qs,t = 200 + 5*Pt-1
Qd,t = Qs,t
   t      Qt        Pt
   0                25.00
   1     325.00     67.50
   2     537.50     46.25
   3     431.25     56.88
   4     484.38     51.56
   5     457.81     54.22
   6     471.09     52.89
   7     464.45     53.55
   8     467.77     53.22
   9     466.11     53.39
  10     466.94     53.31
  11     466.53     53.35
  12     466.74     53.33
  13     466.63     53.34
  14     466.68     53.33
  15     466.66     53.33
  16     466.67     53.33
```

17	466.66	53.33
18	466.67	53.33

As expected, a negative supply shock results in a reduction of the quantity traded and in a increase of the equilibrium price.

(b)
```
Cobweb model
```
```
Qd,t = 900 - 10*Pt
Qs,t = 250 + 5*Pt-1
Qd,t = Qs,t
```

t	Qt	Pt
0		25.00
1	375.00	52.50
2	512.50	38.75
3	443.75	45.62
4	478.12	42.19
5	460.94	43.91
6	469.53	43.05
7	465.23	43.48
8	467.38	43.26
9	466.31	43.37
10	466.85	43.32
11	466.58	43.34
12	466.71	43.33
13	466.64	43.34
14	466.68	43.33
15	466.66	43.33
16	466.67	43.33
17	466.67	43.33

In this case a negative demand shock results in a decrease in both quantity and price equilibria.

(c) Both processes are divergent since $|-\frac{b}{a}| \geq 1$, as depicted in Figure B.1. Note that, for both cases, the maximum number of iterations allowed is reached (100).

2. (a) Perform the following steps: (i) replace the expression for P_t^e into $Q_{s,t}$; (ii) equalise $Q_{s,t}$ to $Q_{d,t}$; (iii) use the previous relation to obtain P_t. To obtain P_t as a function of P_0, recursively replace P_{t-1} into P_t, P_{t-2} into $P_{t-1}, \ldots, P_0$ into P_1.

(b)
```
Qd,t = 1000 - 10*Pt
Qs,t = 250 + 5*PEt
PEt = P(t-1)+0.5*(50-P(t-1))
Qd,t = Qs,t
```

t	Qt	Pt
0		25.00

224 Appendix B

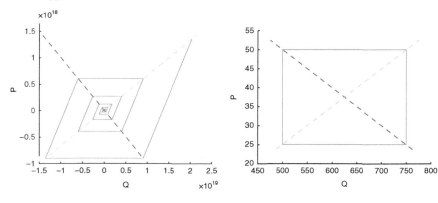

Figure B.1 Divergent processes ($|-\frac{b}{a}| \geq 1$).

```
1    375.00    56.25
2    531.25    48.44
3    492.19    50.39
4    501.95    49.90
5    499.51    50.02
6    500.12    49.99
7    499.97    50.00
8    500.01    50.00
9    500.00    50.00
```

Due to the presence of a normal price, convergence is faster. The convergence rate for $\alpha = 0.5$ is ruled by $|-5/10 * (1 - 0.5)| = 0.25 < 1$.

(c) For $\alpha = 0$, as stated, the original Cobweb model is recovered.

```
------------------------------------------------
Cobweb with normal price expectations
------------------------------------------------
Qd,t = 1000 - 10*Pt
Qs,t = 250 + 5*PEt
PEt  = P(t-1)+0*(50-P(t-1))
Qd,t = Qs,t
   t      Qt         Pt
   0                 25.00
   1     375.00      62.50
   2     562.50      43.75
   3     468.75      53.12
   4     515.62      48.44
   5     492.19      50.78
   6     503.91      49.61
   7     498.05      50.20
```

```
8     500.98   49.90
9     499.51   50.05
10    500.24   49.98
11    499.88   50.01
12    500.06   49.99
13    499.97   50.00
14    500.02   50.00
15    499.99   50.00
16    500.00   50.00
17    500.00   50.00
18    500.00   50.00
```

For $\alpha = 0.2$, the convergence is slower than that of $\alpha = 0.5$; the rate of convergence is $|-5/10 * (1 - 0.2)| = 0.4$ (which compares with 0.25).

```
Qd,t = 1000 - 10*Pt
Qs,t = 250 + 5*PEt
PEt  = P(t-1)+0.2*(50-P(t-1))
Qd,t = Qs,t
 t     Qt        Pt
 0               25.00
 1    375.00    60.00
 2    550.00    46.00
 3    480.00    51.60
 4    508.00    49.36
 5    496.80    50.26
 6    501.28    49.90
 7    499.49    50.04
 8    500.20    49.98
 9    499.92    50.01
10    500.03    50.00
11    499.99    50.00
12    500.01    50.00
13    500.00    50.00
14    500.00    50.00
```

Finally, for $\alpha = 1$ the adjustment process is immediate (the code requires always at least 2 iterations):

```
Qd,t = 1000 - 10*Pt
Qs,t = 250 + 5*PEt
PEt  = P(t-1)+1*(50-P(t-1))
Qd,t = Qs,t
 t     Qt        Pt
 0               25.00
 1    375.00    50.00
 2    500.00    50.00
```

3. (a) Perform the following steps: (i) from the supply function obtain P_t^e; (ii) take the expectations equation and replace P_t^e and P_{t-1}^e with the previous relation to obtain $Q_{s,t} = (1-\beta)Q_{s,t-1} + \beta b P_{t-1} + \beta \overline{Q}_s$; (iii) Equalise $Q_{s,t}$ to $Q_{d,t}$ and solve the resulting expression to obtain P_t. To find P_t as a function of P_0, recursively replace P_{t-1} into P_t, P_{t-2} into P_{t-1}, ..., P_0 into P_1.

(b)
```
Cobweb with adaptative expectations

Qd,t = 1000 - 10*Pt
Qs,t = 250 + 5*PEt
PE,t = PE(t-1)+0.5*(P(t-1)-PE(t-1))
Qd,t = Qs,t
    t     Qt        Pt
    0               25.00
    1     375.00    43.75
    2     468.75    48.44
    3     492.19    49.61
    4     498.05    49.90
    5     499.51    49.98
    6     499.88    49.99
    7     499.97    50.00
    8     499.99    50.00
    9     500.00    50.00
```
With regard to the original model, now the convergence process is faster due to learning induced by the adaptative expectations. The convergence rate is now ruled by $|1 - 0.5(1 + \frac{5}{10})| = 0.25 < 1$.

(c) With respect to the previous exercise, now β was reduced from 0.5 to 0.2. This means that more weight is given to the expected price and less to the difference between the effective and expected prices at the previous period of time. The convergence rate is $|1 - 0.2(1 + \frac{5}{10})| = 0.97 < 1$, which is close to 1 and so convergence is very slow.

```
Cobweb with adaptative expectations

Qd,t = 1000 - 10*Pt
Qs,t = 250 + 5*PEt
PE,t = PE(t-1)+0.2*(P(t-1)-PE(t-1))
Qd,t = Qs,t
    t     Qt        Pt
    0               25.00
    1     375.00    32.50
    2     412.50    37.75
    3     438.75    41.42
```

Solutions

```
 4    457.12   44.00
 5    469.99   45.80
 6    478.99   47.06
 7    485.29   47.94
 8    489.71   48.56
 9    492.79   48.99
10    494.96   49.29
11    496.47   49.51
12    497.53   49.65
13    498.27   49.76
14    498.79   49.83
15    499.15   49.88
16    499.41   49.92
17    499.58   49.94
18    499.71   49.96
19    499.80   49.97
20    499.86   49.98
21    499.90   49.99
22    499.93   49.99
23    499.95   49.99
24    499.97   50.00
25    499.98   50.00
26    499.98   50.00
27    499.99   50.00
28    499.99   50.00
```

Since $\beta = 1$ the original Cobweb model is recovered.

```
Qd,t = 1000 - 10*Pt
Qs,t = 250 + 5*PEt
PE,t = PE(t-1)+1*(P(t-1)-PE(t-1))
Qd,t = Qs,t
  t      Qt        Pt
  0                25.00
  1    375.00      62.50
  2    562.50      43.75
  3    468.75      53.12
  4    515.62      48.44
  5    492.19      50.78
  6    503.91      49.61
  7    498.05      50.20
  8    500.98      49.90
  9    499.51      50.05
 10    500.24      49.98
 11    499.88      50.01
 12    500.06      49.99
```

228 *Appendix B*

```
13    499.97    50.00
14    500.02    50.00
15    499.99    50.00
16    500.00    50.00
17    500.00    50.00
18    500.00    50.00
```

Duopoly

Chapter 7

1.  ```
    Cournot:      Q1* = Q2* = 300
    Stackelberg:  Q1* = 450; Q2* = 225
    ```
    The Cournot equilibrium is, by definition, the same for both firms. It stays between the Stackelberg equilibrium (for the leader and the follower firms). It is relevant to stress that the Cournot equilibrium was already computed as the result of the recurrence relation for the discrete dynamics Cournot duopoly game.
2. Now, since the initial quantity is higher than the equilibrium one, there is an oscillating but decreasing behaviour. The equilibrium is the same, as expected.

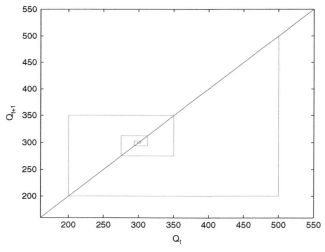

3. For $n=2$, both eigenvalues are less than 1 in magnitude.

    ```
    A =           0    -0.5000
            -0.5000          0

    eigenvalues of A:
        -0.5000
         0.5000
    ```
    ```

(a) For $n = 3$, one eigenvalue is -1:

```
A =            0     -0.5000    -0.5000
         -0.5000          0     -0.5000
         -0.5000    -0.5000           0

eigenvalues of A:
   -1.0000
    0.5000
    0.5000
```

(b) For $n = 4$, one eigenvalue has magnitude greater than 1.

```
A =            0     -0.5000    -0.5000    -0.5000
         -0.5000          0     -0.5000    -0.5000
         -0.5000    -0.5000          0     -0.5000
         -0.5000    -0.5000    -0.5000          0

eigenvalues of A:
   -1.5000
    0.5000
    0.5000
    0.5000
```

(c) For any $n > 3$ it is easy to infer that the largest eigenvalue in magnitude is $\lambda_n = -\frac{n-1}{2}$, and thus $|\lambda_n| > 1$.

```
n=4:    -1.5   0.5   0.5   0.5
n=5:    -2.0   0.5   0.5   0.5   0.5
n=6:    -2.5   0.5   0.5   0.5   0.5   0.5
n=7:    -3.0   0.5   0.5   0.5   0.5   0.5   0.5
n=8:    -3.5   0.5   0.5   0.5   0.5   0.5   0.5
         0.5
...
n=n:   -(n-1)/2  0.5   0.5   0.5   0.5   0.5   0.5
         0.5 ...  0.5
```

4. Equilibrium: Q1 = 0.688796 and Q2 = 0.839568
Note that the two equilibria quantities are not equal since for this exercise costs are different for the two firms.

SP–DG

Chapter 8

1. **disp** 'exercise 1'
   %% SP–DG Model
   % Disinflation (cold turkey and gradual) version

230 Appendix B

```
% Implemented by: T. Andrade, G. Faria, V. Leite, F. Verona,
% M. Viegas, O. Afonso, P.B. Vasconcelos
disp('-------------------------------------------------------');
disp('SP-DG Model: Disinflation (cold turkey and gradual) 
    version');
disp('-------------------------------------------------------');
clear;

% parameters
alpha = 0.5; % SP slope curve
lambda = 0.5; % expectations speed of adjustment
tol = 1e-3; % tolerance for stopping criterium

%% Cold Turkey Strategy
% initialization
itmax = 100;
inflation = zeros(itmax,1); output_gap = zeros(itmax,1);
inflation(1) = 12; expected_inflation(1) = 12;
output_gap(1) = 0; output_growth(1) = 0;
demand(1) = 12; demand_gap(1) = demand(1)-output_growth(1);

% shock
t = 2; demand_gap(2) = 3;
inflation(t) = 1/(1+alpha)*(lambda*inflation(t-1)+...
   (1-lambda)*expected_inflation(t-1)+...
   alpha*(output_gap(t-1)+demand_gap(t)));
expected_inflation(t) = lambda*inflation(t-1)+...
   (1-lambda)*expected_inflation(t-1);
output_gap(t) = output_gap(t-1)+demand_gap(t)-inflation(t);

% loop for ouput gap and inflation rate
while abs(output_gap(t))>tol && t<itmax
    t = t+1;
    demand_gap(t) = demand_gap(t-1);
    expected_inflation(t) = lambda*inflation(t-1)+...
       (1-lambda)*expected_inflation(t-1);
    inflation(t) = 1/(1+alpha)*(lambda*inflation(t-1)+...
       (1-lambda)*expected_inflation(t-1)+...
       alpha*(output_gap(t-1)+demand_gap(t)));
    output_gap(t) = output_gap(t-1)+demand_gap(t)-inflation(t);
end

output_gap_CT = output_gap; inflation_CT = inflation;
clear output_gap inflation;

%% Gradual strategy
% initialization
inflation = zeros(itmax,1); output_gap = zeros(itmax,1);
inflation(1) = 12; expected_inflation(1) = 12;
output_gap(1) = 0; output_growth(1) = 0;
demand(1) = 12; demand_gap(1) = demand(1)-output_growth(1);

% loop for ouput gap and inflation rate
```

```
for t = 2:10
    demand_gap(t) = demand_gap(t-1)-1;
    inflation(t) = 1/(1+alpha)*(lambda*inflation(t-1)+...
        (1-lambda)*expected_inflation(t-1)+...
        alpha*(output_gap(t-1)+demand_gap(t)));
    expected_inflation(t) = lambda*inflation(t-1)+(1-lambda)*...
        expected_inflation(t-1);
    output_gap(t) = output_gap(t-1)+demand_gap(t)-inflation(t);
end

t = 10;
while abs(output_gap(t))>tol && t<itmax
    t = t+1;
    demand_gap(t) = demand_gap(t-1);
    inflation(t) = 1/(1+alpha)*(lambda*inflation(t-1)+...
        (1-lambda)*expected_inflation(t-1)+...
        alpha*(output_gap(t-1)+demand_gap(t)));
    expected_inflation(t) = lambda*inflation(t-1)+(1-lambda)*...
        expected_inflation(t-1);
    output_gap(t) = output_gap(t-1)+demand_gap(t)-inflation(t);
end

output_gap_G = output_gap; inflation_G = inflation;
clear output_gap inflation;

%% show the solution for both strategies
tmax = 30;

subplot(1,2,1);
plot(output_gap_CT(1:tmax),inflation_CT(1:tmax),'r.-',...
    output_gap_G(1:tmax),inflation_G(1:tmax),'b.-'); hold on;
xlabel('Output gap'); ylabel('Inflation rate');
legend('Cold Turkey','Gradual');

subplot(1,2,2);
time_axis = linspace(1,t,t);
plot([0 tmax],[inflation_G(tmax) inflation_G(tmax)],'k:',...
    [0 tmax],[output_gap_G(tmax) output_gap_G(tmax)],'k:');
hold on;
plot(time_axis(1:tmax),output_gap_G(1:tmax),'b—',...
    time_axis(1:tmax),inflation_G(1:tmax),'b-',...
    time_axis(1:tmax),output_gap_CT(1:tmax),'r:',...
    time_axis(1:tmax),inflation_CT(1:tmax),'r-.');
xlabel('Time'); ylabel('Output gap and Inflation rate');
legend('Output gap (Gradual)','Inflation rate (Gradual)',...
    'Output gap (Cold Turkey)','Inflation rate
    (Cold Turkey)');
```

2.
```
----------------------------------------------
SP-DG Model: permanent demand shock
----------------------------------------------
execution with:
 precision      : 1.0e-03
```

232 Appendix B

```
maximum iter.  : 100
alpha          : 0.30

policy adjustment process:
  demand shock  : 3%
  lambda=0.00   : 100 periods
  lambda=0.20   : 67 periods
  lambda=0.80   : 65 periods
  lambda=1.00   : 64 periods
```

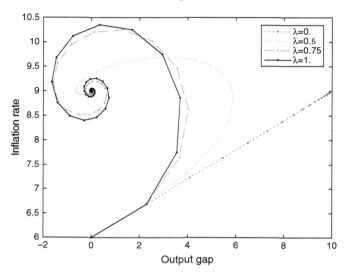

For $\lambda = 0$ there is no convergence; although the inflation rate reaches the target, the output gap does not tend to zero. Differently, for all other values of λ the iterative process converges, π_t to 9 per cent. The stronger the economy inertia in the expectations adjustment process is (lower values of λ) the slower the convergence towards the new steady state.

3. --
```
SP-DG Model: permanent demand shock
     (positive and negative)
```

```
execution with:
  precision     : 1.0e-03
  maximum iter. : 100
  alpha         : 0.30

policy adjustment process:
  demand shock  : 3%
  lambda=0.25   : 71 periods
```

```
lambda=0.50    : 66 periods
lambda=0.75    : 67 periods
lambda=1.00    : 64 periods
demand shock   : -3%
lambda=0.25    : 71 periods
lambda=0.50    : 66 periods
lambda=0.75    : 67 periods
lambda=1.00    : 64 periods
```

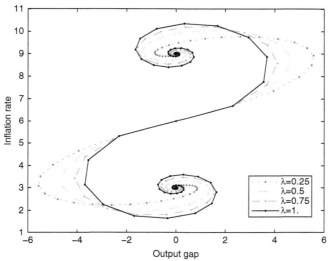

The figure illustrates the long-run equilibrium for both positive and negative demand shocks: the results are as expected and the figure shows a nice symmetrical stylised treble clef kind of representation. The number of iterations towards convergence does not change for symmetrical shocks, yet the inflation rate converges to 9 per cent under a 3 per cent demand shock and to 3 per cent under a −3 per cent demand shock.

4.
```
-------------------------------------------------
SP-DG Model: (temporary) supply shocks
-------------------------------------------------
execution with:
  precision       : 1.0e-03
  maximum iter.   : 100
  lambda          : 0.50
  alpha           : 0.50

policy adjustment process:
  neutral         : 45 periods
  accommodative   : 44 periods
  extinguishing   : 45 periods
```

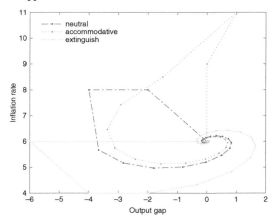

Under a neutral policy, in the first period after the shock, a negative supply shock increases the inflation rate to 8 per cent and decreases the output gap to −2 per cent (for a positive supply shock, inflation rate decreases and the output gap increases). The initial equilibrium is restored. To generate the respective path, a supply shock of 3 in two consecutive periods was considered: `zd = 6; zs = [0,3,3,0];`.

Under an accommodating policy, supply shock has no impact on output gap during the first period. It results from the simulations that the effect on the inflation rate is the strongest, considering all the possible policymaker strategies. A negative supply shock implies an increase of the inflation rate to 9 per cent against 8 per cent for the neutral policy strategy. To generate the respective path `zd = [6,9,12,6]; zs = [0,3,3,0];` was considered.

Under an extinguishing policy, during the first period, a supply shock has no impact on the inflation rate. A negative supply shock implies a decrease in the output gap to −6 per cent against −2 per cent for the neutral policy strategy. The simulation was performed for `zd = [6,0,6]; zs = [0,3,3,0];`.

Solow

Chapter 9

1.  ```
    disp 'exercise 1'
    clc; clear;

    % parameters
    s = 0.4; A = 1; alpha = 0.3; delta = 0.1; n = 0.01;

    % steady-state
    kss = (s*A/(delta+n))^(1/(1-alpha));   % analytical solution
    k0 = 0.5*kss;

    % numerical solution
    odesolow = @(t,k) s*A*k^alpha -(delta+n)*k;
    ```
    ```

```
[T,y] = my_euler(odesolow,[0,100],k0,1);
plot(T,y,'bo'); xlabel('t'); ylabel('k');

% analytical solution
hold on;
ana_solow = @(t) (s*A/(delta+n)+(k0^(1-alpha)-s*A/(delta+n))*...
    exp(-(1-alpha)*(delta+n)*t)).^(1/(1-alpha));
plot(T,ana_solow(T),'r')

legend('numerical solution','analytical solution')
```

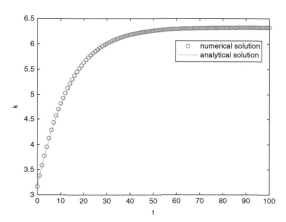

2. (a) The increase in s shifts the sy curve upwards to $s_{new}y$. At the previous current steady-state value k^*, the per capita investment exceeds the amount required to k constant, and therefore the economy begins capital deepening again. This capital deepening continues until $s_{new}y = (\delta + n)k$ and k reaches a higher steady-state value. From the production function, this higher level of k will be associated with higher y; the economy is now richer than before.

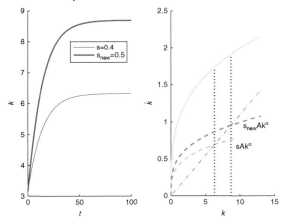

236 Appendix B

(b) In this case, the $(\delta + n)k$ curve rotates up and to the left to the new curve $(\delta + n_{\text{new}})k$. At the previous current steady-state value k^*, the per capita investment is no longer high enough to keep the capital–labour ratio constant in the face of rising population numbers, and therefore the capital–labour ratio begins to fall. It continues to fall until the point at which $sy = (\delta + n_{\text{new}})k$ and k reaches a smaller steady-state value. From the production function, this smaller level of k will be associated with smaller y; the economy is now poorer than before.

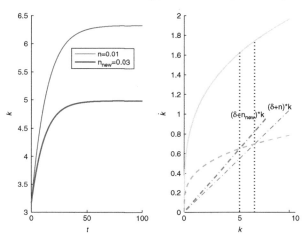

3. (a) **disp** 'exercise 3a'
   % Solow diagram

   % parameters
   s = 0.4; A = 1; alpha = 0.3; delta = 0.1; n = 0.01;

   hold on;
   f = @(k) A*k.^(alpha);
   kss = (s*A/(delta+n))^(1/(1 - alpha));
   k = 0:0.05:2*kss;
   plot(k,f(k),'b'); **text**(k(**end**),f(k(**end**)),'f(k)');
   plot(k,s*f(k),'r—'); **text**(k(**end**),s*f(k(**end**)),'sf(k)');
   plot(k,(delta+n).*k,'m-.'); **text**(k(**end**),(delta+n)*k(**end**),
       '(\delta+n)k');
   plot([kss,kss],[0,f(kss)],'k:','LineWidth',2);
   if ~**exist** ('OCTAVE_VERSION', 'builtin')
       text(kss,0,'k^*','Interpreter','LaTex');
   else
       text(kss,0,'k^*');
   end
   set(gca,'XTick',[]); **set**(gca,'YTick',[])
   hold off;

(b)

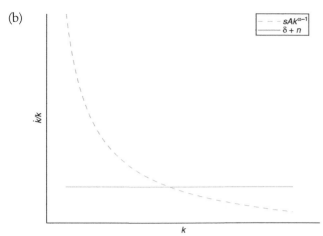

(c) **disp** 'exercise 3c'
% Golden rule

```
exercise3a % perform the Solow diagram
hold on;
kgr = (alpha*A/(delta+n))^(1/(1-alpha));
sgr = alpha;
plot(k,sgr*f(k),'r—','LineWidth',2); % plot sgr*f(k)
text(k(end),sgr*f(k(end)),'s^{gr}f(k)');
plot([kgr,kgr],[0,f(kgr)],'k:','LineWidth',2);
if ~exist('OCTAVE_VERSION','builtin')
   text(kgr,0,'$k^{gr}$','Interpreter','LaTex');
else
   text(kgr,0,'k^{gr}');
end
set(gca,'XTick',[]); set(gca,'YTick',[]);
hold off;
```

(d) **disp** 'exercise 3d'
% Direction field

```
% parameters
s = 0.4; A = 1; alpha = 0.3; delta = 0.1; n = 0.01;

% numerical solution
odesolow = @(t,k) s*A.*k.^alpha-(delta+n).*k;
kss = (s*A/(delta+n))^(1/(1-alpha));

hold on;
% compute path for k0 < kss
[t,k] = ode45(odesolow,[0,80],0.1*kss);
plot(t,k,'LineWidth',2); % t-y plane

% compute path for k0 > kss
[t,k] = ode45(odesolow,[0,80],1.5*kss);
```

238 *Appendix B*

```
        plot(t,k,'m—','LineWidth',2); % t-y plane
        plot(t(end),kss,'ro'); % steady state

        % direction field
        nn = 20;
        aux1 = linspace(0,100,nn);
        aux2 = linspace(0.1,10,nn);
        [t,k] = meshgrid(aux1,aux2);
        dk = odesolow([],k);
        dt = ones(size(dk));
        n_f = sqrt(dt.^2+dk.^2);
        dku = dk./n_f; dtu = dt./n_f;
        quiver(t,k,dtu,dku,'k');

        % legends
        if ~exist ('OCTAVE_VERSION','builtin')
          xlabel('$t$','Interpreter','LaTex');
          ylabel('$k$','Interpreter','LaTex');
          legend('path for $k_0<k^*$','path for $k_0>k^*$','$k^*$');
          set(legend,'Interpreter','LaTex');
        else
          xlabel('t'); ylabel('k');
          legend('path for k_0<k^*$','path for k_0>k^*','k^*');
        end
        axis tight;
        hold off;
```

4. exercise 4
    (a) (1- s)*f(kss) = 1.04337
    (b) (1-sgr)*f(kss) = 1.21726
    (c) (1-sgr)*f(kgr) = 1.07607

5.
```
    %% Solow model
    % Neoclassical growth model (exogenous growth model)
    % Implemented by: P.B. Vasconcelos and O. Afonso
    disp('—————————————————————————————————');
    disp('Solow model: exogenous growth model            ');
    disp('—————————————————————————————————');

    % parameters
    s     = 0.4;  % savings rate
    A     = 1;    % technological progress (Hicks neutral)
    alpha = 0.3;  % capital share in production
    delta = 0.1;  % depreciation rate
    n     = 0.01; % population growth rate
    fprintf('   s       A     alpha   delta    n\n');
    fprintf('%6.2f %6.2f %6.2f %6.2f %6.2f\n',s,A,alpha,delta,n);

    % steady-state and numerical solution
    odesolow = @(t,k) s*A*k^alpha-(delta+n)*k;
    kss = fsolve(@(k) odesolow([],k),10);
    [t,y] = ode45(odesolow,[0,100],0.5*kss);
    plot(t,y);
    if ~exist ('OCTAVE_VERSION','builtin')
```

```
% labels for MATLAB
  xlabel('$t$','Interpreter','LaTex');
  ylabel('$k$','Interpreter','LaTex');
else
  % labels for Octave
  xlabel('t'); ylabel('k');
end
```

Skill-biased technological change

Chapter 10

1. (a) Due to the increase in l, the R&D directed to L-technology becomes more profitable. This heightens the technological-knowledge bias in favour of L-intermediate goods. Such bias increases the supply of L-intermediate goods, thereby increasing the number of final goods produced with the L-technology and lowering their relative price. Thus, relative prices of final goods produced with L-technology drop continuously towards the constant steady-state levels. This path of relative prices implies that, when compared with the baseline case, the technological-knowledge bias increases less (and at a decreasing rate) until it reaches its new steady state D_{new}. An increase of l causes an immediate drop in the H-premium, at time $t = 0$. The H-premium falls instantly due to the rise in l without new endogenous technological-knowledge progress and so without change in technological-knowledge bias. In turn, by reason of complementarity between inputs in the production function, changes in the H-premium are closely related to the technological-knowledge bias. Thus, after the immediate effect on the H-premium, there is a transition dynamics towards the new steady state, which is increasing at decreasing rates.

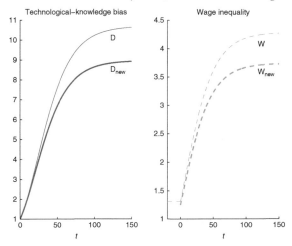

(b) The increase in A affects the R&D profitability of both the L-technology and the H-technology. As a result the technological-knowledge bias is only slightly affected during the transitional dynamic phase. Consequently, there is no an immediate level effect on the H-premium at time $t = 0$. Moreover, the path of the H-premium is driven by the endogenous technological-knowledge bias.

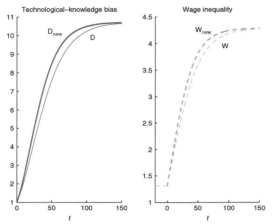

(c) A decrease in q (which implies a decrease in α) favours the R&D directed to H-technology. This reinforces the technological-knowledge bias in favour of H-intermediate goods. The consequent effect on relative prices implies that, when compared with the baseline case, the technological-knowledge bias increases more (and at a decreasing rate) until it reaches its new steady state D_{new}. Since q and α do not affect W directly, there is no level effect at time $t = 0$. However, since the H-premium is driven by the technological-knowledge bias, D, the path of W leads the H-premium for a higher steady-state level.

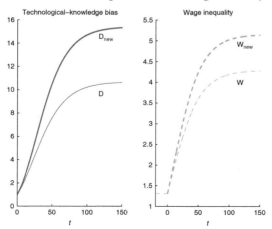

2. ```
function [t,y] = my_meuler(f,tspan,y0,h)
%Modified Euler method with tspan=[t0 tf] and fixed step size to solve
% the IVP y'=f(t,y), y(t0)=y0
% input:
%   f   : function to integrate (f=@(t,y))
%   tspan : integration interval [t0,tfinal]
%   y0   : initial condition at t0
%   h   : (constant) step size
% output:
%   t : specific times used
%   y : solution evaluated at t

t0 = tspan(1); tf = tspan(2);
t = t0:h:tf; y = zeros(1,length(t));
y(1) = y0; yn = y0; tn = t0;
for n = 1:length(t)-1
    k1   = f(tn,yn);
    k2   = f(tn+h/2,yn+h/2*k1);
    yn   = yn+h*k2;
    y(n+1) = yn;
    tn   = tn+h;
end
end

function [t,y] = my_ieuler(f,tspan,y0,h)
%Improved Euler method with tspan=[t0 tf] and fixed step size to solve
% the IVP y'=f(t,y), y(t0)=y0
% input:
%   f   : function to integrate (f=@(t,y))
%   tspan : integration interval [t0,tfinal]
%   y0   : initial condition at t0
%   h   : (constant) step size
% output:
%   t : specific times used
%   y : solution evaluated at t

t0 = tspan(1); tf = tspan(2);
t = t0:h:tf; y = zeros(1,length(t));
y(1) = y0; yn = y0; tn = t0;
for n = 1:length(t)-1
    k1   = f(tn,yn);
    k2   = f(tn+h,yn+h*k1);
    yn   = yn+h/2*k1+h/2*k2;
    y(n+1) = yn;
    tn   = tn+h;
end
end
```

3. Just change the solver to

   ```
   [t,y] = ode45(@ode_sbtc,tspan,y0);
   ```
   ```

242 Appendix B

4. **disp** 'exercise 4'

```
% problem data
global beta zeta q alpha l h A L H sigma
beta = 1.6; zeta = 4.0; q = 3.33; alpha = 0.7; l = 1.0;
h = 1.2; A = 1.5; L = 1.0; H = 0.7; sigma = H/L+1;
y0 = 1.0; tspan = [0 150]; interv = tspan(2)-tspan(1);

% use ode45 to obtain a reference solution
options = odeset('RelTol',1e-13,'AbsTol',1e-16);

% computes error at t=1/3,2/3,3/3 of the interval
error=zeros(1,3);
h_values =[1.,0.1,0.01,0.001];

fprintf('\t h \t error (t=50) \t error (t=100) \t error (t=150)\n')

disp('Euler method')
for i=1:length(h_values)
  h=h_values(i);
  [ts,ys] = ode45(@ode_sbtc,tspan(1):h:tspan(2),y0,options);
  [t,y] = my_euler(@ode_sbtc,tspan,y0,h);
  w = 1/3*interv/h; error(1) = abs(y(w)-ys(w));
  w = 2/3*interv/h; error(2) = abs(y(w)-ys(w));
  w =     interv/h; error(3) = abs(y(w)-ys(w));
  fprintf('   %5.1e \t %5.3e \t %5.3e \t %5.3e\n',...
          h,error(1),error(2),error(3));
end

disp('Implicit Euler method')
for i=1:length(h_values)
  h=h_values(i);
  [ts,ys] = ode45(@ode_sbtc,tspan(1):h:tspan(2),y0,options);
  [t,y] = my_ieuler(@ode_sbtc,tspan,y0,h);
  w = 1/3*interv/h; error(1) = abs(y(w)-ys(w));
  w = 2/3*interv/h; error(2) = abs(y(w)-ys(w));
  w =     interv/h; error(3) = abs(y(w)-ys(w));
  fprintf('   %5.1e \t %5.3e \t %5.3e \t %5.3e\n',...
          h,error(1),error(2),error(3));
end

disp('Modified Euler method')
for i=1:length(h_values)
  h=h_values(i);
  [ts,ys] = ode45(@ode_sbtc,tspan(1):h:tspan(2),y0,options);
  [t,y] = my_meuler(@ode_sbtc,tspan,y0,h);
  w = 1/3*interv/h; error(1) = abs(y(w)-ys(w));
  w = 2/3*interv/h; error(2) = abs(y(w)-ys(w));
  w =     interv/h; error(3) = abs(y(w)-ys(w));
  fprintf('   %5.1e \t %5.3e \t %5.3e \t %5.3e\n',...
          h,error(1),error(2),error(3));
end
```

```
disp('RK4 method')
for i=1:length(h_values)
  h=h_values(i);
  [ts,ys] = ode45(@ode_sbtc,tspan(1):h:tspan(2),y0,options);
  [t,y]  = my_rk4(@ode_sbtc,tspan,y0,h);
  w = 1/3*interv/h;  error(1) = abs(y(w)-ys(w));
  w = 2/3*interv/h;  error(2) = abs(y(w)-ys(w));
  w =     interv/h;  error(3) = abs(y(w)-ys(w));
  fprintf('   %5.1e \t %5.3e \t %5.3e \t %5.3e\n',...
          h,error(1),error(2),error(3));
end
```

```
      h      error (t=50)  error (t=100)  error (t=150)
Euler method
   1.0e+00    5.419e-04    1.194e-02    4.529e-03
   1.0e-01    4.504e-04    2.246e-04    1.079e-04
   1.0e-02    5.382e-05    1.573e-05    4.521e-06
   1.0e-03    5.365e-06    1.253e-06    2.442e-07
Implicit Euler method
   1.0e+00    4.442e-04    2.386e-04    7.195e-05
   1.0e-01    4.561e-07    2.037e-07    9.040e-08
   1.0e-02    7.381e-09    2.029e-09    5.453e-10
   1.0e-03    7.834e-11    1.797e-11    3.415e-12
Modified Euler method
   1.0e+00    2.149e-05    1.038e-04    4.742e-05
   1.0e-01    5.273e-07    2.354e-07    1.038e-07
   1.0e-02    7.713e-09    2.132e-09    5.785e-10
   1.0e-03    7.929e-11    1.821e-11    3.474e-12
RK4 method
   1.0e+00    3.001e-08    1.435e-08    4.402e-09
   1.0e-01    2.071e-13    8.041e-14    2.945e-14
   1.0e-02    2.665e-15    2.602e-16    3.001e-16
   1.0e-03    8.049e-16    5.204e-16    1.804e-16
```

For this exercise, since we do not have access to the analytical solution, we use ode45 (Dormand–Prince RK presented in Chapter 11). The aim is to illustrate the order of convergence of the Euler, modified Euler, improved Euler and RK4 methods. Considering an interval from 0 to 150, we compute, for different integration step values, the error (difference between the approximation and the reference approximation given by ode45, in absolute terms) at three points: $t = 50$, $t = 100$ and $t = 150$.

For the Euler method, error is roughly proportional to the integration step size h: whenever the step is divided by 10, the error is reduced by 10. For modified and improved Euler methods, the error is proportional to h^2: whenever the step is divided by 10 the error is reduced by 10^2. For a k-order method the error scales as h^k: for RK4, error scales with h^4

244 Appendix B

(not so evident to see in the table since the error was computed taking an approximation as the exact solution).

Just note that the error analysed is the so-called global error, error at a given time. The local error, error per step, is the one that results from the truncation of the Taylor series: for instance, for the Euler method, the local error is of order h^2.

Technological-knowledge diffusion

Chapter 11

1. (a) An increase in labour endowments in the South leads to a stronger convergence.

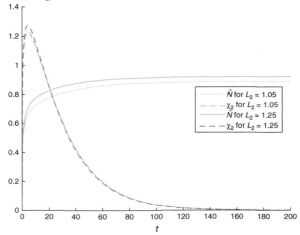

(b) As expected, the effect is opposite to the previous shock.

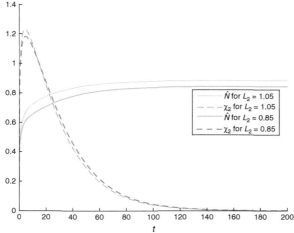

2. (a) Better institutions in the South allows for a closer approximation to the Northern technological progress.

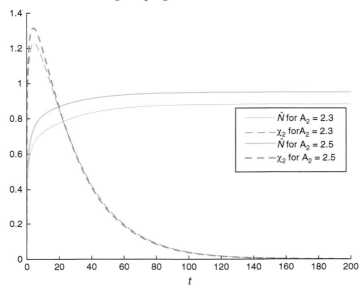

(b) As expected, the effect is opposite to the previous shock.

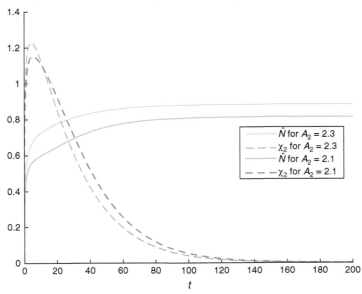

3. (a) The assumption cancels the mechanism of the model by which the cost of imitation is lower than the cost of innovation, although growing. Thus, a high fixed innovation cost in the South leads to a lower

economic growth rate. If this rate is smaller than the one in the North, then countries diverge.

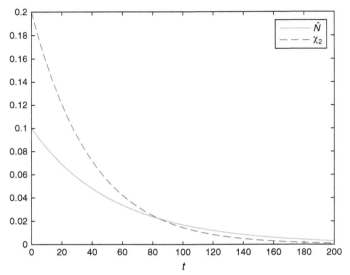

(b) As in the previous exercise, the model's mechanism is destroyed. Now, since the fixed innovation cost in the South is low, its economic growth rate is always higher than the one in the North, which is not economically realistic. At the limit, the South surpasses the North.

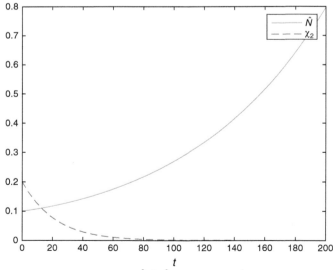

4. (a) $\pi_2 = (\alpha + \beta)(1 - \alpha - \beta)^{\frac{2-\alpha-\beta}{\alpha+\beta}} (A_2 L_2^\alpha G_2^\beta)^{\frac{1}{\alpha+\beta}}$.

(b) The system of differential equations is as follows.

```
function dydt = ode_tkd_G(~,y,...
                nu2,L2,A2,G2,alpha,beta,gamma1,theta,sigma,rho)
% ode system of equations for tkd_G model
% parameters
ab = alpha+beta; mab = 1-alpha-beta;
Pi_2 = ab*mab^((2-ab)/ab)*A2^(1/ab)*G2^(beta/ab)*L2^(alpha/ab);
aux = A2^(1/ab)*G2^(beta/ab)*L2^(alpha/ab)*...
      (mab^(2*mab/ab)-mab^(2/ab));
% ode system
dydt = [y(1)*(...
        (nu2*y(1)^sigma)^(-1)*(aux-y(2))-gamma1 ...
        ); ...
        y(2)*(...
        1/theta*Pi_2*(nu2*y(1)^sigma)^(-1)+...
        sigma/theta*(nu2*y(1)^sigma)^(-1)*aux -...
        sigma/theta*y(2)*(nu2*y(1)^sigma)^(-1)-...
        sigma/theta*gamma1-rho/theta -...
        (nu2*y(1)^sigma)^(-1)*aux +...
        y(2)*(nu2*y(1)^sigma)^(-1)...
        )...
        ];
```

(c) Just set $\beta = 0$ in the system of equations and compare with the one developed in the chapter. The use of $\beta = 0$ in the code should provide the same solution as the results shown in the chapter.

(d) For this comparison and with α constant, the share of intermediate goods in production decreases, which penalises the R&D imitative activity.

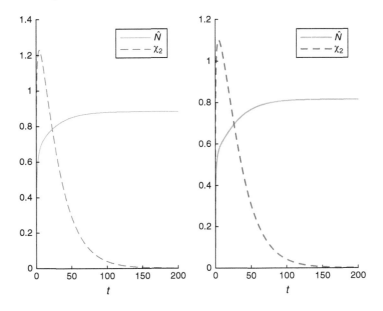

248 *Appendix B*

(e) In this case β is fixed. When G_2 increases the Southern R&D imitative activity becomes more profitable (see the expression for pi_2) and thus the South improves its convergence to the North.

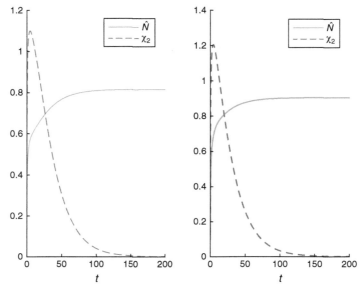

(f) Southern convergence is now stronger than before since $G_2 > L_2$.

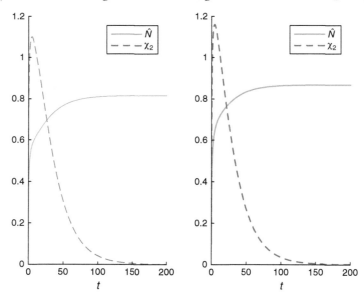

Ramsey–Cass–Koopmans
Chapter 12

1. Just replace bvp4c by bvp5c. The answers provided by the solvers are identical.

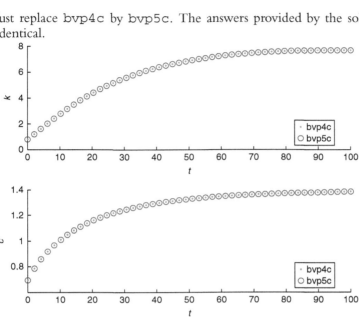

2. (a) % Golden rule

```
function rck_golden
disp 'exercise 2a'
clc; clear;

%% Parameter values
% Baseline parameters from [1,p.78]
global alpha delta rho n gx theta kss css k0
alpha = 0.3; delta = 0.05; rho = 0.02;
n = 0.01; gx = 0.03; theta = 3;

%% Equilibrium point
% Find the intersection point of the 2 curves (f and g)
ktil = fsolve(@(k) f(k)-g(k),10); % avoid 0 (trivial sol)

% plot
figure(1); xlabel('k'); ylabel('c'); hold on
max_k = 1.1*ktil; k = linspace(0,max_k);
plot(k,f(k),'k');
plot(k,g(k),'k—');
plot(ktil,f(ktil),'k.','markersize',20);
xlabel('$k$','Interpreter','LaTex');
ylabel('$c$','Interpreter','LaTex');
```

250 Appendix B

```matlab
%% $\dot{k}=0$ and $\dot{c}=0$
% plot kdot=0
max_k = 1.1*ktil; k = linspace(0,max_k/2);
plot(k,f(k)-g(k),'k:');
% plot cdot=0 (straight line)
plot([kss,kss],[0,2*css],'k-.');

%% Golden rule
% Note that for this case, $k$ for the golden rule is known:
%
% $$k_{g}=(\alpha/(n+\delta+gx))^(1/(1-\alpha))$$
k = linspace(0,max_k);
gold_c = max(f(k)-g(k)); % find initial approximation
[gold_k,gold_c] = fminunc(@k_locus,gold_c);
gold_c = -gold_c; % due to maximization procedure

plot(gold_k,gold_c,'md','markersize',7); % plot golden rule

%% Steady state values
F = fsolve(@(y) ode_bvp([],y),[1 1]); kss = F(1); css = F(2);

plot(kss,css,'ro','markersize',5);
legend('gross production f(k)',...
       'depreciation (n+\delta+gx)k',...
       'eq. point','kdot=0','cdot=0','golden rule',...
       'steady-state','Location','SouthEast');
box off;

%% Numerical solution of the model
k0 = 0.1*kss; % shock at $k$.
nn = 100; % time span
solinit = bvpinit(linspace(0,nn,5),[0.5 0.5]);
sol = bvp4c(@ode_bvp,@bcs,solinit);
xint = linspace(0,nn);
Sxint = deval(sol,xint);

plot(Sxint(1,:),Sxint(2,:),'m','Linewidth',2);
legend('gross production $f(k)$',...
       'depreciation $(n+\delta+g)k$',...
       'eq. point','$\dot{k}=0$','$\dot{c}=0$',...
       'golden rule','steady-state',...
       'net production','Location','SouthEast');
set(legend,'Interpreter','latex');
hold off

% Production function: Cobb-Douglas
function y = f(k)
global alpha;
y=k.^alpha;

% Depreciation function
function y = g(k)
global n delta gx;
```

```
    y = (n+delta+gx).*k;

    function y = k_locus(k)
    % kdot=0, i.e, f-g=0
    y = f(k)-g(k); y = -y;

    % Boundary conditions
    function res = bcs(ya,yb)
    global css k0
    res = [ya(1)-k0; yb(2)-css];

    % Differential system speciification
    function dydt=ode_bvp(~,y)
    global alpha delta rho n gx theta
    dydt = [...
        (y(1)^alpha-y(2)-(n+delta+gx)*y(1)); ...
        (y(2)*(alpha*y(1)^(alpha-1)-...
            (delta+rho+gx*theta))/theta); ...
        ];
```

(b)
```
    % Phase diagram
    function rck_phase_diagram

    disp 'exercise 2b'

    %%% parameters
    global alpha delta rho n g theta kss css k0
    alpha = 0.3;   % elasticity of capital in production
    delta = 0.05;  % depreciaton rate
    rho = 0.02;    % time preference
    n = 0.01;      % population growth
    g = 0.00;      % exogenous growth rate of technology
    theta = (delta+rho)/(alpha*(delta+n+g)-g);

    %%% Steady state values and shock
    kss = ((delta+rho+g*theta)/alpha)^(1/(alpha-1));
    css = kss^alpha-(n+delta+g)*kss;
    k0 = 0.1*kss;

    %%% Numerical solution
    nn = 100;
    solinit = bvpinit(linspace(0,nn,5),[0.5 0.5]);
    sol = bvp4c(@ode_bvp,@bcs,solinit);
    xint = linspace(0,nn,50);
    Sxint = deval(sol,xint);

    %%% Plot the phase diagram
    plot(Sxint(1,:),Sxint(2,:),'b','LineWidth',2); hold on;
    [k,c] = meshgrid(linspace(1,12,20),linspace(0.4,2,20));
    dk = zeros(size(k)); dc = dk;
    for i = 1:size(k,1)
        for j = 1:size(k,2)
            yprime = ode_bvp([],[k(i,j),c(i,j)]);
            dk(i,j) = yprime(1); dc(i,j)=yprime(2);
```

252 *Appendix B*

```
            end
      end
      quiver(k,c,dk,dc,1.0,'k')
      xlabel('$k$','Interpreter','LaTex');
      ylabel('$c$','Interpreter','LaTex');

      % plot kdot=0
      k = linspace(0.5,12);
      plot(k,k.^alpha-(n+delta+g).*k,'r:','linewidth',2);
      % plot cdot=0 (straight line)
      plot([kss,kss],[0.5,2],'m-.','linewidth',2);

      %% Boundary conditions and ode
      function res = bcs(ya,yb)
      global css k0
      res = [ya(1)-k0; yb(2)-css];

      function dydt=ode_bvp(~,y)
      global alpha delta rho n g theta
      dydt = [...
         (y(1).^alpha-y(2)-(n+delta+g).*y(1)); ...
      %ode: k
         (y(2).*(alpha.*y(1)^(alpha-1)-(delta+rho+g*theta))./theta);
             ... %ode: c
             ];
```

3. (a) The less patient – i.e. the higher the value of ρ – the smaller the steady-state growth rate.

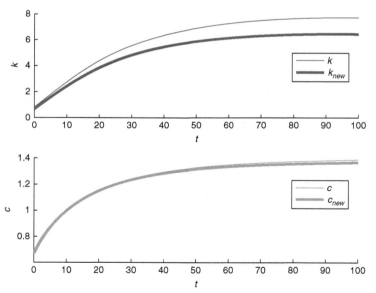

(b) A higher α, in a context with capital accumulation, increases the steady-state growth rate.

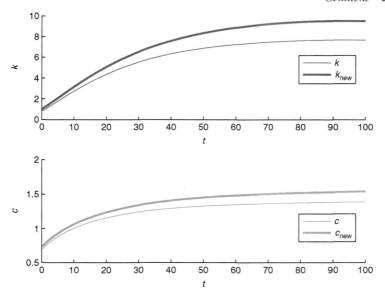

4. An increase in g changes the steady state for both variables of interest, which becomes higher. Furthermore, there is an immediate level effect at $t = 0$.

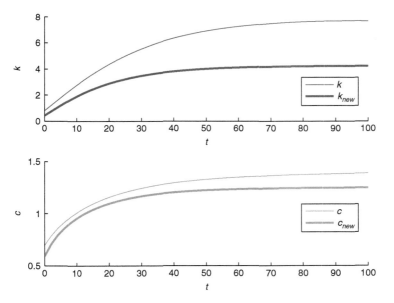

5. ```
% Ramsey-Cass-Koopmans model
% Solves the Ramsey-Cass-Koopmans model, and performs
% the outputs provided in R. Barro and X. Sala-i-Martin,
% Economic Growth, MIT Press, 2004, p.117
function exercise5
```
```

```
disp 'exercise 5'
global alpha delta rho n g theta kss css k0
alpha_v = [0.3; 0.75];
alpha_c = {'-.','-'};
delta = 0.05; rho = 0.02; n = 0.01;
g = 0.02; theta = 3;

% solve the model twice for alpha=0.3 and alpha=0.75
for i = 1:2
  % steady state
  alpha = alpha_v(i); % peak one of the values for alpha
  type_line = alpha_c{i}; % peak type of line
  kss = ((delta+rho+g*theta)/alpha)^(1/(alpha-1));
  css = kss^alpha-(n+delta+g)*kss;
  k0 = 0.1*kss;

  % approximate solution
  nn = 300;
  solinit = bvpinit(linspace(0,nn,5),[0.5; 0.5]);
  sol = bvp4c(@ode_bvp,@bcs,solinit);
  xint = linspace(0,nn);
  Sxint = deval(sol,xint);
  k = Sxint(1,:); c = Sxint(2,:);

  % values per unit of effective labor of the capital stock
  subplot(3,2,1); hold on
  plot(xint,k/kss,type_line);
  axis tight;
  xlabel('$t$','Interpreter','LaTex');
  ylabel('$\hat{k}/\hat{k}^*$','Interpreter','LaTex');
  if i==2, legend('$\alpha=0.3$','$\alpha=0.75$'); end
  set(legend,'Interpreter','latex');
  legend('boxoff');

  % values per unit of effective labor of the consumption
  subplot(3,2,3); hold on
  plot(xint,c/css,type_line);
  axis tight;
  xlabel('$t$','Interpreter','LaTex');
  ylabel('$\hat{c}/\hat{c}^*$','Interpreter','LaTex');

  % values per unit of effective labor of the output
  subplot(3,2,5); hold on
  plot(xint,f(k)/f(kss),type_line);
  axis tight;
  xlabel('$t$','Interpreter','LaTex');
  ylabel('$\hat{y}/\hat{y}^*$','Interpreter','LaTex');

  % growth rate per unit of effective labor:
  % gamma_y=yprime/y=k*fprime(k)/f(k)*kprime/k
  subplot(3,2,2); hold on
  dk = zeros(1,length(k));
  for m=1:length(k)
```

```
            temp    = ode_bvp([] , [k(m),c(m)]);
            dk(m)   = temp(1);
        end
        gamma_y = k.*fprime(k)./f(k).*(dk./k);
        plot(xint ,gamma_y, type_line );
        axis tight; ylim([0  0.1]);
        xlabel('$t$','Interpreter','LaTex');
        ylabel('$\gamma_{\hat{y}}$','Interpreter','LaTex');

        % savings rate transitional dynamics:
        % s=1−c(k)/f(k)
        subplot(3,2,4); hold on
        plot(xint,1−c./f(k), type_line );
        axis tight; ylim([0.1  0.5]);
        xlabel('$t$','Interpreter','LaTex');
        ylabel('$s$','Interpreter','LaTex');

        % interest rate:
        % r(k)=f'(k(k))−delta−g*theta
        subplot(3,2,6); hold on
        plot(xint ,fprime(k)−delta−g*theta , type_line );
        axis tight;
        xlabel('$t$','Interpreter','LaTex');
        ylabel('$r$','Interpreter','LaTex');

    end

    %% Functions:

    function y = f(k)
    global alpha;
    y=k.^alpha;

    function y = fprime(k)
    global alpha;
    y=alpha.*k.^(alpha −1);

    function res = bcs(ya,yb)
    global kss k0
    res = [ya(1)−k0; yb(1)−kss];

    function dydt=ode_bvp(~,y)
    global alpha delta rho n g theta
    dydt = [...
        (y(1).^alpha −y(2) −(n+delta+g).*y(1)); ...
        (y(2).*(alpha.*y(1)^(alpha −1)−...
            (delta+rho+g*theta))/theta); ...
        ];
```

6. The less keen individuals are on consumption smoothing (the smaller the value of θ) the higher the steady-state growth rate. For high values of θ consumers start devoting most of their resources to consumption.

256 Appendix B

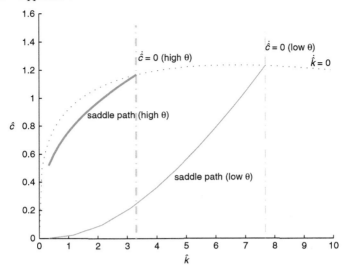

Bibliography

D. Acemoglu. Directed technical change. *The Review of Economic Studies*, 69(4): 781–809, 2002a.

D. Acemoglu. Technical change, inequality and the labour market. *Journal of Economic Literature*, 40(1): 7–72, 2002b.

D. Acemoglu. Patterns of skill premia. *The Review of Economic Studies*, 70(2): 199–230, 2003.

D. Acemoglu and F. Zilibotti. Productivity differences. *The Quarterly Journal of Economics*, 116(2): 563–606, 2001.

O. Afonso. Skill-biased technological knowledge without scale effects. *Applied Economics*, 38(1): 13–21, 2006.

O. Afonso. The impact of government intervention on wage inequality without scale effects. *Economic Modelling*, 25(2): 351–362, 2008.

O. Afonso and P. B. Vasconcelos. Re-examining international technological-knowledge diffusion. *International Economic Journal*, 21(2): 279–296, 2007.

P. Aghion and P. Howitt. A model of growth through creative destruction. *Econometrica*, 60(2): 323–351, 1992.

T. Andrade, G. Faria, V. Leite, F. Verona, M. Viegas, O. Afonso, and P. B. Vasconcelos. *Numerical Solution of Linear Models in Economics: the SP-DG Model Revisited*. FEP Working Papers 249, Porto: Universidade do Porto, Faculdade de Economia do Porto, 2007.

Z. Bai, J. Demmel, J. Dongarra, A. Ruhe, and H. van der Vorst. *Templates for the Solution of Algebraic Eigenvalue Problems: a Practical Guide*, volume 11. Philadelphia, PA: Society for Industrial and Applied Mathematics, 2000.

R. Barro. Are government bonds net wealth? *The Journal of Political Economy*, 82(6): 1095–1117, 1974.

R. Barro. Government spending in a simple model of endogenous growth. *Journal of Political Economy*, 98(5): S103–S125, 1990.

R. Barro. *Macroeconomics, a Modern Approach*. Mason, OH: Thomson South-Western, 2008.

R. Barro and X. Sala-i-Martin. Technological diffusion, convergence, and growth. *Journal of Economic Growth*, 2(1): 1–26, 1997.

R. Barro and X. Sala-i-Martin. *Economic Growth*. Cambridge, MA: MIT Press, 2004.

J. Beath and Y. Katsoulacos. *The Economic Theory of Product Differentiation*. Cambridge: Cambridge University Press, 1991.

M. Burda and C. Wyplosz. *Macroeconomics: a European Text*. New York, NY: Oxford University Press, 2009.

Bibliography

W. Carlin and D. Soskice. *Macroeconomics, Imperfections, Institutions and Policies*. New York, NY: Oxford University Press, 2006.

D. Cass. Optimum growth in an aggregative model of capital accumulation. *The Review of Economic Studies*, 32(3): 233–240, 1965.

A. C. Chiang and K. Wainwright. *Fundamental Methods of Mathematical Economics*. New York, NY: McGraw-Hill, 2005.

A. Cournot. *Recherches sur les Principes Mathématiques de la Théorie des Richesses*. Paris: Hachette (English translation by Bacon, N. T., *Researches into the Mathematical Principles of the Theory of Wealth*. New York, NY: MacMillan, 1927), 1838.

G. Dahlquist and Å. Björck. *Numerical Methods in Scientific Computing*, volume 1. Philadelphia, PA: Society for Industrial and Applied Mathematics, 2008.

O. de La Grandville. *Economic Growth: a Unified Approach*. Cambridge: Cambridge University Press, 2009.

J. W. Demmel. *Applied Numerical Linear Algebra*. Philadelphia, PA: Society for Industrial and Applied Mathematics, 1997.

E. Dinopoulos and P. Segerstrom. A Schumpeterian model of protection and relative wages. *American Economic Review*, 89(3): 450–472, 1999.

A. K. Dixit and J. E. Stiglitz. Monopolistic competition and optimum product diversity. *American Economic Review*, 67(3): 297–308, 1977.

M. Fleming. Domestic financial policies under fixed and under floating exchange rates. IMF Staff Papers, 369–380, 1962.

O. Galor and O. Moav. Ability-biased technological transition, wage inequality, and economic growth. *The Quarterly Journal of Economics*, 115(2): 469–497, 2000.

G. Gandolfo. *Economic Dynamics*. Berlin/Heidelberg: Springer, 2010.

J. Gaspar. *A dynamic aggregate supply and aggregate demand model with MATLAB*. FEP Working Papers 559, Porto: Universidade do Porto, Faculdade de Economia do Porto, 2015.

J. Gaspar, P. B. Vasconcelos, and O. Afonso. Economic growth and multiple equilibria: A critical note. *Economic Modelling*, 36:157–160, 2014.

P. Gil, O. Afonso, and P. B. Vasconcelos. A note on skill-structure shocks, the share of the high-tech sector and economic growth dynamics. *Macroeconomic Dynamics*, forthcoming.

G. H. Golub and C. F. Van Loan. *Matrix Computations*. Baltimore, MD: Johns Hopkins University Press, 1996.

R. J. Gordon. *Macroeconomics*. New York, NY: Prentice Hall, 2011.

G. M. Grossman and E. Helpman. *Innovation and Growth in the Global Economy*. Cambridge, MA: MIT Press, 1991.

R. E. Hall and D. H. Papell. *Macroeconomics: Economic Growth, Fluctuations, and Policy*. New York: WW Norton, 2005.

R. A. Haugen and N. L. Baker. The efficient market inefficiency of capitalization-weighted stock portfolios. *The Journal of Portfolio Management*, 17(3): 35–40, 1991.

A. S. Householder. *The Theory of Matrices in Numerical Analysis*. New York, NY: Blaisdell, 1964.

C. I. Jones. Time series tests of endogenous growth models. *The Quarterly Journal of Economics*, 110(2): 495–525, 1995a.

C. I. Jones. R & D-based models of economic growth. *Journal of Political Economy*, 103: 759–784, 1995b.

L. E. Jones and R. Manuelli. A convex model of equilibrium growth. *Journal of Political Economy*, 98(5): 1008–1038, 1990.

N. Kaldor. A classificatory note on the determinateness of equilibrium. *The Review of Economic Studies*, 1(2): 122–136, 1934.

C. T. Kelley. *Iterative Methods for Linear and Nonlinear Equations*. Philadelphia, PA: Society for Industrial and Applied Mathematics, 1995.

D. A. Kendrick, P. R. Mercado, and H. M. Amman. *Computational Economics*. Princeton, NJ: Princeton University Press, 2006.

T. C. Koopmans. On the concept of optimal economic growth. *The Economic Approach to Development Planning, Pontif. Acad. Sc. Scripta Varia*, 28: 225–287, 1965.

P. R. Krugman, M. Obstfeld, and M. J. Melitz. *International Economics: Theory and Practice*. Addison-Wesley, Boston, 2011.

D. Leite, O. Afonso, and S. Silva. *A Tale of Two Countries: a Directed Technical Change Approach*. FEP Working Papers 539, Porto: Universidade do Porto, Faculdade de Economia do Porto, 2014.

R. E. Lucas. On the mechanics of economic development. *Journal of Monetary Economics*, 22: 3–42, 1988.

N. G. Mankiw. *Macroeconomics*. New York, NY: Worth Publishers, 2009.

H. Markowitz. Portfolio selection. *The Journal of Finance*, 7(1): 77–91, 1952.

A. Marshall. *Principles of Economics*. London: Macmillan and Co., Ltd. [1890] 1920.

A. Mas-Colell, M. D. Whinston, and J. R. Green. *Microeconomic Theory*. Oxford: Oxford University Press, 1995.

Mathworks. Mathworks: Documentation center, 2015. URL Available online at www.mathworks.com/help/matlab/ (accessed 10 February 2015).

R. C. Merton. An analytic derivation of the efficient portfolio frontier. *The Journal of Financial and Quantitative Analysis*, 7(4): 1851–1872, 1972.

M. J. Miranda and P. L. Fackler. *Applied Computational Economics and Finance*. Cambridge MA: MIT Press, 2002.

C. Moler. *Numerical Computing with MATLAB*. Philadelphia, PA: Society for Industrial and Applied Mathematics, 2004.

R. Mundell. Inflation and real interest. *Journal of Political Economy*, 71(3): 739–773, 1963.

R. R. Nelson and E. S. Phelps. Investment in humans, technological diffusion, and economic growth. *The American Economic Review*, 56(1/2): 69–75, 1966.

J. Nocedal and S. J. Wright. *Numerical Optimization*. New York, NY: Springer, 2006.

D. Pachamanova and F. J. Fabozzi. *Simulation and Optimization in Finance: Modeling with MATLAB,@ RISK, or VBA*, volume 173. Hoboken, NJ: John Wiley & Sons, 2010.

B. P. Pashigian. Cobweb theorem. In Lawrence Blume and Steven Durlauf, editors, *The New Palgrave Dictionary of Economics*. New York, NY: Palgrave Macmillan, 2008.

J. M. Perloff. *Microeconomics: Theory and Applications with Calculus*. Boston, MA: Pearson, 2013.

F. P. Ramsey. A mathematical theory of saving. *The Economic Journal*, 38(152): 543–559, 1928.

D. Ricardo. *On the Principles of Political Economy and Taxation*. London: John Murray, 1817.

U. Ricci, Die "synthetische Ökonomie" von Henry Ludwell Moore. *Zeitschrift für Nationalökonomie*, 1(5): 649-668, 1930.

D. Romer. *Advanced Macroeconomics*. New York, NY: McGraw-Hill, 2006.

P. M. Romer. Increasing returns and long-run growth. *The Journal of Political Economy*, 98(5): 1002–1037, 1986.

P. M. Romer. Endogenous technological change. *Journal of Political Economy*, 98(5): S71–S102, 1990.

E. Romero, M. B. Cruz, J. E. Roman, and P. B. Vasconcelos. A parallel implementation of the Jacobi-Davidson eigensolver for unsymmetric matrices. In J. L. Palma, M. Daydé, O. Marques, and J. C. Lopes, editors, *High Performance Computing for Computational*

Science – VECPAR 2010, volume 6449 of *Lecture Notes in Computer Science*, 380–393. Springer Berlin Heidelberg, 2011.

Y. Saad. *Iterative Methods for Sparse Linear Systems*. Philadelphia, PA: Society for Industrial and Applied Mathematics, 2003.

H. Schultz. Der sinn der statistischen nachfragen. *Veröffentlichungen der Frankfurter Gesellschaft für Konjunkturforschung*, 1930.

L. F. Shampine, I. Gladwell, and S. Thompson. *Solving ODEs with MATLAB*. Cambridge: Cambridge University Press, 2003.

R. Shone. *Economic Dynamics: Phase Diagrams and their Economic Application*. Cambridge: Cambridge University Press, 2002.

G. Sleijpen and H. van der Vorst. A Jacobi-Davidson iteration method for linear eigenvalue problems. *SIAM Review*, 42(2): 267–293, 2000.

A. Smith. *The Wealth of Nations*. New York, NY: Random House; 1937 edition, original publication 1776.

D. C. Sorensen. Implicitly restarted Arnoldi/Lanczos methods for large scale eigenvalue calculations. In D. E. Keyes, A. Sameh, and V. Venkatakrishnan, editors, *Parallel Numerical Algorithms*, ICASE/LaRC Interdisciplinary Series in Science and Engineering. Dordrecht: Springer; Volume 4, 119–165, 1997.

R. M. Solow. A contribution to the theory of economic growth. *The Quarterly Journal of Economics*, 70(1): 65–94, 1956.

E. Süli and D. F. Mayers. *An Introduction to Numerical Analysis*. Cambridge: Cambridge University Press, 2003.

G. Tabellini and F. Daveri. Unemployment, growth and taxation in industrial countries. *Center for Economic Policy Research, Discussion Paper*, 1681, 1997.

J. Tinbergen. Bestimmung und deutung von angebotskurven ein beispiel. *Zeitschrift für Nationalökonomie*, 1(5): 669–679, 1930.

H. R. Varian. *Microeconomic Analysis*. New York, NY: W. W. Norton & Company, 3rd edition, 1992.

P. B. Vasconcelos. Economic growth models: Symbolic and numerical computations. *Advances in Computer Science: an International Journal*, 2(6): 47–54, 2013.

W. Zhang. *Differential Equations, Bifurcations, and Chaos in Economics*. Hackensack, NJ: World Scientific, 2005.

Index

Abel-Ruffini theorem 85
Acemoglu, D. 129, 130
AD–AS model 49–63; AD and AS curves together 52; AD curve: aggregate demand 50–1; AS curve: aggregate supply 51–2; diagram 58; dynamic AD–AS model 190–1; MATLAB/Octave code 55–7; numerical results 57–61; numerical solution 52–5; problems and computer exercises 61–3; variables, parameters and functional forms 50
Adams–Bashforth–Moulton family formulas 149
Afonso, O. 129, 145
aggregate demand (AD) *see* AD–AS model
aggregate supply (AS) *see* AD–AS model
Aghion, P. 131, 143, 145
AK growth model 194–7
Andrade, T. 103
Arnoldi method 98
Arnoldi, W.E. 43
autarky, supply–demand model in 4–11

back-substitution 15, 30
backward slash, Gaussian elimination in practice 16
Bai, Z. 93, 98
balance of payments 41
Barro, R. 26, 143, 144, 155, 156, 157, 170
Beath, J. 178
Bertrand model of duopoly markets 93, 95
BiCGstab (stabilised Bi-Conjugate Gradient) iterative method 44, 48, 213–14
bisectional method, nonlinear equations 53
Björck, Å. 4, 26, 49, 113, 130

boundary value problems (BVPs) 119, 163–6
Burda, M. 26, 38, 49
Butcher tableau 148, 149

capital accumulation 113–27
capital mobility 38–9, 44, 180–5
Carlin, W. 26
Cass, D. 156, 170
Cayley–Hamilton theorem 43
centralised equilibrium: Ramsey–Cass–Koopmans model 160–1
CG (Conjugate-Gradient) 44
Chiang, A.C. 79
CIES (Constant-Intertemporal-Elasticity-of-Substitution) utility function 131–2, 161
Cobb–Douglas production function 52, 114, 122, 161
cobweb model 79–92; demand 80–1; demand and supply curves together 81–2; market model with inventory 82–3, 87–90; MATLAB/Octave code 85–8; numerical results 88–90; numerical solution 83–5; plots 90; problems and computer exercises 91–2, 222–8; supply 81; variables, parameters and functional forms 80
cold turkey disinflation strategy 106–8, 110–11
collocation method, solving BVPs 165
condition numbers 31, 44
Constant Intertemporal Elasticity of Substitution *see* CIES
Constant Relative Risk Aversion (CRRA) 161
consumer surplus 6, 9–11, 13, 177
consumer's utility gain 6

262 *Index*

Cournot dynamic duopoly game *see* duopoly model
Cournot equilibrium 94
Cournot, A. 3

Dahlquist, G. 4, 26, 49, 113, 130
Daveri, F. 195
de la Grandville, O. 196
decentralised equilibrium, Ramsey–Cass–Koopmans model 160
demand 4–5; consumption (demand) side skill-biased technological change model 131–2; consumption (demand) side technological-knowledge diffusion model 145; *see also* supply and demand model
demand curve 4–6, 11–13, 18, 21, 80–1, 186
demand shock 103, 231–3
Demmel, J.W. 4, 26, 38, 93
difference equations 79, 83–5, 96–7
differential equations 115, 119, 121, 134, 146–8, 151; ODE problem 149; *see also* boundary value problems
Dinopoulos, E. 129
direct methods, solving linear equations 41
disequilibrium price 6
disinflation 103, 110–11; cold turkey strategy 106–8; gradual strategy, 106–8
Dixit, A.K. 144
dumped Newton methods 54
duopoly model 93–102; Bertrand model 95, 178; Cournot model 94; discrete dynamics Cournot duopoly game 95–6, 101; dynamic continuous duopoly game 186–8; eigenvalue problem 97–8; iterative methods 98; MATLAB/Octave code 99–100; numerical results 100–1; numerical solution 96–7; problems and computer exercises 102, 228–9; QR algorithm 98; Stackelberg model 94–5
dynamic AD–AS model 190–1
dynamic continuous duopoly game 186–8
dynamic IS–LM model 189–90

efficient frontier 64, 65, 69–70, 71–2, 73
eigenvalues 85, 96–8, 165, 189–91, 203, 228–9; problem 97–8
elementary elimination matrix 30
elementary row operations 15
endogenous variables: AD–AS model 50, 190; IS–LM model in closed economy 27; IS–LM model in open economy 39, 181–3, 185, 189; SP–DG model, 104; supply and demand model 4–5, 11, 14–15, 18, 20–1, 23, 24, 80
Euler equation 132, 133, 145, 158
Euler method 120–1, 134–7, 142, 148, 241–4
exchange rates 38, 41, 180–5
exogenous variables: AD–AS model 50; IS–LM model in closed economy 27, 33; IS–LM model in open economy 40, 44, 46, 181, 182, 189; SP–DG model 104; supply and demand model 4–5, 80
explicit *s*-stage Runge–Kutta methods 136
explicit four-stage and fourth-order Runge–Kutta methods 137
explicit two-stage and second-order Runge–Kutta methods 136–7
exports: IS–LM model in open economy 38–40, 46–7, 180–5; S&D model 11–24, 177–8

Fabozzi, F. J. 65
final goods: skill-biased technological change model 129–34, 140; technological-knowledge diffusion model 143–5
finite difference method, solving BVPs 164
firms: duoploy model 93–102, 186–8; product differentiation model 178–80; Ramsey–Cass–Koopmans model 159–60; skill-biased technological change model 130–4
fixed-point iteration, nonlinear equations 42, 55
fixed-price-level model *see* IS–LM model in closed economy
Fleming, M. 38
forward-substitution 16
free trade 12, 18–24

Galor, O. 129
Gandolfo, G. 79, 93
Gaspar, J. 204
Gauss–Seidel method 42
Gaussian elimination 15–16, 26, 29–30
global minimum variance portfolio 65, 71
GMRES (Generalised Minimum RESidual) method 44, 213–14
golden rule savings rate 118, 162–3
Golub, G.H. 4, 26
Gordon, R.J. 26, 38, 49, 103, 104, 111
government spending: AD–AS model 57–61; IS–LM model 47

gradual disinflation strategy 106–8, 110–11
Grossman, G.M. 130, 143
growth miracles 204
growth, multiple equilibria 204–6

Hall, R.E. 44
Hamiltonian optimal control theory 158, 161
Harrod neutral 128, 128n2, 166, 168, 170, 193
Haugen, R.A. 65
Helpman, E. 130, 143
Hicks neutral technological progress 122, 128
Hicks, John 37
high-skilled labour 130, 140–1, 197–8, 200–1, 203–4
Hotelling model 178
households, RCK model 156–60
Howitt, P. 131, 143, 145

imitator country 143–6
Inada conditions 114, 127n1, 159, 196
inflation: AD–AS model 49, 52, 190; SP–DG model 103–6, 108–11
initial value problems (IVPs) 113, 115, 119–21, 134–8, 147–50
innovative country 143–6
Intellectual Property Rights 145
inter-country convergence 143–6
interest rates: AD–AS model 49–51, 60–1; IS–LM model in open economy 41, 46, 38–48
intermediate goods, skill-biased model 130–4, 140, 197–200, 239–40
international-trade policy 11–24
inventory 82–3, 87–8, 89–90
inverse iteration 98
Investment Saving–Liquidity preference Money supply *see* IS–LM model
IS curve 35, 40, 41; goods and services market equilibrium 27–8
IS–LM model, in closed economy 26–37; IS and LM curves together 29; IS curve 27–8; LM curve 28–9; MATLAB/Octave code 31–3; numerical results 33–7; numerical solution 29–31; problems and computer exercises 37, 209–11; shocks 33–7; variables, parameters and functional forms 27
IS–LM model, in open economy 38–48; dynamic IS–LM model 189–90; IS and LM curves together 41; IS curve 40; LM curve 40–1; MATLAB/Octave code 44–6; numerical results 46–8; numerical solution 41–4; problems and computer exercises 48, 211–14; variables, parameters and functional forms 39–40
iterative methods: eigenvalues 98; linear equations 41–4; nonlinear equations 52–5

Jacobi method 42, 98
Jacobian matrix 54, 163, 165, 189, 191, 202
Jones, C.I. 129
Jones, L.E. 196

Kaldor, N. 79
Katsoulacos, Y. 178
Kelley, C.T. 38, 49
Kendrick, D.A. 68, 75
Keynes, John Maynard 37, 49
Koopmans, T. 156, 170
Krugman, P. R. 4
Krylov subspaces 43, 44, 46, 98

labour, technological-knowledge diffusion model 143–4; *see also* high-skilled labour
Lanczos, C. 43
Law of Demand 4, 80–1
Law of Supply 5, 81
Leite, D. 199, 200
linear equations 14–16, 29–31, 41–3
Lipschitz constant 121
LM curve: money-market equilibrium 26, 28–9, 40–1
Lobatto IIIa formula 165
Lobatto quadrature rules 164
LU factorisation 30–1
Lucas, R.E. 194

Mankiw, N.G. 26, 38, 49
Manuelli, R. 196
Markowitz, H. 64, 65
Marshall, A. 3
Mas-Colell, A. 3
MATLAB commands/functions: bicgstab 44; bvpinit 168; compan(p) 85; disp 8; eig 85, 98, 101; fminsearch 66; fminunc 66; fprintf 8; fsolve 55, 57, 122, 168, 186; fzero 55, 210; gmres 44, 46, 48; my_euler 121, 122, 127, 142; ode_tkd 151; pcg 44; plot 8; quiver 125; rck 168; roots(p) 85; spdg 108–9; special character % 8

MATLAB/Octave codes: AD–AS model 55–7; cobweb model 85–8; Cournot dynamic duopoly game 99–100; IS–LM model in closed economy 31–3; IS–LM model in open economy 44–6; portfolio model 67–72; Ramsey–Cass–Koopmans model 166–8; skill-biased technological change model 138–9; Solow model 121–2; SP–DG model 107–9; supply–demand model 7–8; technological-knowledge diffusion model 150–1
Mayers, D.F. 113, 130, 138, 144
Merton, R.C. 65
migratory movements and directed technical change 199–200
minimum residual approach 44
Moav, O. 129
Moler, C. 150
money spending: increase in 47–8
money supply 26–7, 40–1; AD–AS model 60; decrease in 35–7
Monte Carlo approach: portfolio model with 68–9, 71, 72
Monte Carlo optimisation methods 67
multiple equilibria 204–6
multistep methods (IVPs) 135
Mundell, R. 38, 48
Mundell–Fleming model 44–8, 180–5
mundell_fleming.m script 44

Nelson, R.R. 129
neoclassic growth model, extensions to 191–7; *see also* Solow model
net exports, IS–LM model in open economy 38–40, 46–8, 180–5, 211–12
Newton method 164; nonlinear equations 53, 54
Nocedal, J. 65, 66, 67
non-Ponzi condition 158, 159
nonlinear equations 52–5
nonlinear supply–demand model 186
nonstationary iterative methods 43–4
numerical approximations 67
numerical results: cobweb model 88–90; duopoly model 100–1; IS–LM model in closed economy 33–7; IS–LM model in open economy 46–8; portfolio model 72–3; Ramsey–Cass–Koopmans model 168–70; skill-biased technological change model 139–41; Solow model 122–5; SP–DG model 110–11; supply and demand model 8–11, 16–24;

technological-knowledge diffusion model 151–4
numerical solutions: AD–AS model 52–5; cobweb model 83–5; IS–LM model in open economy 41–4; portfolio model 65–7; SP–DG model 106; duopoly model 96–8; IS–LM model in closed economy 29–31; Ramsey–Cass–Koopmans model 163–6; skill-biased technological change model 134–8; Solow model 119–21; supply and demand model 14–16; technological-knowledge diffusion model 147–50

Obstfeld, M. 11
oligopoly markets *see* duopoly model
one-step (or self-starting) method 134–5
open economy 38–48
optimisation, portfolio model 64–75

Pachamanova, D. 65
Papell, D.H. 44
parameters: AD–AS model 50, 57, 190, 191; IS–LM model closed 27, 33; IS–LM model open 39–40; SP–DG model 103–8; supply and demand model 4, 8, 80
Pashigian, B.P. 79
Perloff, J.M. 3, 93
Petrov–Galerkin approach 44
Phelps, E.S. 129
Pigou effect 49
Pigou, Arthur Cecil 49
pivoting 16, 31, 108
population growth 115, 116, 118, 127, 157, 191–6
portfolio model 64–75; efficient frontier 69–72, 73; MATLAB/Octave code 67–72; Monte Carlo approach 68, 71, 72; numerical results 72–3; numerical solution 65–7; problems and computer exercises 74–5, 218–22; quadratic programming approach 65, 69, 71, 73
poverty traps 204
Powell hybrid method 55
power method 98
preconditioned system 42
problems and computer exercises: AD–AS model 61–3; cobweb model 91–2; duopoly model 102; IS–LM model in closed economy 37; IS–LM model in open economy 48; portfolio model 74–5; Ramsey–Cass–Koopmans model

170–1; skill-biased technological change model 142; Solow model 127; SP–DG model 111–2; supply and demand model 24–5; technological-knowledge diffusion model 154–5
producer surplus 6, 9–12
product differentiation model 178–80
production function 114, 115, 116–7, 124–5, 130, 191–7; *see also* Cobb–Douglas production function
public expenditures and optimal taxes 195–6
public spending, increase in 35
public tax, decrease in 46–7

QR algorithm 98
quadratic programming approach: portfolio model with 65, 69, 71, 73

R&D 129, 131, 239–40; effects of public intervention on wage equality 197–9; equilibrium 133; technological-knowledge diffusion model 143–5, 151–2
Ramsey, F.P. 156, 170
Ramsey–Cass–Koopmans model 156–71; assumptions of the model 157–60; centralised equilibrium 160–1; connection with the Solow–Swan model 163; decentralised equilibrium 160; firms 159–60; golden rule 162; households 157–9; linear approximation 163; MATLAB/Octave code 166–8; numerical results 168–70; numerical solution 163–6; problems and computer exercises 170–1, 249–56; steady state 161
Rayleigh quotient iteration (RQI) 98
real domestic output, AS curve 51–2
Ricardo, D. 3
Ricci, U. 79
Richardson method 42
risk, portfolio model 64–75
Ritz–Galerkin approach 44
Romer, P.M. 26, 143, 194, 195
Romero, E. 98
roots of polynomials 85
Runge, C. 136
Runge–Kutta methods 130, 135–8, 149, 164

Saad, Y. 38
saddle points 163, 165
savings rate 113, 117–18, 156; *see also* golden rule savings rate

Schumpeterian R&D models 131
Schur Form 98
secant method, nonlinear equations 54
Segerstrom, P. 129
Shampine, L.F. 144, 150, 156, 165, 166
shocks: AD–AS model 57–61; IS–LM model in closed economy 33–7; skill-biased technological change model 139–42; SP–DG model 103–12; technological-knowledge diffusion 152–4
Shone, R. 190
short-run expectations augmented Phillips–Demand Growth *see* SP–DG model
Shultz, H. 79
skill premium, *see* skill-biased technological change model
skill-biased technological change model 129–42; equilibrium for given factor levels 132–3; MATLAB/Octave code 138–9; modelling the domestic economy 130–2; numerical results 139–41; numerical solution 134–8; problems and computer exercises 42, 239–44; R&D equilibrium 133; Runge–Kutta methods 135–8; steady-state equilibrium 133; Taylor series based methods 135; transitional dynamics 134
skill-structure, high-tech sector and economic growth dynamics model 200–4
Sleijpen, G. 98
Smith, Adam 3
social welfare 6, 11
Solow model 113–27, 191–7; diagram 115–17; Euler method 120; golden rule 118; ingredients 114–15; linear approximation 118–19; MATLAB/Octave code 121–2; numerical results 122–5; numerical solution 119–21; problems and computer exercises 127, 234–9; stability of equilibrium points 121; steady state 117–18
Solow, R. 113, 125, 156
Solow–Pitchford AK model 196–7
Sorensen, D.C. 98
Soskice, D. 26
southern transitional dynamics 146–7
SP–DG model 103–12; algorithm 106; DG curve 105; disinflation process 110–11; expected inflation rate curve 104; global equilibrium 105; MATLAB/Octave

266 *Index*

code 107–9; numerical results 110–11; numerical solution 106; problems and computer exercises 111–12, 229–34; SP curve 104–5; variables, parameters and functional forms 103–4
stability of equilibrium points 121, 165
Stackelberg equilibrium 94–5
static equations, IS–LM model 26, 38
stationary iterative methods 42–3
steady state 117–18, 161–3
steady-state equilibrium 133, 145–6, 161
Successive Over-Relaxation method 42
Süli, E. 113, 130, 138, 144
supply: productive (supply) side skill-biased technological change model 130–1; productive (supply) side technological-knowledge diffusion model 144–5; *see also* supply and demand model
supply and demand dynamics *see* cobweb model
supply and demand model 3–25; curves for all markets 18, 19, 21; demand 4–5; demand and supply curves together 5–6; economic model in autarky 4–6; economic model with international-trade policy 11–14, 177–8; export subsidy 14; four basic laws 6; free trade vs restricted trade 19–24; Gaussian elimination 15–16; MATLAB/Octave code 7–8; matrix representation 15; nonlinear supply–demand model 186; numerical results 8–11; numerical solution 14–16; problems and computer exercises 24–5, 207–9; social welfare 6, 11; supply 5; tariff imports 13–14; variables, parameters and functional forms 4
supply curve 5–6, 81
Swan, T. 156

Tabellini, G. 195
tariff on imports 13–14; free trade vs. restricted 19–24
taxes, decrease in 33–5
Taylor series expansion 135, 136, 163

technological knowledge, labour-augmenting 193–4
technological-knowledge bias 130, 133, 134, 140–1, 197–8, 200, 201, 239–40
technological-knowledge diffusion model 143–55; consumption (demand) side 145; MATLAB/Octave code 150–1; numerical results 151–4; numerical solution 147–50; problems and computer exercises 154–5, 244–8; productive (supply) side 144–5; southern transitional dynamics 146–7; steady-state equilibrium 145–6
technological-knowledge gap 199–200
technological-knowledge-absorption effect 130, 131, 134, 140–1
Tinbergen, J. 79
trade policy 11–24
transformation methods 98
transversality condition 158–61, 200
trapezoidal rule 164
trust-region methods 55

unemployment and economic growth 195

van der Vorst, H. 98
Van Loan, C.F. 4, 26
variable-price-level model *see* AD–AS model
Varian, H.R. 3, 93
Vasconcelos, P.B. 156

wage inequality 134, 141; effects of public intervention on 197–9
wages: AD curve 51; RCK model 156–7, 160
Wainwright, K. 79
Wright, S.J. 65, 66, 67
Wyplosz, C. 26, 38, 49

Zhang, W. 189
Zilibotti, F. 129, 130

An environmentally friendly book printed and bound in England by www.printondemand-worldwide.com

This book is made of chain-of-custody materials; FSC materials for the cover and PEFC materials for the text pages.

#0096 - 291015 - C0 - 234/156/16 [18] - CB - 9781138859654